T0419473

A WAR OF THEIR OWN

FULRO: The Other National Liberation Front, Vietnam 1955–1975

William H. Chickering

CASEMATE
Pennsylvania & Yorkshire

Published in the United States of America and Great Britain in 2025 by
CASEMATE PUBLISHERS
1950 Lawrence Road, Havertown, PA 19083
and
47 Church Street, Barnsley, S70 2AS, UK

Hardcover Edition: ISBN 978-1-63624-560-7
Digital Edition: ISBN 978-1-63624-561-4

A CIP record for this book is available from the British Library

Printed and bound in the United Kingdom by CPI Group (UK) Ltd, Croydon, CR0 4YY

Typeset in India by Lapiz Digital Services, Chennai.

For a complete list of Casemate titles, please contact:

CASEMATE PUBLISHERS (US)
Telephone (610) 853-9131
Fax (610) 853-9146
Email: casemate@casematepublishers.com
www.casematepublishers.com

CASEMATE PUBLISHERS (UK)
Telephone (0)1226 734350
Email: casemate@casemateuk.com
www.casemateuk.com

Cover image: (Front, left) Engraving of a Jarai warrior from 1891. (Cupet, P., "Chez les Populations Sauvages du Sud de l'Annam," Le Tour du Monde, Vol. 65, nos. 1681–1685, Paris (1893): 177–256; (Front, right) Image of Kpa Doh, 1966. (William Chickering, courtesy of SGM Robt Ramsey)

Back flap: Photo by Sacha Chickering.

Author's note: To anyone who knows more of this story, even bits and pieces of it, that posterity ought to know—please email me at author@montagnardhistory.com.

for Bénédicte

This Conference indignantly rejects … the so-called humanitarian mission that the imperialist powers have given themselves, against the consent of even the peoples involved …, of preserving a World called "free," [a mission that] in Indochina has meant indescribable suffering and loss of innumerable human lives.

March 1965, from the declaration of principles at the Indochina Peoples' Conference, probably penned by Sihanouk (author's translation).

From April 17 to May 26 1975
this gate that enclosed
the Embassy of France in Cambodia
was opened then closed again
on an indescribable pain
and on the death of millions of Cambodians.

Inscription referring to the horrors of the Khmer Rouge on a marble slab at the heart of current French Embassy grounds in Phnom Penh, near the original grille of the 1975 embassy gate (author's translation).

Contents

Acknowledgements

Y-Bhan Kpor, Y-Tlur Eban, K'Briuh, Kok Ksor, Meidine Natchear, Bob Ramsay, Maud Y-Bun Sur, Sen Tith, Nara Vija, Françoise Demeure, Chuck Darnell, Rong Nay, Steve Sherman, Youk Chhang, Hannafiah, Intan Kosem, Merle Pribbenow, Alan Schapira, Seth Mydans, Jonathan Padwe, Jean-Pierre Chazal, and Louis Y-Pen Bing.

Y-Blim Adrong, Y-Dhe Adrong, Y-Ghak Adrong, Ro'o Bleo, Y-Jut Buon To, Cil Te, Siu Hiupp, Puih Hloanh, Kpa H'mian, Hip Ksor, Y-Cam Hwing, Y-Ton Hwing, Y-Pri Nie, Y-Hin Nie, DinhNieu, Paul Nur, R'com Ali, R'com Jimmy, and Ksor Wol.

Edward Abse, Justin Adams, Harry Amos, Sabu Bacha, Elizabeth Becker, Mike Benge, Charlie Benoit, Bob Best, Long Botta, Richard Boyle, Patrick Cabanes, Lynn Cavage, Elizabeth Cavanaugh, Song Chhang, Chhay Born Lay, Nick Chickering, Pierre-Yves Clais, Sara Colm, Ken Conboy, Phil Courts, Patrice de Beer, Arnaud de la Grange, Po Dharma, Jean Dominique, Saorun Ellul, Roger Faligot, Rocky Farr, Jack Fischer, Jean-Michel Filippi, Daniel Ford, Cristophe Maria Froeder, George (Speedy) Gaspard, Gene Hall, Irv Hamberger, Steve Heder, Michael Hayes, Fritz Hoffecker, Haney Howell, John Howell, Peter Iseman, Jake Jacobelli, Juris Jurjevics, Ibrahim Keo, Larry Kerr, Harris Kosem, Denny Lane, Nils Larsen, Thibault Ledeq, Harry Le Fever, Marcia Lèbre, Henri Locard, Peter Maguire, Crews McCulloch, Mac McNamara, Caroline Monnier, Jim Moody, Jim Morris, Nick Palmer, Les Naser, Roland Neveu, Nguyen Quoc Thanh, Ysa Osman, Thomas Pearson, Bob Pierson, François Ponchaud, Euless Presley, Douglas Porch, David Quammen, Martin Rathie, Jean-Pierre Riedel, Carl Robinson, Martin Robillard, Al Rockoff, Doug Sapper, Jay Scarborough, Sydney Schanberg, Catherine Scheer, Rob Schwab, Ing Sera, Guy Simon, Clyde Sincere, Pat Smith, Farina So, Steve Spoerry, Ed Sprague, Kathryn Statler, Ken Swain, Nate Thayer, Yvette Truong, Champa Um, Michael Vickery, Gary Webb, and Brian Zittel.

Introduction

Early in the Vietnam War, a group of mountain tribesmen, called Montagnards, rebelled against Saigon with the goal of winning a country of their own in the Central Highlands. They saw all Vietnamese, including communists, as invaders of their homeland and named their movement FULRO, an acronym for liberating their peoples from oppression (*Front Uni pour la Libération des Races Opprimeés*, Liberation Front for Oppressed Races).[1] Operating from sanctuary just across the border in Cambodia, they played a shadowy role for a few years, then faded away. They resurfaced in Phnom Penh near the end of the war, where they and their families flickered into history's spotlight as they walked toward certain death, then were gone.

Until now, this was essentially all that was known about them. What follows, the story of FULRO, is one of the last significant stories of the war still untold. It is unlike anything you have ever read or heard about Vietnam. It is the story of the *other* national liberation front. Held up to a certain light, it is a tragedy in the classic sense of the word, even though its protagonists—five mountain tribesmen and one Cham from Cambodia—were the very opposite of high-born—in stilt huts, with only one foot in the modern world.

A storm was coming to Indochina; they saw in it a chance to save their peoples from extinction. They also heard something in the rising wind that modern men might not, a call to defy fate. With little education and zero political tradition, they tried to get the attention of the world with a bloody revolt, but they only became the focus of secret manipulation by Washington, Paris, and Hanoi. For a long moment, they stood alone against those powers.

Then, spying one slim chance to show their potential as allies instead of pawns, they leapt at it.

***

In 1973, I met four of FULRO's Montagnard leaders in Phnom Penh (the fifth having been murdered years before). I also met briefly with the Cham and his wife.

Without those meetings, I never could, or would, have written this book.

Being photographed next to FULRO's revered older leader (see p. 73) turned out, decades later, to be a bona fide like no other in getting Montagnards to open up to me about FULRO.

From spending several days with one young leader, I was infuriated years later to find him depicted as a coward in a 2004 book about the fall of Phnom Penh, which set me on a two-year quest to learn the Montagnards' fate at the hands of the Khmer Rouge.

Having known, and liked, a second young leader took me metaphorically back into Vietnam combat, where I finally understood FULRO's reasons for fighting alongside Americans.

Giving my address to a third leader—the only one to survive—resulted in his entering my life so completely that he eventually became like an exotic uncle to my children, drawing me in so deeply to the FULRO story that I spent 16 years researching it all over the world, even moving to Phnom Penh. He could not, or would not, answer one question, however: why FULRO had suddenly faded away. It looked to be unanswerable.

Then, 45 years after having met, the Cham's widow gave me access to FULRO's secret papers.

The book's narrative thus follows the history of my search, but only Chapter Five is pure memoir. I have otherwise kept myself out of this because it is, above all, a history of the Montagnards' and Chams' fight for a country of their own.

***

The Vietnamese are villains in this book because FULRO saw them that way. To the extent that fear and disdain towards Montagnards was woven into the Vietnamese cultural fabric, and to the extent that the Vietnamese will bring about the cultural extinction of the Montagnards, FULRO was correct in seeing them as the enemy.

But the fact that anti-Montagnard racism had been around for millennia makes those Vietnamese individuals who fought against it, at risk to their jobs and often lives, that much more extraordinary. They are mostly unsung because the world has moved on. I cannot sing their praises now as I have for specific Montagnards because I knew no Vietnamese like that; however, looking back, I can wonder whether a racism of my own blinded me to heroism before my eyes.

From a larger perspective, many Vietnamese today will appreciate how the FULRO story makes a necessary case to history that, in that war, there was more than one idea of country that good and patriotic men could fight and die for.

Note

1 *Lutte* (struggle) was sometimes used instead of *Libération*, with a more leftist ring.

CHAPTER I

Beginnings

Rebellion

The night of September 19, 1964, Captain Chuck Darnell,[1] commander of a six-man team of American Green Berets, was making rounds on his camp's perimeter. Passing the fire arrow, a contraption of gasoline-soaked sand to be lit and swiveled toward the enemy in case of attack, to be seen from the air, he was thankful the weather had been unseasonably clear, with no monsoon rains borne up from the Gulf of Thailand, and no thousand-foot-thick layers of mist sitting like a cold, wet washrag on the face. Isolated on the Vietnam–Cambodia border, the camp was dependent on airpower if attacked.

He found several Montagnard soldiers asleep on guard duty. They probably knew better than he that the enemy would not come on such a clear night. The highlanders knew war, having fought almost 20 years—on both sides.

He was more puzzled by the absence of ammo belts in two of the perimeter's machine guns. It was as though the guns were to be carried.

Only later did he realize the men had been feigning sleep.

Shortly after midnight, he woke to his name being called softly from outside. Through an acetate window that warped and sickened the scene, he made out his top sergeant and a large number of highlanders—all strangely motionless. He felt the first tug of the current about to sweep all of them away. The sergeant's rifle was lowered. The highlanders had their rifles raised.

One of them approached, addressing Darnell as "sir." It was his interpreter and constant companion over the eight weeks since the Americans had arrived from Okinawa. His usual grin was gone.

"Tonight is the night we kill the Vietnamese."

The shock was the specificity. "The Vietnamese" could not mean the enemy, the faceless Viet Cong. It could only mean the Vietnamese Green Berets in camp—his counterparts, his allies.

He knew there was tension in camp. The Vietnamese were thought to be skimming the highlanders' pay. But this?

Americans got on well with the highlanders, much like the French before them. But three Special Forces camps had fallen in the previous year, one from treachery within (Plei Mrong); its Montagnard defenders had included a number of Viet Cong.

The fire arrow was not designed for that.

***

"We want your weapons, sir," said Darnell's interpreter. Darnell liked the man and tried to dissuade him. But the young man shook his head. "If we take your weapons, the Vietnamese can't blame you later."

Darnell spotted another of his sergeants under guard but still in possession of his carbine. Having no choice, he told his men to turn over their arms. Immediately, a group of highlanders rushed past Darnell into the team house. Collecting all rifles, grenades, and radios, they woke the remaining Americans and moved everyone into the team's mess hall.

Gunfire broke out. One of the Vietnamese Special Forces soldiers ran toward them, seeking refuge with the Americans. He suddenly pitched forward onto his face, almost at their feet, and convulsed, the static of a dying brain.

Hunched below sandbagged walls, they listened to the firing. Darnell thought it lasted about 45 minutes. A young American civilian, there to teach animal husbandry, thought it lasted two hours. In any case, Darnell recognized it for what it was—an execution, not a gunfight.

After it was over, Darnell inquired as to the safety of two young Vietnamese nurses who had midwifed many highlander births. They had been spared but were shaking with terror when brought into the mess hall. Thirteen Vietnamese Green Berets had been killed.

The question now, for Darnell, was what—who—might be next. "Overrun" was the word, meaning no prisoners taken, dreadful in its banality. No fire arrow prevented being overrun from within. One of Darnell's sergeants was almost undone with fear.

Around 3:00 am, the situation shifted toward the surreal when two unknown leaders arrived. One was light skinned and goateed, wearing unfamiliar camouflage fatigues and a *krama*, a Cambodian checkered scarf. The other was tall and well built, with almost Polynesian features and striking eyes, wearing shirt and slacks and carrying an incongruous briefcase. Both were in their early thirties and seemed well educated, addressing the Americans courteously in French, which Darnell's interpreter translated to English. The tall one revealed himself to be Rhadé by speaking to some soldiers in that dialect. With others, who were Mnong, he spoke French. Over time, it became evident he was in charge, but that his companion was a Cham and more hardline. An American photojournalist who arrived the next day assumed from the Cham's anger that he was Viet Cong.[2]

Along with a curved pipe, the tall Rhadé pulled a mimeographed document and three-starred flag out of his briefcase, and, draping the flag over his knees, began to read from a manifesto.

The killings were the first act of a rebellion. The rebels belonged to FULRO (*Front Uni pour la Libération des Races Opprimeés*, Liberation Front for Oppressed Races), which claimed the ancient territory of Champa on behalf of the Cham people and their linguistic brothers, the Rhadé and Jarai.[3] For the Mnong and all other Montagnard groups, FULRO claimed "Northern Cambodia" and, for ethnic Cambodians living in Vietnam's Delta, "Southern Cambodia." All were one race.

"FULRO's struggle," he explained, "is to save our ancestral lands and to keep our race intact. We have been forced to take up arms by our enemy's murderous acts, to show them our determination to stay forever as we are and not, in any way, turn into Vietnamese."

When the Rhadé paused to relight his pipe, putting down the papers, the young American International Voluntary Service worker was close enough to scan them and see references to American imperialism the Rhadé had skipped, also long, legalistic paragraphs mentioning the United Nations Charter.[4]

The Rhadé was justifying the violence. "Because we are independent of both Vietnamese camps, and because our policy aims for self-government, our struggle conforms to international law. From the beginning we tried to negotiate, to avoid armed conflict, but we could not." In this lantern-lit hut, he was aiming his message to reach the world and win support from lovers of justice everywhere. But one might still imagine a tremor in the night, liquid in the door.

After first light, Darnell was allowed outside and saw four bodies laid out on the ground. He was told they had "resisted." He saw more bodies in the dry pit of a new latrine being dug next to the old. When he came back, he instructed the young IVS civilian to stay away from the area, using the back wall as a latrine.

Later, this got distorted into a story that the dead, or dying, Vietnamese had been stuffed down into the filth of a latrine. In some versions, a grenade was tossed in after.

From his young interpreter, Darnell learned that simultaneous rebellions were occurring at five Special Forces camps. This camp (Buon Sar Pa), plus three others, would soon send troops to converge on the capital of Darlac province, Ban Me Thuot, in order to capture it on signal at 7:00 am. A Vietnamese Army division was in town, but help would come from Montagnard soldiers within the division. The fifth camp (Bu Prang) was to capture Gia Nghia, a smaller provincial capital far to the south.

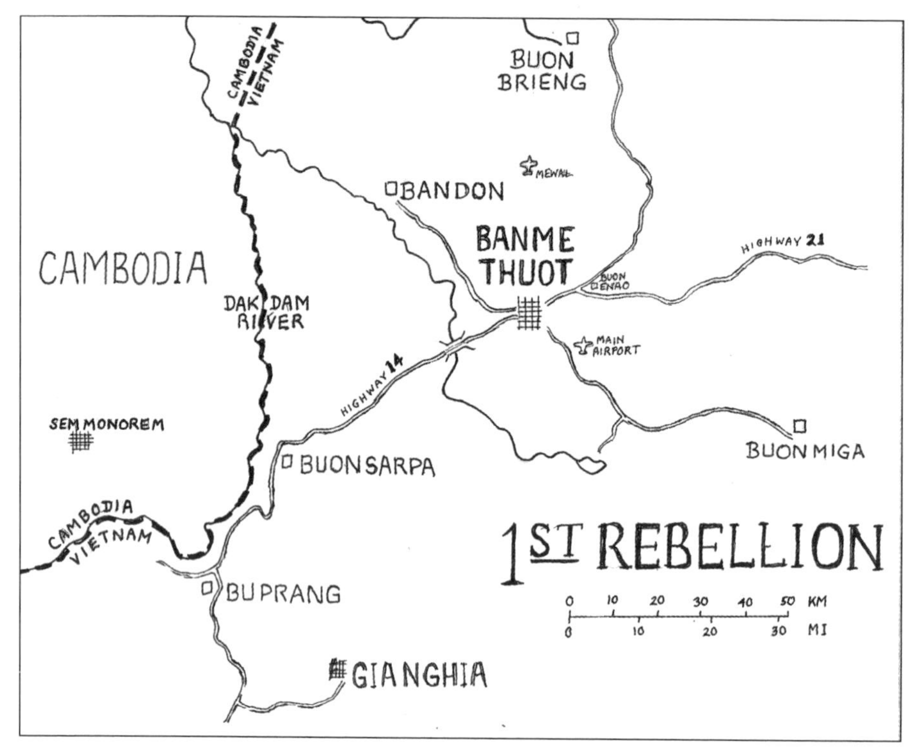

First Rebellion, September 1964, camps involved. (Map by author)

Darnell pointed out to the interpreter that, once all this got going, the camps would be open to attack by the Viet Cong. The man shook his head. One company of soldiers would stay behind at each camp. Plus, he added, the communists had been told not to interfere.

The latter was as disturbing to Darnell as reassuring.

Troops had been loading the camp's ammunition onto trucks; Darnell spotted the two machine guns. An advance party began to move out. The interpreter hoisted the FULRO flag on the camp's pole. Already there was disagreement among the rebels about what the stars stood for. To men like the Rhadé leader, aware of the need to have the broadest possible coalition, the stars stood for Montagnards, Chams, and Cambodians. However, to many of the younger troops, the stars represented the three main Montagnard provinces of Vietnam.

Shortly after 6:00 am, the rebels tuned a shortwave radio to the Ban Me Thuot station. When the broadcast suddenly cut off, they grinned, taking it as the sign of success. Many more troops began to move out. But when an advance party took the capital's radio station, they found its crystals missing, pulled by the Vietnamese radio operators before they escaped. FULRO had been silenced.

***

Elsewhere, too, the rebellion was not going as planned.

At Buon Mi Ga, to the southeast, the Montagnard rebels disarmed the American team, then, out of its sight and hearing, executed the 10 Vietnamese Special Forces soldiers. This was probably the template for all the camps, with the Americans kept separate but on hand as hostages if necessary. Meanwhile, the camp's main force descended on Ban Me Thuot but failed to block the airport because the absent start signal had delayed or cancelled help from Montagnard units in town. As a result, Vietnamese paratroopers were able to fly in the next day.

Things went worse at remote Bu Prang to the southwest. The Vietnamese Green Berets got wind of what was about to happen and slipped away in trucks crucial to the rebels' plans. Unable to move onward to the second targeted province capital, the rebels killed 15 Vietnamese irregular soldiers in camp, then moved on to a fortified district outpost; gaining admission on trust, they slaughtered 19 more Vietnamese including the district chief, his wife, and their daughter. The American team was unaware of all this, hearing nothing, even the murders in camp. Bu Prang's troops were Mnong. The district outpost was only 6 kilometers (4 miles) from where the Mnong—perhaps including grandfathers of the Bu Prang men—had famously murdered a French official in 1914, reacting to his invasion of their territory. This had been exactly 50 years before. The Mnong were again reacting to invasion, this time by Vietnamese settlers. (Today, if you look down at the Vietnam–Cambodia border by satellite, you can see what they feared: patchwork fields on the Vietnamese side of the border, solid forest green on the Cambodian side, though here and there ominous pseudopods intrude.)

Back at Buon Sar Pa, sometime before dawn, the Rhadé leader contacted Bu Prang's rebels by radio. Darnell remembers him cursing. Was it anger at what they had done—killing civilians—or about the missing trucks?

From the point of view of whoever planned the rebellion, however, the highlanders' deference to Americans was a problem as consequential as the absent start signal.[5] Despite a mutual affinity, the deference was one-way, inevitable given vastly different levels of sophistication. It had been the same with the French.

At Ban Don, to the north, a young American lieutenant named Jack Fischer had been practicing his West Point French over the previous month with a grizzled highlander supply-sergeant, an *ancien tirailleur* (rifleman) with the French.[6] They had become friends over cigars. When screams of terror brought him rushing outside the team house, he found the Vietnamese Green Berets bound and kneeling, a highlander behind each man with a gun to his head. He confronted the rebels' leader but noted the man kept looking past him. Turning, he found his gray-haired friend. Over the course of many hours, Fischer finally convinced the older man the Americans would not, could not, support FULRO, thus the Vietnamese should be let go. Meanwhile, 700 men had left Ban Don to attack Ban Me Thuot, their mission to take the ammunition dump on the northwest edge of town. But they, too, were ultimately dissuaded by Americans, who then led the highlanders back to camp.

At Buon Brieng, to the north, a Green Beret captain named Vernon Gillespie stopped the rebellion in its tracks by taking command of the camp by threat of US force. In rapid succession, he sheltered the Vietnamese team, forbade highlander troop movement, and, just in case, ordered the surreptitious disabling of trucks and wiring of the ammo dump for detonation. By chance, an American photojournalist was in camp overnight and documented all this, depicting the highlander commander, Y-Jhon, as swayed by Gillespie's reasoning and dominant presence. Photos show Y-Jhon to be a small, delicately handsome man with an anxious look.

However, Y-Jhon already had reason to wonder who was behind the rebellion. A force of Montagnard Viet Cong was rumored to be poised to join FULRO in attacking Ban Me Thuot. Its leader was a man whose greater allegiance was assumed to be the highlander cause, not communism. Yet Y-Jhon had just received intelligence that Vietnamese Viet Cong might be standing by as well. Perhaps this was wrong. If not, it was thoroughly confusing.[7]

Y-Jhon was a *métis*, with a French father, marginalized in Rhadé society to begin with. In any case, his apparent deference to Gillespie doomed him. He was accompanying Gillespie to other camps to defuse the rebellion when Gillespie was suddenly whisked away to Saigon to brief General Westmoreland and Henry Luce of *Time/LIFE*, and, just as quickly, Y-Jhon was snatched by the Vietnamese Security Police. Upon his release days later, he was mumbling, with an empty stare, whether from beatings or shame or both. US Army psychologists in Nha Trang could do nothing for him; likewise, shamans brought in by his Rhadé mother. Several weeks later, he laid himself face down in the mud of a busy road in Ban Me Thuot to die. Taken home to be nursed, he disappeared. A month after that, he was seen one last time, standing by a road in Mnong country—evidently banished from Rhadé territory—splattered with chicken-blood.

***

Back at Darnell's camp, by midmorning the Rhadé leader and the Cham were preparing to make the 60-kilometer trip north to Ban Me Thuot. They asked Darnell to join them, ostensibly to mediate if they ran into the Vietnamese division outside the town. He agreed and sat hulkingly between two Montagnard soldiers in an enclosed jeep, looking like a hostage—probably what the Rhadé intended.

He had never crossed this no-man's land before without a lot of firepower. Now they were unescorted, in four unarmed jeeps, but it soon began to feel like a parade. Small groups of highlanders dotted the roadside, waving and cheering. Either news travelled fast, or the population had known beforehand that something would happen.

After crossing an iron bridge at the Sre Pok river, they brazened past a couple of Vietnamese Army roadblocks, but the last was barred. Despite angry shouts from Vietnamese in half-tracks looking down the sights of .50-caliber machine guns, the Rhadé leader calmly lifted the barrier, got back in his jeep, and they drove on.

At Ban Me Thuot's outskirts, they turned into the Montagnard ghetto and pulled up in front of a wooden longhouse with a small porch at the end. The Rhadé called out. A middle-aged man emerged, wearing civilian trousers and suit jacket, and bid goodbye to his wife and six children.

From introductions, Darnell learned this was Y-Bham Enuol, Rhadé president of FULRO. The younger Rhadé, the rebellion's leader, was Dhon,[8] FULRO's vice-president.

They all got back into the jeeps and crossed back over the main road, arriving at a small church after a kilometer. From his jeep, Darnell watched Y-Bham Enuol and Dhon walk 60 meters to meet three bearded Caucasians in dark civilian clothes, with lots of handshakes and laughter, like a meeting of old friends, that lasted about ten minutes. The Cham stayed with Darnell.

Returning south, they stopped en route to let Dhon and the Cham off at a rebel command post just beyond the iron bridge. Rebel troops there were now defending what they considered to be liberated Montagnard territory, south of the river. But Americans had started showing up, each one with news of another pillar of the rebels' plan knocked away. An American Green Beret major arrived on foot, leading the highlanders who had fruitlessly taken the radio station. An American colonel arrived, fluent in French and gusting on his moment in history, to get the rebels to negotiate with a Vietnamese general, but Dhon refused, leaving shortly afterward for Cambodia.

Darnell remembers Y-Bham Enuol as both warm and impressive, with the bearing of a leader and the clear devotion of his soldiers. Back in Darnell's camp, the Montagnard leader asked as to the safety and wellbeing of Darnell's team, who were in effect still hostages, and explained in a quiet voice the reasons for the uprising, mentioning he had just gotten out of prison. Then, indicating his men were waiting, he too left for the Cambodian border, four kilometers away.[9]

That evening, the Americans received a message in broken English from Dhon, conveying his apologies to the Vietnamese general for being "unable to meet, too busy cooking rice for dinner"—an enormous insult.

From this point on, the rebellion was essentially smothered by Americans. Darnell's interpreter became its de facto leader at age 22 because he spoke English, French, and Rhadé, plus some Mnong and Vietnamese. On instructions from across the border, he used hostages to draw things out for almost a week in hopes of getting the world's attention. But the issue had been decided on the first day. The world did pay attention for a week to "The Revolt of the Tribesmen," then moved on.[10]

Seventy-three Vietnamese had been killed in the camps. The American brass, including civilian higher-ups at the embassy, immediately suspected the communists because of the FULRO pamphlets referring to American imperialism; those lower down were not sure. A number of signs pointed to the French, most strikingly the three bearded Caucasians at the church. However, though they sounded like French priests, they could equally have been American evangelicals. The distinction was crucial. Both the French and American clerics were close with their country's secret services. The meeting looked collegial and congratulatory, meaning—maybe—that either France's SDECE[11] or the CIA had countenanced, perhaps encouraged, maybe even directed, the cold-blooded killing of 73 Vietnamese.

Darnell had been too far from the church to make out details. He could only say the three men's dark clothes were not cassocks. But he was certain of the route they had taken to the church and that it was about one kilometer from Y-Bham Enuol's house.

The question was—was the church Catholic or Protestant?

***

Immediately after the rebellion, Y-Bham Enuol, Dhon, and a large security guard set up headquarters 2–3 hours' walk from the border, in one of the few cement buildings in a small, windswept town called Sem Monorom, the remote capital of Mondulkiri, Cambodia's easternmost province.

Two days later, 16 men gathered to sign a decree creating the national flag of Champa: seven Montagnards (six Rhadé and one Mnong), seven Cham from Phnom Penh, and two colonels from the Cambodian Army. One colonel was a Cham central to this story (Les Kosem), the other an ethnic Cambodian from the Mekong Delta (Um Savuth). The 16 thus represented all three groups mentioned in Dhon's lantern-lit FULRO manifesto.

This was like the Declaration of Independence for Montagnards—except that, given that the Chams were already calling the country Champa, the simile might be more apt if Lafayette and Rochambeau had been signers in 1776 and started calling the new country Gaul.

Situated on a bare rise above the forests, Sem Monorom had an airstrip. When Y-Bham Enuol's wife and children arrived a week later, it was generally assumed they had been flown in by the French Secret Service.[12]

Some 100–200 men had crossed into Cambodia—Rhadé from Buon Sar Pa and Mnong from Bu Prang who knew the cross-border area well and had relations there.

The Cambodian border was a river, walled by jungle. From the air, even from low-flying aircraft, it was hard to see, slicing through forest that resembled broccoli, cushiony, familiar, until one looked down into the river's cut and saw the darkness, veined with slender tree trunks, a reminder that there was another border here, between sky and earth. The rebels were conscious of that border too. Unable to guess how the United States would react to their rebellion, they chose a site invisible from the air, under double canopy, with only tiny chinks of blue visible far above. They referred to it as Nam Lyr, because it was south of a mountain by that name that rises like a dark castle keep from the plain.

Within weeks, some of the rebels' wives and children arrived, and they all began constructing huts with thatch roofs and bamboo walls, each long enough to house 4–5 families, each family with its own entrance and hearth. The huts were on the ground, Mnong-style, as opposed to on pilings, because no one expected to stay long. Rumor had it Cambodia's Prince Sihanouk was going to give them land and water buffaloes to farm with.

Periodically, Cambodian soldiers—who were Cham, speaking a language similar to Jarai (less so to Rhadé)—arrived by truck to deliver rice, dried fish, and salt, which the Montagnards supplemented by foraging, hunting, fishing, and raising chickens. As time passed, they planted vegetables, especially pumpkins and several varieties of eggplant. It was never enough, though—because, as word of the Montagnard rebellion spread through the highlands, more and more soldiers and families crossed the border to join the cause.

Malaria

Nothing explains the spontaneity and intensity of Montagnard ethnonationalism in the 1950s so much as the fact that complete freedom and sovereignty over their highlands were still a living memory for them.

Only 60 years before, on meeting Jarai warriors (one of whom is on this book's cover), a French explorer guessed from their arrogance that they had never submitted to any power, never paid any tribute. If true, this is remarkable because their plateau[13] had long been sandwiched between aggressive lowland states, most notably Angkor and Champa.

Scholars assume that the explorer was wrong and that, in fact, Champa at one time colonized the plateau.

But I believe he was right—that until the late 19th century, the Montagnards had never been dominated and that their core lands had never been colonized.

If so, the principal reason for this was malaria.

In Vietnam, *falciparum* malaria—the worst kind—was highland malaria, to which only Montagnards were immune and which, combined with topography, effectively kept lowlanders out. One would expect ruins of brick or stone, especially of temples, where colonies had been, yet only one small temple has been identified on the high plateau itself. Four other temples are known but on the plateau's flanks. Two of these are close together on the eastern flank in *the only semi-arid valley in the entire Central Highlands*; the other two are on the western flank in areas of low rainfall and clear forest, inhospitable to malarial mosquitoes. Even the temple on the plateau sits in a bald area of rare prairie.[14] Their sites' common denominator appears to have been that they were free of tall forest and relatively dry, thus malaria-free.

My hypothesis, then, is that malaria was largely responsible for keeping Montagnards free, thus was essential to the origin of FULRO. To understand this, we need to take a brief detour into the Montagnards' prehistory.

***

More than two thousand years ago, an emperor of China learned an extremely rare and desired incense, called eaglewood, could be found in a land "south of the sun."[15] At that moment, the China luxury trade was born, and with it the bygone land called Champa.

Champa consisted of several kingdoms separated by mountain spurs touching the sea. One kingdom would dominate for a few centuries then yield to another further down the coast. Powerful at sea for a millennium, their capitals fell again and again over 800 years to the slow, southward push of the Vietnamese.

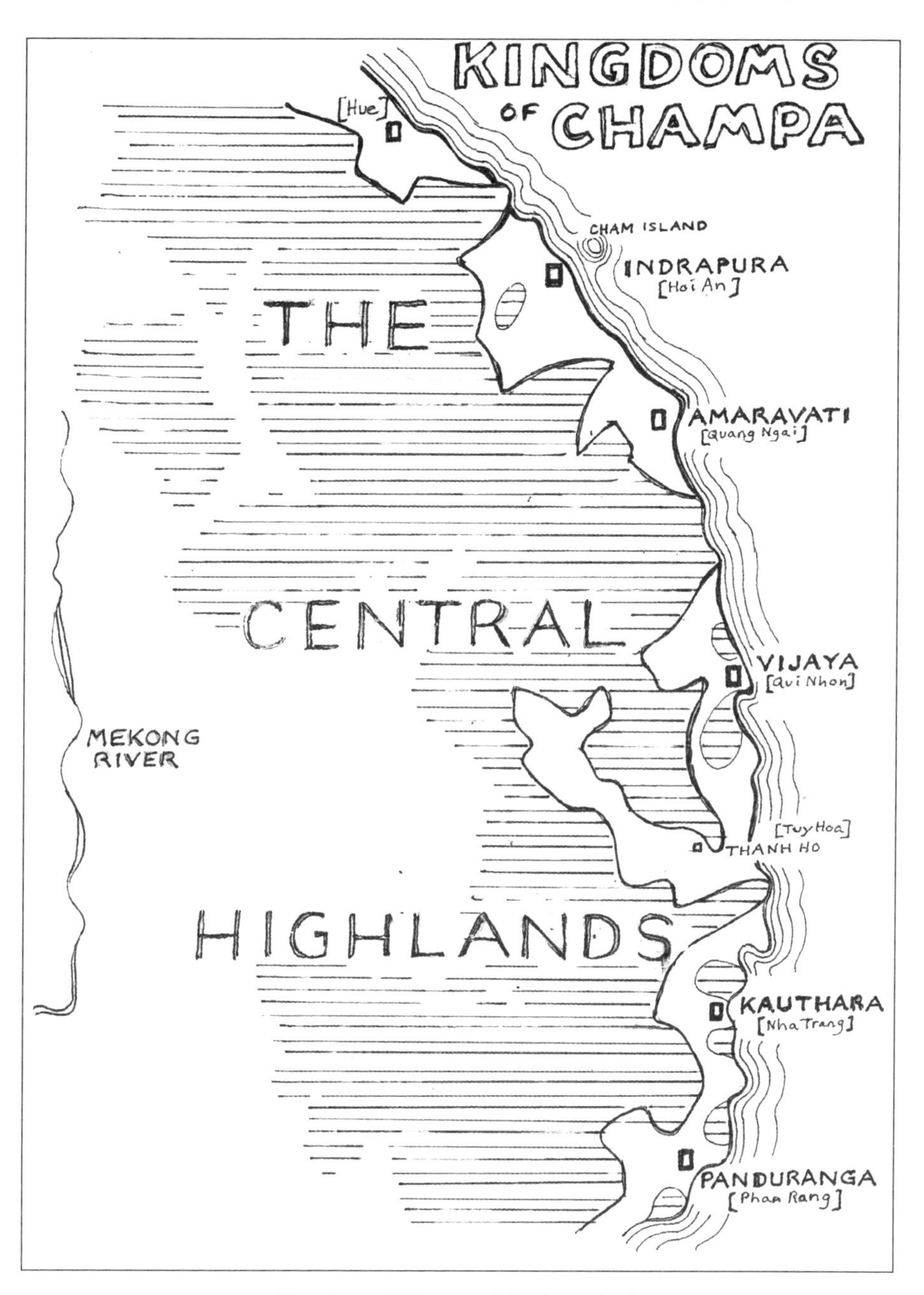

Kingdoms of Champa. (Map by author)

It was fortunate for Champa that the Chinese believed the South China Sea to be shallow. Navigators in slow-moving junks would hug the coast, stop in for fresh water, and find a world beyond imagining, with gifts to delight their sovereign and memories to polish and repolish like jewels into their old age. Over the first millennium, which Cham kingdom rose and which kingdom fell depended on the winds, and reach, and dynastic change in far-off China.

The original inhabitants of those coastal kingdoms were probably a people who looked and spoke a Mon-Khmer language like today's Cambodians. Then Malay seafarers from Southeast Asian islands brought a culture and language so powerful that the coastal people adopted them. Waterborne trade, and piracy, became part of their culture. Then gold seekers and gurus from southern India, the latter invited by early Cham rulers to bring Hinduism and erudition to their courts, added their genes and culture to the mix, creating today's Cham,[16] who remain a riverine or coastal people in both southern Vietnam and Cambodia.

Eaglewood has many qualities, but two stand out—its scent, unsurprisingly said to be sexually arousing, and its extreme rarity. Found only in highland tropical forest, the *Aquilaria* tree has to suffer a wound in order to produce eaglewood.[17] Normally trees close their wounds with a puffy scar of unremarkable wood, but if *Aquilaria* fails at this, it has a second line of defense: it secretes a chemical barrier of resinous wood—the eaglewood—that grows larger year by year as long as the wound stays open. What keeps a wound open is probably a fungus. The process needs an undetermined combination of light and humidity, most often found on rocky outcroppings. The uncertainties are what have kept eaglewood from being commercially farmed.

Champa was soon fabled throughout the ancient world for its exports, not just its eaglewood but its sandalwood and other aromatics, its gold, its rhinoceros horns and elephant tusks, beeswax (both yellow and white), gamboge, peacocks, ocellated pheasants, betel nut, cinnamon, cardamom, cubeb—all found only in tropical forests, which, in Vietnam, are only found in the highlands. At some point, slaves joined the list. The highlanders, despite rumors of having tails, were a handsome and able people.

Today, the influence of ancient Chams on the highlands is still evident in the matrilineal culture of two tribes, the Rhadé and the Jarai, and in their Chamic language, which can be understood in Malaysia and the Philippines and is resonant as far away as Madagascar and Easter Island.[18] The highland tribes to their north and south, who are less advanced, speak Mon-Khmer languages and are mostly patrilineal.

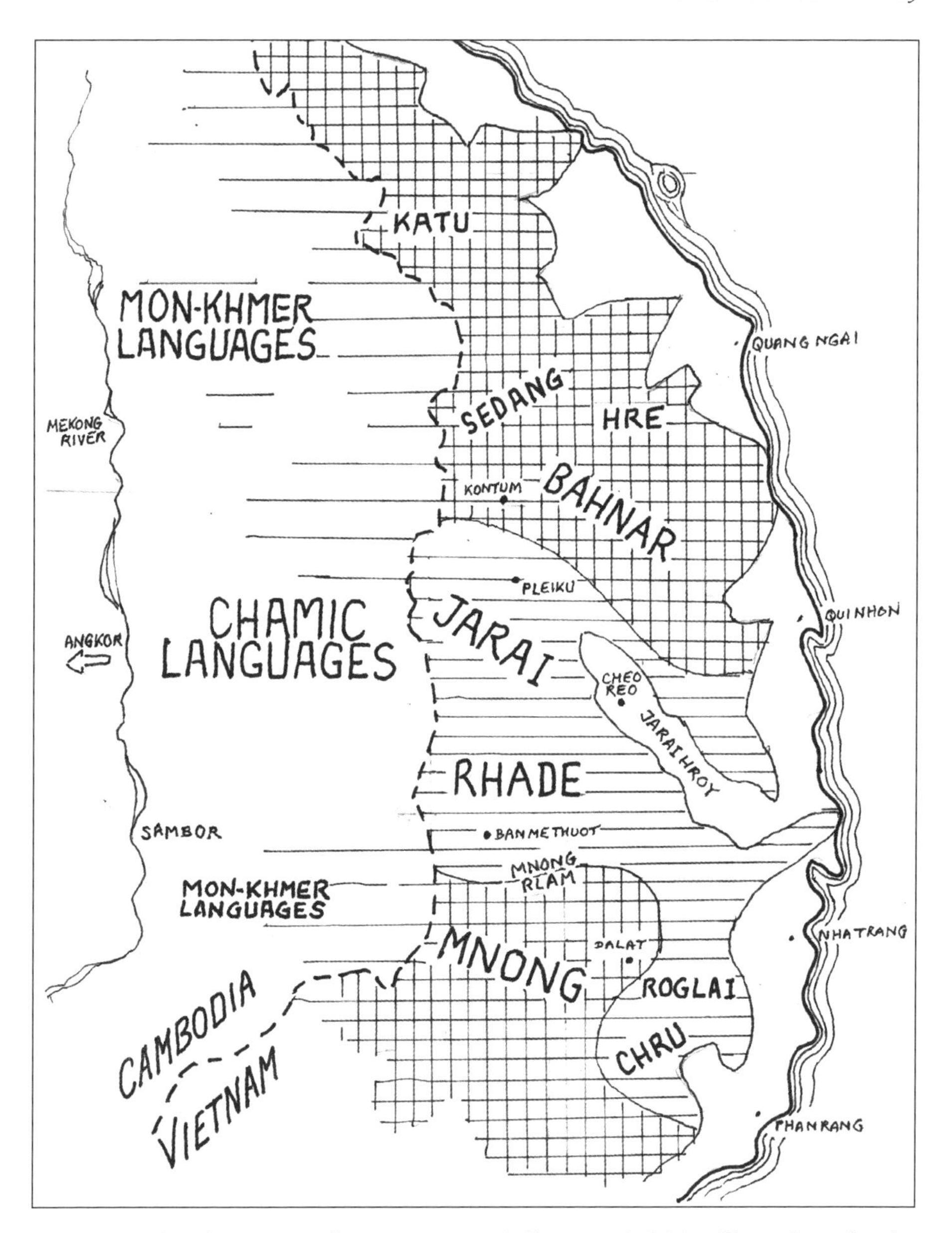

Languages within the two main language groups, 1) Chamic and 2) Mon-Khmer (note that the Chamic languages occupy the Indochina Saddle). (Map by author)

The topography of approaches to the plateau from the east tells us that there were two main routes connecting the coast with the plateau; from there it is less clear, but it appears that a northern branch ran through Jarai territory toward Angkor and that a southern branch ran through Rhadé territory toward one of Anglor's predecessors, Sambor. (See Best Routes map, p. 22) The "Chamicization" of the Jarai and Rhadé must have been related to this, but there is reason to think that it was by cultural diffusion, not conquest.[19]

***

There is nothing subtle about malaria, either the experience of having it,[20] or, in the case of *falciparum* malaria, its death toll. It has always affected choices and lives, even massively, but its historical footprint is indistinct, if not invisible, because, until modern times, death by fever was terribly common and the vector role of mosquitoes was beyond imagining.[21]

To appreciate how severe malaria could be even if not fatal, one has the experience of Father Dourisboure, missionary to the highlands in the 1850s:

> Forest-fever often struck him while travelling, forcing him to stop where he was, far from human help, to wait for the crisis to end or for death ... Once, he and another missionary only had time to confess each other and to give each other extreme unction before falling, one after the other, into a coma.[22]

This awaited *anyone* from the lowlands, not just Westerners.[23]

Malaria in Vietnam is carried by *Anopheles dirus* (pronounced like "virus"), a mosquito that prefers the humid gloom of canopy forest and literally dandles on the forest's breath,[24] swirling like motes in thin shafts of sunlight. Such forest grows only in the wet highlands.[25]

We do not know the exact extent of such forest 500 years ago, though presumably it is much less now than it was then because of human activity. Certainly, there were open expanses, but most Montagnards were farmers of the forest, even if their village was in the open. Entire families would go into the nearest forest for days to cut, burn, then cultivate a field, constantly exposing themselves to malaria. According to a study from early 1950s, three-quarters of the children in the home village of one of the protagonists of this story (Bhan) had active malaria.[26]

Where forest fever lurked was hard to grasp because there were two scenarios: In scenario #1, infectious mosquitoes were everywhere and inescapable, like Bhan's home village or its nearby forests. As a consequence, up to 40 percent of children under the age of five died and the remainder suffered repeated fevers throughout childhood, but then those individuals who made it into adolescence were generally immune and healthy. In scenario #2, in areas where malaria was spotty or intermittent, e.g., where tall, humid forest existed only in copses or where malaria surged only during wet times of the year, no one got enough infectious bites to ever develop complete immunity, thus both adults and children kept getting sick with fever. Areas like this gave malaria its name, forest-fever, though paradoxically areas of forest far worse looked to be healthy and safe.

If malaria's spatial distribution was hard to figure out, it had a temporal trick up its sleeve, too. Because the large parasite is far more capable of confusing our immune system than a virus or bacteria, it takes years to develop immunity to it but as little as *six months* to lose it. In 1864, Dourisboure's superiors in Paris took pity on him and ordered him to spend *seven* months in Saigon. We do not know what happened to him on return to his Kontum mission, but individuals who completely lose their immunity do *worse* when they return to a malarial area.[27] This "you can't go home again" aspect would have been particularly discouraging to voluntary colonization of the highlands by lowlanders.

None of this would have kept them off the plateau entirely, of course. The lure of gold and rubies had been drawing them for millennia.[28] And soldiers could be commanded to take the risk. In the 11th century, Champa and Mekong kingdoms began attacking each other, sending armies across the plateau.[29]

Initially, both Chams and Cambodians would have used Montagnards as guides. No doubt the Montagnards made the most of their secret knowledge. (They would have known the areas where sickness reigned, and they probably had some idea that even healthy-seeming forest could be dangerous to outsiders.) We might expect the lowlanders to have learned over time to thread their own way across the plateau, but apparently this never happened. Over 500 years later, the King of Cambodia was still asking the Jarai, almost plaintively, to "guard well the mountain trails and forests." (See p. 21).

***

To recap, my argument that the Chams never colonized the high plateau is based on its emptiness. A vast area—the upper reaches of the Mekong Basin from Kontum down to M'Drak/Ban Me Thuot—has no sign of permanent structures other than the ruins of one small temple east of Pleiku.[30]

As mentioned previously (p. 10), the idea that fear of malaria kept the Chams off the plateau is supported by where they put their temples in relation to rainfall. (Presumably, areas with the lowest rainfall had little-to-no malarial forest.) A map of annual rainfall shows that the high plateau itself had no such

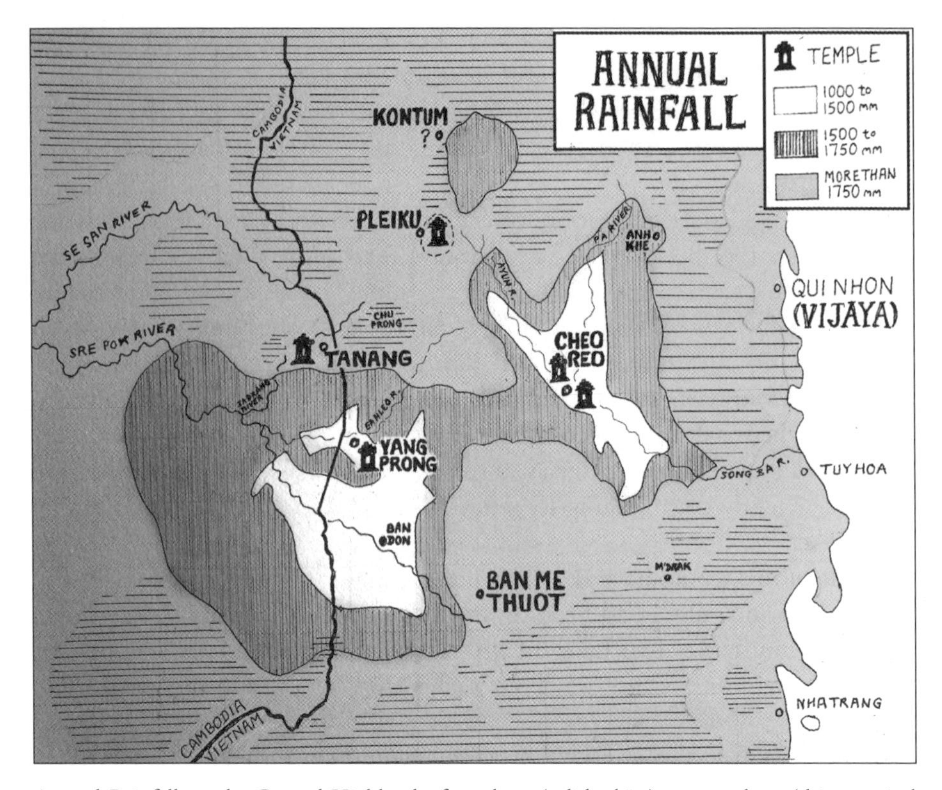

Annual Rainfall on the Central Highlands, from least (solid white), to next least (thin, vertical lines within the dog-shaped silhouette), to moderate-to-heavy (solid gray everywhere else in the highlands).[31]

areas except a narrow band crossing it (the neck of the dog-shaped silhouette), while the flanks of the plateau—the dog's head and body—were relatively dry compared to the entire rest of the Highlands. Three of the temples are clearly in areas of lowest rainfall. A fourth (Ta Nang) appears to be just outside a low rainfall area, but I have been there and suspect that it is in the rain shadow of Chu Pong massif. (Where data is averaged like this, small anomalies do not show up.) The fifth temple, near Pleiku, is located in an area today of prairie-steppe vegetation, possibly an anomaly also—though I suspect that it marks a different sort of settlement than colonization (see p. 201).

The Annual Rainfall map has one other item of interest: the Chams also needed rivers, ideally headwaters, as temple-sites. Two here are downriver on the Ayun, one is on the Ea Hleo, one is on the Ia Drang, and—surprisingly, because at first glance far away—the Pleiku temple is on a tiny northern fork of the Ayun.

***

Anthropologist Gerald Hickey thought that "given the kind of relationships that the Cham had with [the Rhadé and Jarai] over a long period of time, it is curious that they did not have a greater impact," adding that, "in many respects the Cham presence in the highlands seems to have been as ephemeral as the morning fog."[32]

If the Cham never successfully colonized the plateau, then it is likely the spread of Cham culture and language occurred largely through voluntary adoption and imitation—with the ancestors of the Jarai and Rhadé coming down off the plateau for short periods to trade their forest products with the Cham at malaria-free entrepots where they learned to speak Cham and adopted Cham customs. These traders became an elite, who were then increasingly imitated by others back home.[33]

The most likely entrepot was Cheo Reo, in Jarai country.

***

The Cheo Reo valley is a liminal place.

It is a topographical threshold. Fanning out from the upper end of a long, gently inclined corridor from the coast, it lies only 150 meters below the lip of the high plateau. Two routes from the coast converge here then separate again to climb into the highlands (see map on p. 22).[34]

Shiva at the Danang Museum. (Alamy Images)

The valley's semi-aridity is due to being in the partial rain shadow of both annual monsoons. If it indeed was malaria-free in the past, it was an epidemiologic threshold to the highlands, too.

And it feels to be a threshold of memory. In the harsh light of post-communist, uber-capitalist Vietnam, a lingering sense of the valley's past, of what once was, is about to vanish like a dream. The process began in the 1930s, when the French effectively erased all Cham artefacts there, removing statuary and tearing down two temples for their brick, one to build a guard post. (Fortunately, a few of the statues ended up in museums, like the magnificent 700-year-old Shiva on the preceding page.)

The process went to warp speed during three decades of war, when a cacophony of urgent voices proclaiming a better future through Marx, Jesus, or the American Way drowned out old men talking of the past, and war's tyranny of the here-and-now stood tradition on its head. Today, the valley is one large Vietnamese truck farm. The Jarai still live in their own communities, recognizable by houses on stilts, but have been largely assimilated. Their one remaining distinction from the Vietnamese is ironically a cultural import, a stubborn evangelical Christianity.

Even the echoes have died. No Jarai clan still cremates its dead or obeys the cow taboo, vestiges of Brahmanism via the Chams. Legends of Cham presence in Cheo Reo exist mainly on paper now, in musty French archives. The site of the dismantled temple may still be sacred to a few aging Jarai but for most now, it is the scar of a forgotten wound.[35]

Nonetheless, a vision of Cheo Reo's past can be conjured—from topography and epidemiology, and indirectly from written sources, beginning with Chinese imperial archives and epigraphy on Cham ruins.

Around 1280, Kublai Khan, in the process of consolidating Mongol rule over China, demanded his predecessor's vassals, rulers of neighboring countries, present themselves in person at his court to deliver tribute. The aging king of Champa balked at the 2,000-mile journey and stalled. His son, Harijit, was openly hostile. Kublai Khan ordered a punitive expedition.

In 1283, hundreds of Chinese junks disembarked troops near Vijaya (today's Qui Nhon), who were met by thousands of Cham. The battle lasted six hours. Eroded Sanscrit writing on stone brings it alive: soldiers marching to the cadence of conches, followed by a corps of war elephants, "often a thousand head," "battlefields darkened by the dust thrown up by horses in their haughty trot, by their rapid and hard hooves," "fields … blood-red like the *ashoka* flower," "shattered by the noise of bowstrings vibrating from both armies," and by "the rumble of war drums and the trumpeting of gigantic elephants."[36] Cham soldiers fought as teams of five. If one fled, the other four were punishable by death. Sometimes, the five tied themselves together.[37]

But the Chinese prevailed.[38] The Cham king and his son, Harijit, withdrew to the mountains, where they were beyond reach. For this to succeed, they would have needed the loyalty and secrecy of Montagnards.

Foreshadowing the French and American experience seven centuries later, the Chinese were disastrously ambushed whenever they entered the forest (a Montagnard art),[39] so they created palisaded camps and brought in more troops and weapons and supplies from China. This failed.

Chinese annals record that the country had "a damp climate, [was] swampy and … rich in miasmas and epidemics."[40] Chinese desertions mounted. Replacements were "prisoners, the worst assassins, parricides, and others."[41] Officers were transferred to the Champa front as punishment. Stalemated, Kublai Khan tried to send an army overland through Vietnam, but the Vietnamese emperor beat it back, conscious that a Chinese victory over Champa to his south would put him in pincers.

Kublai Khan finally called off his Champa campaign in 1285. Harijit came down from the mountains to rule Vijaya for another 22 years.

We can guess where he and his father had taken refuge, because in his dotage Harijit ordered construction of Yang Prong temple, like Ta Nang, on the dry western flank—see map on p.16.

***

Traders crossed the plateau in both directions, eastward from Angkor and Sambor as well as westward from Cheo Reo (see maps on pp. 13 and 22). While more factors than simply rainfall and vegetation (e.g., rivers) must have played a role in determining routes, it seems clear from the rainfall map that at least one route connected Sambor to Cheo Reo via Yang Prong and that another route connected Angkor to Cheo Reo via Ta Nang.

Ta Nang only recently became known to the outside world (around 2010?). The first Westerners to see it may well have been a six-man American recon team in 1967 whose mission was to locate concentrations of the enemy without being seen, then withdraw and call in an airstrike. They paid the temple little heed; most likely it was covered by undergrowth.[42] Today it has been reverently cleared by local Jarai. Its tiered roof has crumbled, but the *lingam*, symbol of the life force, is crisp (photo, p. 21). According to one recent estimate, Ta Nang was built in a Cham style of the *ninth* century, or 1200 years ago.[43] More conservatively—it may be one of the way-stations mentioned by Chinese diplomat Zhou Daguan in the early 14th century, thus be as little as 700 years old.[44] In either case, its edges seem way too sharp to be that ancient— until we remember that the Chams probably chose its site because there was so little rain.

Like milestones on forgotten roads, the two temples point toward Cheo Reo.

We also have early accounts by Westerners that mention Cheo Reo by another name, Ayunapar—for its two rivers, the Ayun and Apa—as the rumored location of two fabled Jarai kings, the King of Fire and the King of Water.

Yang Prong Temple. (Alamy Images)

Westerners first heard of the kings in 1663 from Guiseppe Filippo de Marini, a Jesuit missionary to the Vietnamese court. Their names alone sparked the imagination. In Europe, they might have joined Prester John in creating yearning for the Orient had they not been known to be pagan.[45] In Southeast Asia, they were widely believed to have catastrophic powers of lightning, fire, and flood. Their inaccessibility was part of their aura.

For centuries, the plateau was a world apart. On the east was a scarp and malaria. On the west was malaria, too, but to the north and to the south. The middle was open, a long, dry stretch of savannah forest. Early European maps, compiled from hearsay, label the western approach with "SOLITUDE and DESERT, without water, without anything of life."[46] Despite being only 200 kilometers (125 miles) across, with an ancient track that allowed ox carts most of the way, the traverse was said to take three months. Something else was at play here, a mix of dreads perhaps, of what lay beyond—deadly fever and, according to those early maps, wild barbarians—and of that SOLITUDE itself. Even today the forest is uncanny, like an empty pillared hall in every direction. It is so still that one expects the broom grass to turn to ash on walking through it.

Ta Nang Temple. (Photo by author)

A Cambodian document from 1601 describes an ancient exchange of tribute between the King of Cambodia and the Kings of Fire and Water, every three years across this wasteland. The ritual is dressed up as relations with a vassal. However, in exchange for a caravan's worth of precious goods, the lowland monarch received a hunk of beeswax in return, with the King of Fire's fingerprints. Its charter, an exhortation to the Jarai to "guard well the mountain trails and forests," sounds more like a request/bribe to an ally.

By the end of the 19th century, however, the plateau had been penetrated enough—by Thai slave traders, Vietnamese conmen, and other frontier riff-raff—that the truth was out that the "kings" were spiritual leaders only, shamans-in-chief, and not political ones. They had even been seen tilling their own fields for a living.

The first European to meet one of them, French Captain P. Cupet in 1891, knew this but had read about them as a boy. He was bound to be disappointed, and he was. "Nothing distinguishes [the King of Fire] from the other savages."

He did not like the Jarai, who openly threatened him. He correctly called them the terror of their neighbors. He was surprised that, despite being

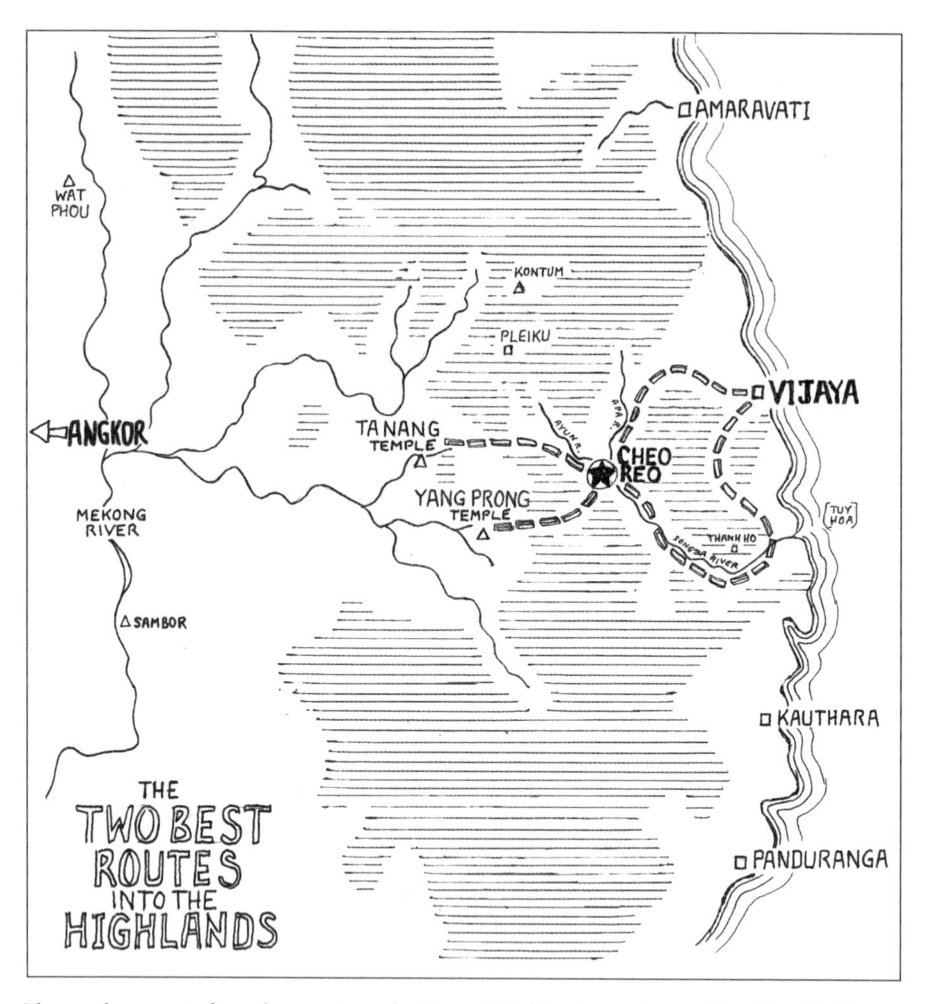

The two best routes from the coast into the Central Highlands, crossing at Cheo Reo (Ta Nang is the small temple, Yang Prong is the large one). (Map by author)

"savages," they had figured out the French were trying to block the Laotians and Thais from claiming the western slope of the plateau. He added that, "until now," they had never submitted to any power, never paid any tribute. The words of one warrior, whom he quoted at length, could have come from a North American Comanche:

> We did not call you here. We count more on our lances, our bows and our poisoned arrows than on you [to hold off] the Laotians. We are more numerous than they are, we know how to set up ambushes in the forest and, if they come, not one will return to Laos.

Cupet saw none of this as admirable. His attitude toward highlanders in general was largely negative, a glass half empty. Like the French missionaries at Kontum from whom he got much of his ethnographic detail,[47] he regarded them as slaves to superstition and fear. In his eyes, even their "thirst for independence" and dislike of authority was a fault, responsible for an ugly fractiousness.

He concluded:

> When I hear that [civilization] only brings obstacles to freedom, I think about these poor people whom one assumes to be free because they do not obey anybody, but whose entire life is threatened and whose every act is enclosed in a narrow circle of fears, prejudices, and superstitions ... One thing is certain, if I ever had the slightest desire to become an anarchist, I would have come back [from my expeditions] totally cured of it.[48]

Our ears are deaf to this, but contemporary readers would have caught it: Cupet was using the highlanders to make a point in the nascent left–right debate of his day, one that, in different forms, is still with us.

Plus ça change, plus c'est la même chose.

There is another way of looking at this.

***

The Art of Not Being Governed, by anthropologist James C. Scott, is a marvelous book—so daring and original that it invites pot-shots, but its larger ideas feel intuitively true.[49]

Scott theorizes that many aspects of the cultures of Southeast Asian highlanders were adaptations to avoid being governed, which in turn came from their having fled over the millennia from the ills of lowland civilization like conscription, forced labor, and taxes, or—more resonant now perhaps—bad rulers, epidemics, and economic collapse. (I use the past tense because Scott insisted his theory only applied up to 1950.)

Their zones of refuge were protected by physical difficulty of access. In the case of the highlanders, it was altitude and rugged topography.

Their cultures repelled the State in two ways, either by escaping the grasp of its tax collectors, press gangs, and slavers, or by preventing a State from arising in their midst.

Scott is most thought provoking in explaining the escape aspects. Swiddening (aka, slash and burn) was "escape agriculture." Crops grown in evanescent forest clearings, especially if root crops, were invisible and unpredictable to tax collectors, the exact opposite of paddy rice, which concentrated crop and people in one spot at the same times every year, all the better to be exploited by greedy rulers. (For anyone who has ever worked for a boss too interested in "productivity," this book is a pleasure to read. One can transpose the imagined squeals of frustration from the palace to the executive suite.)

The highlanders' dislike of authority noted by Cupet was a social adaptation to keep their own society from turning into a State. This had an escape function, too. Having no permanent headmen meant outside powers could find no one to suborn or coerce.

Scott's anti-State, anti-lowlander thesis was immediately seen by some to threaten Hanoi's efforts to establish a harmonious, multi-ethnic state, and the knives came out. One critic felt only a bourgeois white man could have written it. Another well-known Marxist scholar dismissed it as "romantic."[50]

That said, Scott does not mention malaria, which I suspect was a barrier so complete that it kept the flow of escapees to a trickle. With no boluses, much less waves, of immigrants from the lowlands, highland culture would have remained relatively static and homogenous for centuries.[51] If I am right, the malaria-barrier calls into question Scott's idea that direct exaction/taxation of crops by lowlanders was a threat. It seems more likely the highlanders practiced swidden farming because it produced a better nutritional bang-for-the-labor-buck than traditional farming.[52]

Instead, the main threat would have been from within, from highlanders themselves becoming middlemen to lowlanders and serving as a tax farmers or slavers. As a cultural adaptation against this, egalitarianism, beyond keeping everyone's head down, would have enforced group solidarity.

The threat of sellout, as well as of physical invasion, would have been greatest where highlanders met with lowlanders for trade—Cheo Reo, which happens to be the location of the Kings of Fire and Water.[53] We can wonder if the kings were cultural adaptations to reduce both threats, but particularly the threat of rogue behavior. In a rigidly egalitarian society, external controls could not arise. The only check on individual behavior had to be internal—conscience, fear, or both.

Perhaps it was exactly because the kings were so ordinary, one of the people, that their potential powers as guardians of social order were so frightening. Perhaps images of lightning bolts from the fingertips of one of your own were the next best thing to an inner voice.

Notes

1 Charles B. Darnell Jr., whom I knew personally from serving with him in 1967 in Project Omega, was the source of most of the rebellion info. Telephone interview, January 18, 2016. Most of the rest of the information came, if not otherwise noted, from Steve Sherman, dedicated historian of the US Army Special Forces, in telephone interviews from 2010 to 2023.

2 This was Howard Sochurek, in his "American Special Forces in Action in Vietnam." *National Geographic*, January 1965, Vol. 127, No. 1: 38–65.

3 Two much smaller groups also speak a Chamic language, the Chru and Roglai. See map on p. 13.

4 Tracy Atwood, interview with author, January 28, 2014.

5 A sixth Montagnard force, at Buon Enao just outside Ban Me Thuot, was kept from participating in the revolt by the failure of a prearranged signal of three mortar rounds. (Petersen, (1988): 77).

6 John E. Fischer interview with author, March 15, 2015.

7 A patrol from Buon Brieng heard brief but loud explosions and firing to their west the night of September 19/20. On return to camp hours later, the patrol leader fired long-range mortar rounds at the suspected site and later was told by Montagnards he had hit a Viet Cong assembly area. This does not really make sense, however. Like much real-time intelligence, it is fileable under "fog of war." Robert W. Jones Jr., "A Team Effort: The Montagnard Uprising of September 1964," *Veritas* 3 (2007).

8 His full name was Y-Dhon Adrong, with the prefix "Y" indicating a male Rhadé. Because another protagonist is named Y-Bhan Kpor, easily confused with Y-Bham Enuol, I use the full name only for the latter.

9 The question as to whether Y-Bham Enuol went willingly to Cambodia or was kidnapped by the militants used to be of great import. Darnell's testimony, plus the content of documents we will discuss later, suggest it was completely voluntary. However, there is no evidence either way as to his thoughts about the killing that had just taken place.

10 First notice was a squib on page 8 of the September 21 *New York Times* about Montagnards raiding Ban Me Thuot but, from September 24 through 28, the rebellion at Bon Sar Pa occupied a spot on the *Times*' lower front page. Once the rebellion was over, coverage switched to the harm it was doing to US–South Vietnamese relations.

11 *Service de Documentation Extérieure et de Contre-Espionnage* (External Documentation and Counter-Espionage Service)—France's version of the CIA but even more "muscular," to use Douglas Porch's term, meaning given to covert action.

12 Barry Peterson, *Tiger Men: A Young Australian Soldier Among the Rhade Montagnards of Vietnam* (Bangkok: Orchid Press Publishing Ltd, 1994), 94. They had been seen leaving Ban Me Thuot in an old Peugeot driven by "Cambodians." The car was later found abandoned near the private airstrip of Mewal plantation, run by a Corsican associated with the French secret service.

13 For simplicity, I refer to a single plateau. Geologically, there are three, Kontum, Pleiku, and Darlac, all basaltic, relatively flat, tilted toward the Mekong. Darlac in the south (Rhadé country) is largest and lowest, then Pleiku in the middle (Jarai country) is slightly smaller and higher, with Kontum (Bahnar country) an extension off the north of Pleiku plateau. (Politically, the corresponding names today are Kontum, Gia Lai, and Dak Lak.) What I call the Indochina Saddle—self-explanatory—is Darlac plus the lower hslf of Pleiku. Total habitable area of the plateaus is difficult to ascertain but probably around 20,000 square kilometers. (Schmid, *Végétation du Vietnam*, 34, 43.)

14 Schmid, *Végétation du Vietnam,* p. 19. This temple, 10 kilometers (6 miles) east of Pleiku, was two piles of bricks when Parmentier and Dournes saw it (*Inventaire Descriptif* (1909), Vol I, 558 and *Potao* (1977), 95), but archeologists now think it was a small Cham temple (Travel Tourism News online February 25, 2022). https://dulichvn.org.vn/index.php/item/thap-rong-yang-gia-lai-phe-tich-cham-o-pho-nui-49185. Accessed December 2024. (Thanks to Kon Ngok for finding this.) It is <3 kilometers from the headwaters of the Ayun.

15 Maspero, Georges. *The Champa Kingdom.* Translated by Walter E. J. Tips. Bangkok: White Lotus Press, 2002, 141. Meaning below the Tropic of Cancer, which is at 23° N. There, the sun stands directly overhead on June 21st. In lands below that, sunlight comes from the north at least part of the year. The Chinese were fascinated that house entrances in those lands could face north instead of south.

16 By comparing the matrilineal and patrilineal DNA of today's coastal Cham, we know that both the Malay and the Indian input was from men only, i.e., raiders, traders, priests, prospectors—*not* immigrants with wives and daughters. Peng, M-S., et al. (2010), and He, J-D., et al., (2012).

17 Eaglewood production peaked after the Vietnam War, for unknown reasons. (Interview with Thibault Ledeq, Director, SE Asia Forestry Program, World Wildlife Fund Cambodia, April 20, 2015.) More projectile wounds? Or lots of industrious Vietnamese living for months/years in the high mountain forests?

18 The Jarai word for sunset implies descent into the sea, but the nearest sea is 100 kilometers to their *east.* (Nakamura (1999), 21).

19 The Jarai appear to have been more Chamicized than the Rhadé. The process likely started earlier in the north because Vijaya (and Indrapura?) were dominant earlier than Panduranga. Also, as I elaborate below, Cheo Reo was an ideal entrepôt. I suspect that more southern routes to the plateau from the coast, e.g., via M'Drak, played a later role in the Chamicization of the Rhadé but I was unable to travel those myself the way I did the Cheo Reo–Song Ba route.

20 Some years ago, after working for several weeks in the clinic of a small Guatemalan town, I thought to ask why I was not seeing any patients with acute malaria. "Because," I was told, "they're too sick to get out of bed." (Note that Guatemala's form of malaria is considerably milder than *falciparum.*)

21 The ancients did make a connection between swamps and air, at least, as we will see below with the Chinese. The name "mal-aria" comes from Italian for evil air.

22 Father Pierre Dourisboure (1825–90), https://irfa.paris/missionnaire/0591-dourisboure-pierre/. The quote is from the original archives at http://archives.mepasie.org/fr/notices/notices-biographiques/dourisboure. Accessed June 2015.

23 Over the last half of the 19th century, quinine—initially called "Jesuit bark" after those who first brought it back from Peru—enabled the scrabbling roots of empire to gain increasingly deeper hold in soft, steaming lands worldwide, condemning them to near destruction when those roots were finally ripped out.

24 The trees' transpiration humidifies the air and their shade lowers temperature, increasing precipitation.

25 M. W. McLeod, "Indigenous Peoples and the Vietnamese Revolution, 1930–1975," *Journal of World History,* 10 (1999): 2, 357–58, mentions malaria in this context but misconstrues why it is highland malaria, attributing that fact to fast-flowing streams (as opposed to stagnant pools in the lowlands). It is the opposite. In the mosquito's larval stage, the larva hangs from water's surface to breathe. Much like a snorkeler, rough water drowns it. *Anopheles dirus* finds still water in highland forests in hollows in trees.

26 M. E. Farinaud, "The Use of Anti-Malarial Drugs as Adjuvants to DDT in Malaria Control in Vietnam," paper presented at the WHO Malaria Conference for the Western Pacific and

SE Asia Regions, Taipei, WHO/MAL/106, 1954. The village was Buon Ea Ktur, southeast of Ban Me Thuot, which, we will see at the very end of this book, is still playing a role in this story.

27 One of this book's protagonists, Bhan, raised in the village mentioned above, spent his mid-twenties as an army officer in the lowlands before returning to the highlands, where he had an episode of cerebral malaria that almost killed him. He claims he awoke from a coma in a blanket, about to be carted off for burial.

28 Maspero, *The Champa Kingdom*, 137. The Cham knew how to divert rivers to look for gold. Rattanakiri, a Cambodian province, means "Mountain of Precious Stones." Today, men still dig pits there resembling 12-foot-deep foxholes to mine for zircons. However, in the context of whether Champa colonized the highlands, it should be noted that the current mining area is on the plateau's *flank*.

29 In 1074, Champa's armies seized Sambor on the Mekong, presumably by traveling west overland. In 1147, Khmer armies came east to seize Vijaya, Champa's northern capital (near Qui Nhon). In 1176, the Chams tried to cross west with chariots but failed. In 1177, seeing the light and being more comfortable on water anyway, the Chams took boats down the coast, up the Mekong and onto Cambodia's great inland lake, to sack Angkor.

30 Kontum has some "ruins" that indicate a one-time Cham presence but are too insignificant to suggest colonization. Even if one believes that there was once a temple there, Kontum, too, is a comparatively low rainfall area.

31 The Annual Rainfall map is adapted from the map, "*Precipitation annuelles*" on p. 16 of Schmid, *Végétation du Vietnam.* Only the Cheo Reo region merits the designation "semi-arid" (map named "*Climats*" on Schmid's, p. 24).

32 Hickey, *Sons of the Mountains* (1982a), 120. He was speaking culturally, but, in my opinion, this is true archeologically as well.

33 Over the centuries some military outposts or, as we will see below, places of royal refuge, might have become permanent enough for a generation of Cham to be born in the Highlands, thus becoming immune. These children—most likely born of Rhadé or Jarai mothers—could not journey to the lowlands and return, thus would eventually have become "Cham highlanders." Whether this contributed significantly to the Chamicization of the Rhadé and Jarai could be determined by population genetic studies. These are politically impossible in today's Vietnam, but many individuals of 100 percent Rhadé and Jarai blood still exist today in North Carolina.

34 Another route ran from the earliest Cham kingdom in the north, Indrapura (today's Hoi An), to Kontum and down thru Pleiku, then westward. I know the terrain personally, and it must have been worse than the high plateau in terms of malarial forest.

35 Hip Ksor, interview with author, August 15, 2013.

36 Maspero, *The Champa Kingdom*, 17, 49, 55. This is a composite picture, from other battles too, to try to get a feel for, especially, the noise.

37 Ibid., 17, 135.

38 Ibid., 158. War elephants were less effective than one might imagine. Despite shielding, their mahouts were exposed to arrows. Defenders dug narrow, deep pits camouflaged with grass—leg traps—that could wreak havoc with the adrenalized beasts. Also from Michel Jacq-Hergoualc'h, "L'Armee du Campa au Début du XIIIe Siècle," in *Le Campa et le Monde Malai: Actes de la Conférence Internationale Organisée à l'Université de Californie 30–31 Août 1990* (1991).

39 Ibid., 200.

40 Ibid., 25.

41 Ibid., 85.

42 Fred Lindsey, *Secret Green Beret Commandos in Cambodia* (Bloomington: AuthorHouse, 2012), 111.
43 Heng, *Landscape, upland-lowland, community"* (2022), p 16. (Thank you to Catherine Scheer for finding this.)
44 Bourotte, *Essai d'histoire*, 27.
45 Unwittingly, I must have first read about them as a restless 18-year-old freshman in my college library stacks, where I devoured Sir George Frazer's 1890 *The Golden Bough*, a book that fed my hunger to drop out. At the time of Frazer's writing, they still had not been seen by a Westerner.
46 Harold E. Meinheit, "Captain Cupet and the King of Fire: Mapping and Minorities in Vietnam's Central Highlands," *The Portolan*, Fall issue (2012). "*SOLITUDE et DESERT*," in French, is derived from the Latin *solitudo* on Portuguese maps, said to mean "wilderness." That seems a prosaic translation. I wonder if "God forsaken" might not be better, capturing more of the existential horror we once felt, and can still feel, in the presence of too much nature.
47 Most of it, we can guess, from his exact contemporary and friend, the warrior-priest J-B Guerlach, who once led 1,200 Bahnar in battle against the Jarai. Guerlach was a type whose own total immersion in an alien culture and willingness to share their knowledge enabled passers-by to do good or ill. In Guerlach's case, his reputation suffered when he endorsed one adventurer too many, the Baron de Mayrena, who declared himself King of the Sedang. Mayrena might have gotten away with it—creating a country of his own, even issuing postage stamps—but when he declared it an officially Catholic country, this raised the ire of anti-clericals back in France, spelling his doom and almost bringing Guerlach down with him.
48 P. Cupet, *Among the Tribes of Southern Vietnam and Laos*, translated by Walter E. J. Tips (Bangkok: White Lotus Press, 1998), p. 48 for "Nothing distinguishes the King of Fire", p. xi for "We did not call you here", and p. 140 for anarchism.
49 James C. Scott, *The Art of Not Being Governed*, (Yale University Press, New Haven, CT, 2009).
50 The "romantic" comment was from Michael Vickery, I can no longer find the other source, the "critic."
51 That is, until the last half of the 19th century when sudden growth in the slave trade seems to have penetrated the malaria barrier and begun to degrade highlander society.
52 Victor Lieberman, "A Zone of Refuge in Southeast Asia? Reconceptualizing Interior Spaces," *Journal of Global History*, 5 (2010): 333–46.
53 There was a third king as well, less important, the King of Air. They were only missing a King of Earth to be intriguingly Aristotelian.

CHAPTER 2

Y-Bham Enuol

Born circa 1920, Y-Bham Enuol was the oldest of this story's protagonists, old enough to have heard talk around the hearth about the time before the French and before the Vietnamese when Montagnards still ruled the highlands. For his ethnic group, the Rhadé, this had come to an end around the turn of the century when they "submitted" to the French, but the Rhadés' neighbors to the south, the Mnong, were still fighting, still *insoumis* (unpacified).

He must have heard too about the Mnongs killing Henri Maître, less than a decade before he was born.

***

In late July 1914, as war ignited Europe and *La Belle Epoque* collapsed in incandescent ash, a young Frenchman named Henri Maître was about to die for his country on the far side of the world.

French colonial official, explorer, and one of the first ethnographers of the highlanders, Maître was responding to tribal unrest among the Mnong, inhabitants of the forests of eastern Cambodia.[1] A rebellious band had communicated its willingness to give up. He had come with native soldiers to accept their submission and had found the tall jars of rice wine waiting, gongs sounding another drunken celebration of stasis. To refuse to drink was out of the question, worse than openly refusing to shake hands in Western culture. As always, he had to consume three horns' full, every swallow watched.

Perhaps the jars had extra-potent mash. By the time the band's chief suggested consecrating everyone's weapons with pig's blood, it must have seemed a most reasonable suggestion. Maître handed over his pistol, his men their carbines.

One native soldier escaped. Everyone else got speared. By one account, Maître's head was cut off. By another, not necessarily a contradiction, his murderers buried him with gentle respect, a kapok pillow beneath his head, from which a large kapok tree grew—which he would have identified as *Bombax malabaricum.* It is said to be there today.

To his killers, he personified invasion. Highlanders had no problem swearing oaths of submission, even letting foreigners pass through their territory. But the Mnong could not tolerate signs of settlement like the French penetration trails or, worse, the small post Maître had established.[2]

Exactly 50 years later and 6 kilometers (~4 miles) away, the Mnong rose murderously again, this time alongside the Rhadé, to forestall a different invasion.

***

At the time of Y-Bham Enuol's birth, another Frenchman was having a very different effect on the Rhadé, 80 kilometers (50 miles) to the north in a small town central to this story, Ban Me Thuot.

From a lower-class background, Leopold Sabatier had paid his own way to Indochina, toiled in the ranks of the colonial administration, then grabbed a chance to be on his own at a remote post in the highlands. Like other administrators, Sabatier saw the highlanders as children needing protection from harmful outsiders, but, unlike the others, he had some respect for their culture, learned to speak Rhadé, and believed the outsiders to be fended off included not just the Vietnamese but his fellow Frenchmen, planters and priests alike.

Creating his own small protectorate, he instituted an early village health-worker program, enlisted young warriors in a militia, and, most importantly for this story, started a primary school in 1915 for highlanders, most of whom were boarders. Instruction was in French until Sabatier and a dedicated young teacher named Antomarchi devised an alphabet for Rhadé; then instruction was given in both languages. Seven decades later, an aging highlander remembered that the school principal, who by 1941 was a Rhadé, would regularly exhort the students in assembly to "preserve their characters"—a reference to four letters/sounds unique to the Rhadé language—meaning to keep and defend their culture.[3]

Sabatier lived his dream for 13 years, then lost it in 1926, pushed out because the automobile and World War I had driven up the price of rubber, rendering the plateau's red earth, and its easily gulled workforce, too valuable to let languish in one prickly dreamer's preserve.[4]

***

The fact that Y-Bham Enuol was more than a decade older than the other protagonists was a fateful distinction, leading to his becoming the highlanders' Mandela. If he did not exactly arise out of the mist, his early years are little known.

He started Sabatier's school at age 15, in 1935, possibly attending bible school at some point with American evangelicals.

Both his late start in school and his sampling of Protestantism may have been due to the same phenomenon, highlander dismay at the arrival of rapacious French colonists after Sabatier's removal in 1926. For parents, sending their children to be stripped of their culture could not have been easy in any case; now they had reason to mistrust the French. Hundreds of students dropped out between 1926 and 1930, possibly greater numbers failed to enroll. In 1934, newly arrived American missionaries would have looked good by comparison, though Y-Bham Enuol's schooling with them was likely brief.[5] It can only be speculation but the tension about whether, and where, to start school anticipated the central challenges of Y-Bham Enuol's life—how to reconcile the traditional and the modern, and whether to trust the French or the Americans.

Education was a *sine qua non* for FULRO to arise. All five Montagnard protagonists of this story attended the Ban Me Thuot school or the middle school that grew out of it. For all of them, education was that most achingly hopeful gift but, for each of them personally, it was like a dagger turned inward.

Y-Bham Enuol thrived at school and was one of the first highlanders to seek education beyond 6th grade.[6] In 1941, this meant traveling 200 miles to attend the only middle school open to highlanders, at Qui Nhon on the coast. (Old men in North Carolina today, Montagnard refugees, say "Y-Bham Enuol was the first" as though that explains everything.) In 1943, he went north to an agricultural college outside Hanoi. He was due to attend *L'Ecole Superieur* in Hanoi the next year, but the Japanese coup in March 1945 (see below) forced him to return to Ban Me Thuot.[7]

***

A few highlanders like Y-Bham Enuol felt the benefits of French colonialism. Many more felt its growing oppression, especially its labor tax, the *corvée*. This was intended to be relatively benign, only 15 days' work per year on public projects, but, unsurprisingly, it got prolonged and/or privatized. For a people unused to hierarchy, the word "coolie" entered their vocabulary as anathema, *kuli*.[8] Some of the work they did, such as building "penetration roads" into their highlands, must have felt an existential threat.

As had happened often before in threatening times, in 1937, a prophet arose.

First inkling that something strange was going on was a sudden scarcity of small bronze coins called *sous*. Next, fields were empty, even though it was the time of early rains, planting season. Entire villages in the region of Cheo Reo shut themselves within bramble-thicket palisades. Word was that a Jarai man was selling magic rice and water for a *sou*. Only four grains of rice, one planted in each corner of a field, would produce a miracle crop without work. The water would protect its owner during a coming cataclysm.

The Python God had returned.

Believing the water would also protect them from bullets, people were refusing to do their 15 days' labor. If they owned any animals that were white, they were sacrificing them. The latter made the French nervous, a seeming metaphor (though, much later, it was pointed out that highlanders do not see Caucasians as white but simply pale, like corpses).[9] Word spread hundreds of miles. At the periphery of French control, there were attacks on militia posts, and one patrol was never seen again.

The French investigated. The man behind it all was an elderly Jarai named Sambram whose daughter was said to have given birth to a python. The Python God now spoke through Sambram and prophesied that, someday soon, on a brilliant morning when three suns rose after a very long, very dark night, a typhoon would boil up from the Eastern Sea and sweep away all foreigners—French, Lao, and Vietnamese alike—leaving highlanders who possessed the water to live life unmolested again.

The French already knew Sambram as a respected go-between with his people. Raised in a village near the coast, he was probably Jarai Hroi (see map on p. 13, small print near the center), a group of very Chamized Jarai. He spoke Vietnamese in addition to French. He wore Western clothes and, even more remarkably, built his house on the ground (Vietnamese-style, not on pilings). And he had a beard (unusual for a highlander, and with some mythic resonance).

This was a millenarian movement, presumably sprung from a vague, communal feeling of doom. Like many leaders of such movements, Sambram was relatively educated, multi-lingual, and comfortable in several worlds, yet his movement was rooted in his followers' deepest, most-ancient beliefs (indeed, it is hard to imagine a god more primordial than the python). He represented rescue. His total package—magic water/rice, obedience to his proscriptions and prescriptions—promised a way back to a Golden Age.

The French Bishop of Kontum was scathing (and cringe inducing) in his disdain. In a pamphlet entitled, "The Hatching of a New God," he said, "Don't laugh too much, yes, a new god is born there, among the natives."[10]

The secular authorities simply took Sambram away. The highlander version of what happened to him next included repeated miraculous jailbreaks, but no one knew his ultimate fate (which is a common end for messiahs). However, a Jarai in North Carolina today, thoroughly Americanized and modern, has distinct memories from 1949 or 1950 (when he was three or four years old) of Sambram arriving in his village, mounted on a white horse. He had a long white beard, which he combed before washing his face with water from a bowl. Then he poured the remaining water on the little boy's head, saying "You will be a king like me!" Another Jarai in North Carolina corroborates that Sambram was still active as late as 1953.[11]

In 1973, I visited Cheo Reo and asked about Sambram. I received a slightly different story from the one mentioned above:[12] there were two pythons born, both appearing to Sambram as young men who literally glowed—one a Jarai and one Vietnamese—telling him that together they would create the New Human. This may echo communist themes, of harmony between highlander and lowlander and of New Socialist Man. If so, it would not be a total surprise. The Cheo Reo region was shared by both sides in relative peace for the entire war.

***

On March 9, 1945, the Japanese took sudden, full control of Indochina in a coup, capturing French colonial troops and in some cases executing them.[13] There could not be a more poignant metaphor for the lives of Montagnards of my generation than the memory of one aging refugee in North Carolina today of half-tracks and equipment discarded on the road where French soldiers had fled into the jungle, and, at age three, his picking up shiny cartridges and, in imitation of his peasant-farmer parents, planting them like seeds.[14]

Despite the coup, Japan was clearly going to lose the war. Anti-colonial Vietnamese in the lowlands began preparing to take back control of their country when that happened, knowing they would have to prevent a French return. Many of these were pure nationalists, but their core was communist. These were the Viet Minh.

Originally, the few Viet Minh in the Central Highlands were all Vietnamese but, in early 1945, the Viet Minh started organizing Montagnards.[15] In the vacuum following the Japanese defeat in August, they set up Montagnard administrative committees in the main towns (Ban Me Thuot, Pleiku, and Kontum) and prepared to resist the French. This included drilling teenage highlanders with sticks as rifles.[16]

In September 1945, when Ho Chi Minh took power from the Japanese, Y-Bham Enuol was in North Vietnam. Heading back down to Ban Me Thuot, he spent the next three months working as a functionary for the Viet Minh. Years later, he implied that the Viet Minh had forced him to do this after jailing him for a week, but there is no reason to believe that he did not do so voluntarily, as affected by the euphoria of the time as any other thinking/feeling 25-year-old.[17]

As expected, in December 1945, the French returned in force to the highlands to retake their lost colony. Remarkably, despite having armored vehicles and being veterans of war in Europe, they were almost beaten back.

The memoirs of a French combatant describe his column's slow climb into the highlands, halted again and again by road traps and blown bridges, then three ambushes, one "in depth" with enemy firing murderously and unseen from the jungle on either side of the road. Resistance was fierce. Though he took part in only the first half of the campaign, he saw over 300 dead "Viets" and several dead Japanese. The fiercest resistance was in Ban Me Thuot itself, at the ex-prison and at the camp that had housed the *Garde Indigene* (Montagnard Guard).

"*Ils n'en démordent pas*," he said. "They don't let up."[18]

The proportion of Vietnamese opposing them cannot have been large, coming from a very small pool in highland towns and plantations, plus a few ex-political prisoners. At this point, the Viet Minh had had little training and were new to combat. Their tenacity may be explained by exhilarated patriotism, but there must be another explanation for their near success. Japanese deserters, motivated by their own version of anti-colonialism, stiffened their defense but cannot have been central.

More likely, veteran Montagnard soldiers made the difference. The Rhadé colonial infantry had spent the 1930s putting down rebellions by other Montagnards and even fighting the Thais. They knew the French tactics, plus the ambush was a Montagnard art, plus they knew the terrain, expressly including Ban Me Thuot's ex-prison and *Garde Indigène* barracks.[19] General Giap attributed the loss of Ban Me Thuot in part to the fact that "our Rhadé brothers" had been insufficiently organized and that some had been "bought off" by the French. This can be read in the inverse, suggesting Rhadé participation almost beat the French back, keeping them out of Ban Me Thuot.

One of the Viet Minh organizers of his fellow Rhadé was Y-Bih Aleo.

Born around 1902, he had been one of the very first students at Sabatier's school of five grades. Eventually, he joined the *Garde Indigène,* rose to the rank of warrant officer, and served as a prison guard in Ban Me Thuot. After joining the Viet Minh, he helped them seize power in August 1945, then organized a Montagnard militia to oppose the French return, thus must have been at least partly responsible for the fierce resistance.[20] Corroborating this, he was subsequently arrested by the French and sentenced to 20 years' hard labor at the notorious mist-bound mountain prison at Dak Pek. (Also corroborating this, as we shall see, he eventually became leader of the Montagnard Viet Cong.) After eight years, in 1954, he was released by Ngo Dinh Diem, South Vietnam's new president.[21]

Y-Bham Enuol was in Ban Me Thuot at the same time Y-Bih Aleo was organizing its defense. As two of the most educated Montagnards, they already knew each other. Both were Viet Minh (if only temporarily in Y-Bham Enuol's case), and both shared proto-ethnonationalist thinking. They are known to have been, and to have remained, good friends despite divergent political trajectories.

It is very unlikely Y-Bham Enuol participated in the subsequent fighting. Though the returning French jailed him in early 1946, it was only for a month, and then, evidently reassured he was not a true Viet Minh, hired him to work for the next six months as secretary to the French provincial governor.

In Y-Bih Aleo's case, he may have picked up some political ideas from Vietnamese prisoners he was guarding in the 1930s. But an important question is what made other Montagnards join the Viet Minh or, for that matter, the Viet Cong later?

Montagnards were accustomed to being disdained by lowlanders, whether Cambodians or Vietnamese, but the Vietnamese revolutionaries who came to convert them in the late 1940s, filled with ideas for a new world, were different. Not only did party discipline translate into consistently respectful and politic behavior toward the highlanders, but the Viet Minh truly walked the walk of equality between genders and races. In North Vietnam, Montagnards had risen to high ranks, and highlander women were visibly welcome in the proto-NVA (North Vietnamese Army).[22]

This must have been deeply impressive to highlanders on a personal level. Thus, by 1960, when the first North Vietnamese arrived in northeastern Cambodia via the Ho Chi Minh Trail, there was already a revolutionary tradition in the highlands and they found young Jarai whose fathers and uncles had served with the Viet Minh and who could describe the idea of revolution as "beautiful."[23]

In addition, the Viet Minh talked about eventual autonomy for highlanders. (It would be years before Montagnards in the South began to suspect this was a fiction.) Some highlanders may have been attracted to the idealism of

Communism itself—the dignity it offered the poor, or its brawny solidarity with the oppressed everywhere. Some may have resented a disparity of power and riches at the village level, but it seems unlikely many Montagnards related to class struggle. (A possible exception could have been the Jarai, who did have a kind of aristocracy traceable to the Cham.)

As for negative motivations, many highlanders had grown weary of French abuses, whether colonial, like the labor tax, or rapaciously capitalistic, like indentured servitude on plantations, or simply personal. One bitter Montagnard joke ran: "How do the French pay for work done? With a kick in the ass." We can imagine that colonies in the steaming tropics did not attract the highest-quality Frenchmen.[24]

Two decades later, American bombing and forced relocations would begin driving Montagnards into the arms of the communists as well.

***

Over the 11 years following his 1946 job clerking for the French, Y-Bham Enuol bounced down dirt tracks on a bicycle all over the highlands, from hamlet to hamlet, working as an agricultural extension agent.

"Ag agents" were among the world's first development workers, enabling the rural poor to improve their own lives through up-to-date farming methods and seeds. To a people whose methods had not changed for thousands of years, his results were magical; to a people whose land was limited by the boundaries that a matriarch could walk in one day, he was the outside world. As that world grew more threatening, his role changed from interpreter to intercessor, from town crier to priest.

By all accounts, he was a spellbinding speaker, with a practiced eloquence in urging his people toward self-reliance. His oratory may have taken on an edge after he lost some land of his own to Vietnamese settlers, but it was never so sharp as to bring punishment. The government simply moved him to a new post, over and over. Pretty soon he was known throughout the highlands.

Notes

1 Strictly speaking, this group is called Bunong in Cambodia, Mnong in Vietnam, but I have chosen to use only one name here to avoid confusion.

2 The band's chief, N'Trang Lung, also had motives of personal revenge, his wife and daughter having been killed in a French-ordered punitive expedition two years before. Hickey, *Sons of the Mountains* (1982b), 289.

3 Y-Bhan Kpor, handwritten autobiography, author's personal collection, 2008. Written by this story's main protagonist, Bhan, it ties his sense of ethnic and political identity to the Rhadé alphabet. At the end of this document in English, Bhan adds footnoted references to two ethnographic works about Montagnards, in essence acknowledging that his autobiography was ethnographic data. This is as close to a written agreement from Bhan to being written about as exists. He spent so many years as a clearly willing collaborator in my research into FULRO that when I uncovered information from another source he might have wished not to divulge—about a crisis within FULRO's leadership and his role in it—it did not occur to me to ask him for permission to do so, largely because I did not see the information as negative (other than showing him to be human). By the time this did occur to me, his capacity for meaningful consent was gone.

4 Despite opposition by business interests, Sabatier's work was widely admired and imitated by other administrators, particularly his codification of Rhadé customary law. No other Frenchman at his level had as much effect on the lives of highlanders, yet, of all his footprints, those of his feet of clay lasted the longest. In 1973, a Jarai told me Sabatier was remembered for his succession of Rhadé mistresses. Kpa Doh, interview with author, April 1973.

5 The evangelicals' school operated from 1934 through 1935, closed for 1936, then restarted in 1936 or 1937. The idea that his exposure to Protestantism was too brief to have lasting effect is an assumption. In his thirties, he was conducting animist rituals, and, near the very end of his life, when invited to pray by an American pastor, he politely declined. Pastor Gene Hall, interview with author, July 14, 2014.

6 Paul Nur was another, one year ahead of Y-Bham Enuol at Qui Nhon, 1940–43 (interview with author, April 1973). Nur was a Bahnar and a major figure among early Montagnard ethnonationalists, jailed for a year for his Bajaraka activities in 1958, but becoming more moderate with time and eventually becoming South Vietnam's Minister of Ethnic Minorities (1966–71).

7 Y-Bham Enuol, interview with author, April 1973. What he told me does not quite compute. What I recorded was "born 1923, started school at age 15, 6 years primary school ("First in his class"), 2 ½ years at Qui Nhon, 2 years at Ag college, return to his village in March 1945." Of all those data points, the one most likely to be incorrect, for a number of reasons, is his birth year. Info from Paul Nur corroborates 1941 as the year he started at Qui Nhon. Counting backwards, he started school in 1935. If he truly was 15—which fits with Montagnard custom at the time—then he was born in ~1920.

8 Jonathan Padwe, *Disturbed Forests, Fragmented Memories: Jarai and Other Lives in the Cambodian Highlands* (University of Washington Press, 2020), 96.

9 Jacques Dournes, "Sam Bam, Le Mage et le Blanc dans L'Indochine Centrale des Années Trente," *L'Ethnographie, 1978-I* (1978), 91.

10 Oscar Salemink, *The Ethnography of Vietnam's Central Highlanders* (Honolulu, HI: University of Hawai'i Press, 2003), 109.

11 Nay Rong, interview with author, February 17, 2014; Hip Ksor, interview with author, August 15, 2013. They may be referring to imitators. Several of these—though more contemporaneous—were documented. But perhaps not.

12 My informant was Ksor Wol, the King of Fire's representative in a village near Cheo Reo (this was the Jarai version of a village mayor). A 71-year-old veteran of the *Garde Indigene*, 1926–42, he had fought at Dak To against "unpacified" Bahnar and Sedang (some of whose agitation derived from an earlier messianic movement called the Holy Man's Rebellion among the Boloven highlanders in Laos). For this, he picked up a pension of 34,000 piastres twice a year in Kontum. Dournes also lists Ksor Wol as his source about Sambram.

13 The great majority were interned. Some 1,200 were killed in battle or executed. Of the latter, the Japanese beheaded some high-ranking officers. David Marr, *Vietnam 1945: The Quest for Power* (Oakland: University of California Press, 1997), 61.

14 Y-Tlur Eban, interviews with author over a 20-year span, 2003–2023. Y-Tlur (Thomas) Eban played, and plays, an enormous part in making this book possible. We first met in 1967 when he was an interpreter at Project *Omega* (B-50) and I commanded its Mike Force. I was unaware of it at the time, but he had already been a pivotal figure in two FULRO actions, the 1964 rebellion and an April 1966 migration of ~3,000 FULRO partisans from Vietnam to the Mondulkiri base. He had also participated in the December 1965 rebellion in Pleiku. Despite being based himself in Vietnam, he was also present in Cambodia for a fourth major FULRO event, the December 1968 split. I could have written this book from his point of view—which would have taken it into the post-1975 FULRO experience when, Zelig-like, he was *also* present (!)—but chose not to because the narrative involving Dhon/Kosem/Paul/Bhan and Kpa Doh seemed a better vehicle for conveying the history of FULRO from 1955 up to and including the fall of Phnom Penh. I have, of course, included a great deal of information from Y-Tlur, whom I visited in Greensboro over ten times.

15 Marr, *Vietnam 1945*, 189.

16 Y-Thih Eban, interview with author, May 1973. Y-Thih was a sympathetic and important figure, who was Gerald Hickey's primary source. But because he, like Nay Luett, was a moderate who remained in Vietnam, he does not play a role in this story. In 1973, he gave me his biography typed out in carbon, part of his unsuccessful quiet campaign to be appointed minister of ethnic minorities. However, he was a realist about how the war might end; on his nightstand was the book, *Hawaii, The Aloha State*. He was killed in an ambush trying to cross into Cambodia shortly after the fall of Saigon. Hickey, *Free in the Forest*, 258. Includes much info on Y-Thih Eban and the Front for the Liberation of Montagnards (FLM), the organization that preceded Bajaraka (p. 49 onward)

17 Part of this is from Vinh Ngon, *FULRO #1: A Criminal Organization*, translated by Merle Pribbenow, 2015 (Ho Chi Minh City: Cong An Nhan Dan, 1983). This book erects a frame of truth on which to festoon lies. Like the confession under torture referred to in a later chapter, it is too passionate to be trusted. Yet both are too precious in an exhumation like this to be ruled inadmissible.Y-Bham Enuol himself told me in 1973 he had worked three months for the Khmer Rouge, but coerced by a week's house arrest in Ban Me Thuot at the *Hôtel de la Jeunesse* (youth hostel). However, at that time, none of the FULRO leaders would have admitted to an American interviewer they had ever been anything but fiercely anti-communist.

18 Pierre Guinet, adjutant, *Corps Léger d'Intervention Aéroporté*, oral history obtained by Michel El Baze, 2015. http://ea58.free.fr/MichelElBaze/complements/PierreGUINETAveclecorpslegerinterventionaeroporteGUERREindochine1945-1946.html. Guinet's account rings with authenticity, in part because he lists many fellow soldiers by name, including those killed.

19 Rhadé infantry even fought for the French in a small war against the Thais in 1941.

20 Marr, *Vietnam 1945*, 438. Marr's source has it that "Y-Bih was persuaded by the local Viet-Minh [*sic*] to participate in the seizure of power [on August 24th]." It is admirable that in this era a Vietnamese is mentioning a Montagnard, though somewhat lefthandedly. I suspect Y-Bih needed no persuading. The "bought-off" slur had been a leftist trope since the French Revolution, when *La Marseillaise* referred to "mercenary phalanxes." One of this book's points is that, during the Vietnam War, the mercenary trope was used with considerable success as propaganda to discredit both FULRO and especially the CIDG. (I am unable to re-find Giap's comment, I believe that it came from Marr and that I found it online.)

21 It may seem incongruous that Diem would release a Viet Minh but, in 1954, Diem himself was still virulently anti-French, arguably being as much of an anticolonial nationalist as Ho Chi Minh.
22 Marr, *Vietnam 1945*, 180, 515.
23 Henri Locard, *Jungle Heart of the Khmer Rouge*, NIAS Monographs, No. 157, University of Copenhagen (2023), 280.
24 In Cameroon, the people themselves refer to them as *petits blancs* (little whites).

CHAPTER 3

Dhon

Born in 1932, Dhon was about 12 years younger than Y-Bham Enuol, of a generation more exposed to the outside world. Dhon's father farmed like everyone else but also had a small store in their village, a hint of modernity. With a year's hiatus during World War II when schools were closed, Dhon was 17 years old by the time he finished primary school.

In 1947, his father was jailed for suspected Viet Minh activities. Dhon's younger brother claimed French suspicions were mistakenly aroused because, having to push his cart back and forth to Ban Me Thuot, their father had to pay to get his merchandise past the Viet Minh. However, his brother's objectivity may be in doubt, having fought the communists for 22 years.[1] The fact that their father was still in jail, at three years and counting, suggests he was more than a simple shopkeeper who had made a simple mistake. Plus, Dhon's subsequent political beliefs, indeed the trajectory of his entire life, suggest a social justice bent that could have arisen *de novo* but more likely did not.

***

In quick succession, from late 1949 to early 1950, Russia exploded an atomic bomb, Mao took over China, and North Korea set off the Korean War. When Mao recognized Ho Chi Minh's government, the French fight to hold onto its Indochina colonies became, in American eyes, an anti-communist struggle. (Previously the United States had only given France money, but, in September 1950, the Americans set up shop in Saigon and began providing military and civilian aid. Some French saw this as ominous.)[2]

In a great travel book, *A Dragon Apparent*, Norman Lewis described passing through Ban Me Thuot in January 1950, where he met the acting provincial governor, whom he described as one of the last sincere believers in the value of colonialism to native peoples, Monsieur Doustin.

His villains were Corsican planters who trick "miserable-looking … human scarecrows [Montagards]" into putting their thumbprints on work contracts, in effect enslaving them. By contrast, at one jungle outpost, Lewis and a companion ran into a group of Mnong paying a tax in rice. "Splendid in tasselled loin cloths, earplugs, and necklaces of beads and teeth," they are "oblivious" to the Europeans' presence. "We walked round them looking at their ornaments but none so much as glanced at us. We might have been transparent." Lewis continued, "It was a coincidence that [shortly] after this first encounter with the noble savage of Indo-China ... practically untouched by Western influence, native guards brought in a half-crazed creature in rags who had escaped from one of the plantations."

Doustin was evidently a Gaullist appointee, having been with the Free French in England during the war, then colonial service in Mauretania. He was nostalgic for what Lewis "had always thought of as drab [English] provincial towns ... seen now across years of fierce, sunny exile as congeries of quaint pubs, full of tenderly acquiescent maidens and wrapped in a Turner sunset." The book is pure New Journalism—as entertaining, biting, and subjective as anything written by Wolfe or Mailer, so it is a surprise that Lewis is faintly kind to Doustin, whom he found imperturbable, decisive, and efficient.

Like Sabatier, who was his predecessor 25 years before, Doustin is in absolute control of everything in his province (except the planters protected by France's commercial interests). But, unlike Sabatier, who prided himself in having no servants, Doustin had all the trappings. In a town whose main street was still dust, the *Résidence* had been "conceived in the grand manner, with a wide ambassadorial entrance and a flight of steps worthy of an Italian customs house. [Montagnard] sentries ensconced in the bougainvillea woke up and slapped their rifle-stocks furiously at our approach. As soon as we entered the house, white clad [Montagnard] domestics with tamed, empty faces flitted at our heels."[3]

In 1950, because of growing pressure from the Viet Minh, it was "thought necessary to press every available [highlander] into the militia." This would have been Doustin's job.[4]

At the end of the 1949–50 schoolyear, after exams, Monsieur Doustin popped up like the Burning Bush at the Montagnard school, asking the graduating students what they wished to become. Choices available included clerk, medical technician, forester, tradesman (electrician, carpenter, etc.), teacher, and soldier.

Dhon chose soldier, which was surprising. Every one of his contemporaries described him as being the best student of his generation, helping all the others with math at noon recess, always first in his exams, and winning the top two academic prizes in his class. Either he was sincere and under the influence of his people's warrior tradition, or he had figured out what the Frenchman wanted to hear and, beyond that, how their subsequent exchange might play out.

Despite the colony's military manpower needs, Doustin said, "No, no. That's not right for you. With your grades, you ought to be a teacher."

Then he asked Dhon what his father did for a living.

Dhon was ready with a response about his father. It was so forthright as to be almost arrogant in the eyes of his classmates. (This was still an era in which highlanders walking single file along the side of the road would turn and bow to the sound of a motor car, in other words bow to *any* Frenchman. Doustin was at the Olympian pinnacle.)

"I don't want you becoming a soldier," Doustin replied. "I will release your father."[5]

The students could be forgiven for mistaking the *Résident*'s name for *Destin* (Fate). Many other boys in Dhon's class had their life courses set by him. We will hear much more about one of them, named Bhan, initially an unwilling soldier.

***

Father Roger Bianchetti arrived in Ban Me Thuot in 1951, seventeen years after the American Protestants.

He had just finished five years as a combat chaplain with French forces fighting the Viet Minh in North Vietnam, having been wounded and awarded a *Legion d'Honneur.* In his thirties, he was finally living his dream, like Sabatier. Initially hoping at age 15 to become a missionary priest in Africa, he had switched his goal four years later on learning that more missionaries to Asia had been martyred. For his time, place, and family circumstance, becoming a priest was almost the norm. Having made that step, wanting to join the elite, those who really suffered for Christ, made some sense.[6]

He threw himself into learning Rhadé. Initially, no village would let him come live there because the American evangelicals' puritanism had created hostility to foreign clerics among a people whose culture encouraged alcohol excess and, at least among teens, sexual license. Finally, one village did, and then his self-abnegation, living in a tiny stilt house—and his relative Catholic tolerance—won the highlanders over.

Bianchetti had a way with the highlanders. From the French Alps, he joked that their mountains were like elephant-shit balls, nothing compared to his. They loved that.

Bianchetti's flock included some Corsican planters, though usually only their wives attended mass, occupying the two front pews on the right, hand fans aflutter. Among the planters were agents of the SDECE, the French CIA. It seems likely Bianchetti functioned as naturally and unashamedly as an ally of his country's secret service as the American evangelical Protestants did of theirs.

In 1954, he accepted the installation of French nuns, who opened a *foyer* (home) for Rhadé girls. One of these nuns would come to know Dhon and another of this story's protagonists as youths, recalling them with great clarity 60 years later.

***

Dhon went on to middle school, where he excelled, then won a scholarship to a prestigious boarding school in Dalat, a hill station and second home to French colonials. The Lycée Yersin catered to wealthy Vietnamese and a few French, including children of planters. In the early 1950s, the French opened a small number of slots for highlanders.

Father Bianchetti knew how enormous the leap would be for Dhon and tried to fill in some gaps in the younger man's education, teaching him about mosquito nets and bedsheets.

In 1953, the ride from Ban Me Thuot to Dalat was by chicken-bus along 300 kilometers (185 miles) of jungle track. Some of the highlander boys arrived shoeless and in shorts, but Dhon would have found shoes to wear, no matter what.

It was as if the US Government during the early civil-rights era had obliged a New England prep school to accept bright but poorly educated blacks from the Mississippi Delta. Instead of great lawns and brick Georgians to awe them, however, the lycée had a four-story imitation chateau with tower and colonnaded halls.

If any of the highland students did not show awe, it was Dhon. Older than his classmates, he was physically mature as well, taller than most, and played center on the defensive line of the soccer team. His left wing on that line, now an old man in North Carolina, remembers him as a notably aggressive player.[7] He also remembers that, by the next school year (1954–55), enough highlander boys had entered Yersin to rise up together against the hated epithet, "*moi*," that meant "savage/primitive." A gang fight against the Vietnamese erupted down by the lake shore. Someone even brought a knife. Dhon exhibited what another boy described as sangfroid, holding the others steady.[8]

He finished 9th grade expecting to continue through 12th grade and go on to medical school in France. Highlanders had miserable-to-no health care; he would come back and fix that. He was so well known as a high achiever committed to his people that everyone was counting on him, naively, sweetly, to do so.

He underwent catechism to be baptized as a Catholic. He and Father Bianchetti were similar men— energetic and fervently committed to a cause. Initially, at least, their causes ran parallel. Dhon would have been impressed by the Frenchman learning Rhadé, and probably by his asceticism, and, as a young man under the shadow of war, he may have found Bianchetti's personal experience and survival of it magnetic.

Lycée Yersin. (Photo by Diane Selwyn)

Father Bianchetti (far left), Bishop Seitz (hand raised), and Father Dournes (far right). (Photo courtesy of François Demeure)

While at Dalat, Dhon attended a conference of lay Catholics that inspired him to organize a social-work organization back home. Significantly, it aimed at materially improving peoples' lives, not simply helping them grow spiritually.[9]

The partition of Vietnam at Geneva in 1954 gave Vietnamese 300 days to choose which part of the country they wanted to live in. By May 1955, 600,000 Catholic North Vietnamese had come south; 140,000 of them were shunted to the highlands. By the end of 1955, new settlements of Vietnamese dotted the area around Ban Me Thuot, on land highlanders had always considered theirs. Some Montagnards responded by doing what they had always done when crowded—move, usually west. Sometime in Dhon's 9th or 10th grade year at Yersin, his father led half the people of their village to a new site 15 kilometers away.

For all highlanders, the arrival of so many Vietnamese was a shock. For Dhon, this seems to have been a flint-strike moment, lowering the visor, igniting the blowtorch. Gone were dreams of finishing school and becoming a doctor.[10]

The summer of 1956, Dhon attended a conclave for highlander youth at Kontum's seminary on a hill. A sprawling, dark-wood, Victorian structure, it

Bishop's Conclave for Highlander Youth at the Kontum Seminary in 1956. Father Dournes (behind), Dhon (far left, standing), Bishop Seitz, Paul (arms crossed), Nay Luett (far right, standing). (Photo courtesy of Françoise Demeure)

seemed to soar against stormy skies. Bishop Paul Seitz had invited boys and young men from several ethnic groups to promote ethnic unity and pride, aiming to create "*l'homme debout*" ("standing man," though with the idea of acting, not being acted upon). Many were from the Lycée Yersin. For someone like Dhon—already politicized, already proud of being Montagnard—this would have been like rocket fuel.

According to Seitz, highlander ethnonationalism was born at this meeting, but the CIA says its cradle was Lycée Yersin.[11] These conflicting sources are easily reconciled: Dhon was their most likely common denominator. In the conclave's photo (opposite), he is standing at the far left, a little apart.[12] By the end of the conclave, the highlander movement had a name: Bajaraka.[13]

Dhon's occupation-to-be, teaching, was calling him because it would allow him to mold young minds while giving him the time and pretext to do quiet organizing far from the eyes of Diem's Security Police.

Around this time, he married H'Dua Eban, who had been taught to read and been catechized by the French nuns. Anticipating the personalized marriage ceremonies of a much later era, the couple asked Father Bianchetti to marry them with Rhadé verses and an exchange of brass bracelets, a ritual they repeated afterward in their home villages, though without the animal sacrifices that some of their relatives wanted. The newlyweds then moved into one of the small, dark, huts behind Bianchetti's chapel.

H'Dua and Dhon and their two children (with Dhon's adopted brother, Y-Gum, on the right). (Photo courtesy of Françoise Demeure)

Notes

1 Y-Blim Adrong, interview with author, February 2, 2014; and Y-Blim's autobiography, author's personal collection. Born in 1934, he spent 22 years as an officer, first in the French Army, then in the Army of the Republic of Vietnam, rising to the rank of lieutenant colonel, always stationed in lowland areas, wounded once. Hard to read between the lines, but it sounds as if he served under and alongside Vietnamese without problems. He escaped overland through Cambodia in 1986 in a surprisingly mundane fashion, largely by bus. He died in 2017.

2 Kathryn Statler, *Replacing France: The Origins of American Intervention in Vietnam* (Lexington: The University Press of Kentucky, 2007), 39.

3 Lewis, *A Dragon Apparent* (1951), "noble savage," 85, "sunny exile," "sentries," 89.

4 Norman Lewis, *A Dragon Apparent* (London: Jonathan Cape, 1951), 144. His other villains are American evangelical missionaries, whom he savages. I gave a French translation of his book to a 93-year-old French nun who was in Ban Me Thuot four years after Lewis. She thinks his depiction of highlander servitude on plantations has some truth to it, but that his trashing of her ecclesiastical rivals is deeply unfair. How objective she is may be open to debate, but it appears Lewis is no more so. His New Journalistic style makes discerning what is factual, as opposed to his larger poetic or political truth, problematic for the reader. Presumably, accuracy constraints were even weaker with travel writing.

5 Y-Blim Adrong, interview with author, February 2, 2014; and Pierre K'Briuh, interviews with author over a ten-year span, from 2014–2024.

6 Biographical material on Bianchetti accessed at *Mission Etrangères de Paris* website in 2015. Note that the most up to date website is now https://irfa.paris/missionnaire/3700-bianchetti-roger/.

7 His right wing was a Jarai named Kpa Doh, who, like Dhon, would follow his political beliefs into the maelstrom. We will meet him later.

8 Pierre K'Briuh, interviews with author over a ten-year span, 2014–2024. He credits diminutive Nay Luett with being equally impressive in that situation.

9 The Dalat conference was the Legion of Mary, engaged primarily in the performance of spiritual works of mercy, but on return home he chose to organize a chapter of Youths of Good Will, an organization concerned with material aid.

10 Dhon's adopted brother, Gum, partially fulfilled Dhon's dream by becoming the first Montagnard physician in southern Vietnam. He lived to be 81. See photo p. 47.

11 Paul Seitz, *Men of Dignity* (Bar le Duc, France: L'Imprimerie Saint-Paul, 1975), 99; and CIA, *The Highlanders of South Vietnam: A Review of Political Developments and Forces*, CIA-RDP80T01719R000300010003-8 (Washington, D.C., 1966), 19–22. The bishop's exact words are that the movement arose at a "Montagnards' meeting in secret in 1956," but he had reason in 1975 to protect identities and to keep himself out of the picture. He cannot have imagined in 1956 how his efforts to empower these young men would lead some of them toward violence and death. Unlike Protestant missionaries, he was constrained by his large flock of Vietnamese Catholic refugees and would not have encouraged violence against the Vietnamese.

12 The photo has three others of interest here, aside from Bishop Seitz at the center. **Nay Luett,** standing at the far right, was as charismatic as Dhon but less militant. Unlike Dhon, he had early contact with American Green Berets and came to believe his people's only hope lay with Saigon and Washington, subsequently becoming Saigon's minister of ethnic minorities. After 1975, he spent 12 years in a prison camp, then died on coming home of what sounds like a spontaneous hemorrhage in his brain, thus unconnected with external events. **Father Jacques Dournes**, half-hidden near Dhon, was a missionary in Cheo Reo. Rebellious, prickly, solitary, he was a fascinating character who slowly transformed himself into a respected anthropologist while becoming less and less of a priest, eventually looking back with pride at not having converted a single Jarai. By 1970, before being withdrawn to France, he had taken to wearing a loincloth (Françoise Demeure, interview with author, July 2, 2014). (https://irfa.paris/missionnaire/3740-dournes-jacques/. More information about him is easily available online.) **Y-Bun Sur** is the smiling teenager with his arms crossed midway between Nay Luett and the bishop. We will come to know him later in this story as **Paul.**

13 Ba-Ja-Ra-Ka came from the names of four ethnic groups, Bahnar, Jarai, Rhadé, and Koho. To resolve an impasse, Bishop Seitz suggested a north-to-south order, Bahnar first because their homeland was furthest north (Nay Rong, interview with author, August 15, 2013), Mnong were not included, either because their only representative was Y-Bun Sur (Paul) or because the Mnong were considerably less advanced than the other groups (Paul being the exception).

CHAPTER 4

Bhan

One year younger than Dhon, Bhan was the son of a sergeant in the highlander colonial troops that were often deployed in North Vietnam. Because his mother accompanied his father to garrisons (an ancient practice in Southeast Asian armies) and because the Rhadé are matrilineal, Bhan's earliest years were spent in the care of his grandmother.[1]

He left for school in Ban Me Thuot, 25 kilometers (15 miles) away, possibly when eight years old, but would walk home on weekends. His grandmother urged him to fail his exams at school, hoping he would flunk out. It is unclear whether she saw where education would lead him or simply missed the grinning little boy bouncing up and down on the plaited bamboo floor of her longhouse.

But he had done well. Now he could not decide what he wanted to be. He loved to draw, but there was no job for that. He did not like needles, so no to medical technician. He only knew he wanted to keep learning. Becoming a teacher would be ideal except how could he prepare his next day's classes every evening and still play music? Music was his joy. Like many Rhadé males, he played all nine Rhadé instruments, going to a different house every few nights for a jam session. Most longhouses had a set of all nine. His favorite was the *ding nam,* a sort of large pan flute with a calabash from which protrude six bamboo tubes with holes to be fingered.[2]

Then, to his horror, he learned he was slated to become a soldier, along with 20 other boys. The others went docilely, but Bhan bicycled furiously back to his home village, only to learn that Doustin had been out there in his jeep, looking for him. "Son," his mother said, "You have to do this, otherwise you'll go to jail. We'll miss you, in jail. Your father did it. You can do it."

***

Bhan was one of those people to whom the military's seeming absurdities make perfect sense. Over the next two years, he rose from recruit to lieutenant at a French training center for highland soldiers at Ban Don.[3] In the last months of the war, his training unit was transferred to Cheo Reo where it was converted to a combat unit.

***

April 1954—Bhan is a 21-year-old lieutenant in the Third Montagnard Battalion of the Far East. The highlanders have largely sided with the French to battle against independence because they fear rule by lowland Vietnamese.

Seven hundred fifty miles to the north, the decisive battle of the first Indochina War is raging at Dien Bien Phu. The war will be over in three months.

The French officers in Bhan's native unit can be forgiven for losing spirit. Patrols returning from the high mountains with news of enemy movements are met with a shrug, "Leave them. They'll starve out there." But the Vietnamese rebels in the forest are on the attack, mindful of eventual negotiations and elated by the imminence of victory.

Several hours earlier, his platoon joined its first firefight, defending a low hill. Two French warplanes have arrived overhead and await instructions. For any newcomer, combat's roar is terrible, but an unlucky few are paralyzed by the whisper they hear within it that promises to slice and gut any mother's son or burst a braincase fine as Limoges bone ware. Bhan's French officer is white eyed with adrenaline.

Ammunition is low, water too. They have been in a moving firefight for hours. Bhan gives an order in Rhadé to his grenadiers to hold fire until they can actually see the enemy. In sparse woods, this is only 40 meters away.

The arriving planes are still circling, still waiting. Bhan offers to try to direct the planes. He takes the radio handset, talks in French with the pilots overhead. First, he must help them identify his position, then to recognize the attacking force in black. Now they can make repeated bombing runs over the enemy, who eventually withdraws.

He will have other battles, but this first experience of combat will remain his most significant, teaching him his worth, and doing so in a way that can never be diminished, not by a European, not by a Vietnamese, not even by poverty and the frailty of age. For anyone, this is priceless and rare.

***

The war was over, but the French had not yet departed.[4] Bhan was back at Ban Don, living on a French coffee plantation along with the French officers, no doubt an impressive billet. One afternoon, a half-brother of his mother's came to visit, with a pretty girl in tow whom he left sitting under a tree while he bought Bhan a beer. Bhan must have known what was about to happen. By Rhadé matrilineal custom, marriage proposals are made by a man from the woman's family.

"See that girl over there? Do you want to marry her?"

"No. Tell her to go home."

But the man called her over to sit with them, buying her an orange drink, of which she drank little. Her name was H'dak.

Bhan turned to her. "Go home."

"No," she replied, "I have no more home. I am going to sleep and eat with a French officer [meaning marry Bhan]. I will sleep on your doorstep."

For the next five days she did just that. Bhan ignored her. But Bhan's Montagnard troops took pity on her, buying her food and drink.

Finally, she moved in with Bhan.

Looking back, Bhan said, "At the time, I was thinking, 'If a small dog follows you, you kick it.' I should have told her more strongly to go away, but I didn't know how to talk to a woman." He clears his throat. "But I ended up being happy."

By their fifth year of marriage, they still had no children. This was grounds for divorce, easy in Rhadé culture but expensive, costing two water buffaloes if the man wanted it, four if the woman did. "But I didn't want to get divorced," he said. "I loved her." They went looking for a baby to buy.

Because the Rhadé did not sell their children, the baby had to be Vietnamese. After a year of looking, they bought a baby boy for 15,000 piastres ($180, but no doubt a huge sum to them), naming him Huer. They could now address each other as "*Ma Huer*" (father of Huer) and "*Mi Huer*" (mother of Huer), indicating they were now properly integrated in their society, having a child.[5] They raised him as if he were their own. To Bhan, it was unimportant that his son was not of his own blood, unimportant even that the boy's blood was Vietnamese.

Five years later, they had a baby of their own, followed by two more.

***

Following the Geneva Convention of 1954, Ngo Dinh Diem took shaky power in the newly created state of South Vietnam. Boosted by Washington, he was bitterly opposed by Paris because he had been a strong anti-colonialist who hated the French. For 10 months, he fended off challenges from Vietnamese groups loyal to the French, finally coming out on top in 1955 with the help of the CIA in a proxy battle between the CIA and French Secret Service in the streets of Saigon.[6]

To Diem, the highlanders must have looked like another group that would cause problems for him. The French had cultivated them the longest. Even if not, their ethnicity was an obstacle to creating a strong state (a problem for all his successors, including the current government in Hanoi). That the Montagnards might be manipulated by outsiders made it that much more imperative to assimilate them as soon as possible, to turn them into Vietnamese.

First order was to settle the 140,000 North Vietnamese Catholic refugees in their midst. To that end, he abrogated highlander land titles. Then he turned to the highlander schools, forbidding teaching in any language but Vietnamese.

With the settlers came soldiers and administrators. Some were dedicated individuals, sensitive to the highlanders' very different culture, but most were imbued with age-old fear and contempt for highlanders. Incidents multiplied, in fact or imagination. What the highlanders heard, even if not openly said, was "Your French father is gone. We are in power now. The highlands belong to Vietnamese."

***

Particularly disturbing to Bhan were the bulldozers and the poisonings.

A number of highland cemeteries had been razed by Vietnamese settlers. Bhan could imagine the rumbling yellow beasts, chuffing, clanking over graves, body slamming sacred wooden sculptures beneath their treads.

And he had heard of clusters of people sickening and dying. To highlanders, whose forest pharmacopeia contained real poisons, this could have only one explanation. In Pleiku, Vietnamese doctors were supposed to have injected a toxin into bananas still on the trees. Near Ban Me Thuot, something sharp and lethal was said to have been hidden in bars of soap. Such malice could not be blind. The motive had to be revenge for the Montagnards' past support of the French.

He was unaware of his own credulity. Conscious of the need to lead his people into the modern world, he was still only partway there himself.

***

In 1955, along with other highlander officers from the French Army, Bhan was melded into the new Army of the Republic of South Vietnam, echoing the effective integration of blacks into the American military around the same time. But when Bhan reported to his new unit, he discovered he had to rent his own quarters and walk to work, while Vietnamese sergeants, below him in rank, were allotted houses and cars.

The logic of his first major assignment, to a Nung division, was clear. Nungs were hill tribesmen too, but from southwestern China, pushed south over the centuries by the expansionary Han Chinese.[7] Bhan, only 23 years old but a combat veteran, was given a battalion, which would be his next lesson, confirming over time that highlander military units could be commanded solely by highlanders.

They were sent out to reconnoiter the northern fastnesses of South Vietnam where the fiercest battles of the next war would be fought. One extended operation took Bhan up "the old French road" (Hwy 14) into the misty canyons of the Katu, a Montagnard ethnic group that had practiced human-sacrificial blood hunts into the 20th century. There, in the gloom of cathedral forest, he encountered a man and his daughter tending a small fire at the base of a tree. Bhan had never before seen fellow highlanders so emaciated, wearing nothing but loincloths in the mountain cold. He was even more shocked when he looked up and saw a platform with a low thatch roof, dusted white, on which lay the body of the man's dead wife. Not burying the dead struck him as the most primitive thing of all.

It made him realize the enormity of the task ahead, organizing his people politically.

***

The last French soldier left in 1956, though the French had been feeling the Americans' grip on their collar and pants-seat for years, rushing them toward the door.[8]

The remaining French were increasingly bitter at the Americans' overconfidence and heedlessness of French experience, plus the Americans' lack of *mesure* (sense of proportion). For their part, the Americans expected to succeed where the French had failed, largely because of these qualities. Being far stronger militarily and economically than the French, and being fresh, they possessed a can-do spirit the French had apparently lost. They distanced themselves from the French to avoid acquiring colonial stigma. And they were excessive, not simply by inclination but because the science of development was still new. They did things ad hoc, priding themselves on improvising even though this resulted in duplicated effort. Unable to agree with Diem about whether roads should be built for economic or military reasons, they built both. They threw money at everything. Even the mildest French critics noted American stumbles with glee.[9] As the numbers of earnest do-gooders in country swelled, the American presence became overwhelming, easy to tar with a propaganda brush as self-interested imperialism.

Eventually, even Diem started to appreciate the French, finding them a useful counterweight to the Americans. In turn, the French—who had feared he would become an American stooge—warmed to him and stopped purposefully causing him problems.

The Second Indochina War—still called the Vietnam War by Americans—is usually dated from 1957 but Vietnamese started dying in significant numbers as early as 1956. In the South, Diem arrested around 50,000 suspected communist sympathizers and may have executed as many as 12,000.[10] Meanwhile, the communists were murdering as many as 50,000 "class enemies" in the North and would begin assassinating "traitors" in the South in 1957.[11]

Vietnam was largely out of the world's eye, but already the two sides were like grimly silent duelists with their shirttails tied together, slashing away with fish knives.

***

In 1957 or 1958, Bhan invited all his fellow highlander officers to his birthday party.[12] They knew something unusual was afoot when they saw no tall Alibaba jugs of rice wine, only soft drinks.

"How can we salute the flag every morning," he asked them, "when Vietnamese bulldozers are destroying our cemeteries? How can we salute the flag when they treat us as savages, as servants?" He added, "We can talk to the Vietnamese from morning to night, but they're like a tree stump. It won't go away just by kicking it. We have to dig it out, tear it out." This was sedition. At first there was silence, then everyone started talking. They ended by electing him their representative to a growing movement of angry highlanders.

This movement was not Bajaraka but a parallel group of highlanders—less educated than the group at the bishop's conclave and somewhat older—that had founded an organization called the Front for the Liberation of Montagnards (FLM), headed by a childhood friend of Bhan's, a government clerk. His friend had closed an anonymous letter to President Diem that listed highlander grievances with, "You are like a Tiger for parent; when you adopt us, you scratch us."[13]

Bhan and his friend realized the average highlander would never follow young men, thus went looking for an older man to lead their movement, vetting some Rhadé ex-colonels in Laos, then an old school principal ("No, children. Do what you're going to do but don't kill"), then a well-known civil servant, before settling on Y-Bham Enuol.

However, Y-Bham Enuol was only 13 years older (they addressed him as "Elder Brother"). It seems they were really looking for someone who bridged the old and the new better than they did, someone who respected the traditions.

When they came upon Y-Bham Enuol—one of the few Montagnards of his generation with more than elementary school education—wearing only a loincloth and in the gory and atavistic process of sacrificing a water buffalo, they knew they had found him.

The idea that they "settled" for Y-Bham Enuol, a man already with his own considerable following, is likely an intentional slant, reflecting a later political schism.

***

By mid-1958, the two ethnonationalist groups had merged into a single organization, headed by Y-Bham Enuol but keeping the name of one, Bajaraka.

Dhon was the movement's intellectual and its ideologue, more militant than Y-Bham Enuol. He dreamed of an independent country for Montagnards and was already thinking of tactics to win it, starting with seizure of a highland town, and was vowing to fight to the bitter end.[14]

Neither he nor Y-Bham Enuol had any political forbears to emulate. Neither had any political experience beyond grassroots organizing. Both naturally sought advice from foreigners they knew well.

Father Roger Bianchetti convinced Dhon to tone down his demand for independence, changing it to one for political autonomy.

Y-Bham Enuol was in contact with the Americans. His assistants used the Gestetner machine at the Protestant Leprosarium to run off copies of Bajaraka's demands. One visiting evangelical from Idaho went so far as to suggest "picking up a Bible in one hand and a rifle in the other" to defend Montagnard land rights.[15] But Y-Bham Enuol was too practical to listen.

He sent out letters to various foreign embassies in Saigon, detailing highlander aspirations and asking them to intercede with Diem, which was like sending letters to the North Pole. Initially, the United States Embassy even refused to accept the letter. Then he sent two letters in a row to Diem, copying the second to Diem's province chiefs. This was too overt. Diem's Security Police began rolling up Bajaraka's leaders in mid-September.

As he waited for his turn, Bhan considered slipping away into the Laotian forest with 100 men to start a resistance movement but could find no one willing to join him.

He soon found himself in a basement room of a mansion in Dalat, being interrogated every night for 2–3 weeks. His interrogators would hold the muzzle of a Thompson submachine gun hard against his temple after making sure he saw them loading it (they knew that he knew Tommy guns have no safety). Another interrogation was going on in the next room, of an older man. Bhan recognized his voice. It was Y-Bih Aleo. "You can kill me, I don't care," Bhan heard him say, "I do this for my children." Today, Bhan has no doubt Y-Bih was referring to ethnonationalism, not Communism.

Dhon seems to have been off the police radar. Only when he organized a demonstration in Ban Me Thuot of 2,000 highlanders carrying signs and shouting condemnation of Diem's actions did he himself get arrested, beaten, and water boarded.[16] He may also have spent two months in jail. His co-organizer had been Y-Bih Aleo.

***

Bhan spent two more months sunk in a dungeon at a prison in Saigon, then was flown up to Hue where, as far from his ethnic base as possible, he was put to work soldiering again, but under watchful eyes. His skills were too valuable to let rot in a black hole.

From 1959 or 1960 onward, he began to see combat again, now against the Viet Cong (VC) instead of the Viet Minh. He was a one-off: a dark-skinned Montagnard, speaking only broken Vietnamese, in command of men—lowland Vietnamese—who, in other circumstances, would have disdained him. Communicating in French with veteran Vietnamese sergeants who, like him, had served with the French, he was strict but less harsh than the average Vietnamese officer. Most important, his reputation had preceded him: he was "good at war."

He soon proved it. Sent with about 300 men and three tanks to defend a half-built camp on the coast, he raced to erect defenses in the sandy soil. On the third night, sensing imminent attack, he visited the tanks outside the camp to tell the crews they would have to sleep inside their machines this night, despite the heat. At 1:00 am, the attack came. The tanks were silent; their crews had slept in the open and been killed. The fight lasted till dawn, illuminated by flares from aircraft. Twenty-two of his men died, almost everybody else was wounded, including Bhan, who had continually roamed the camp under fire, repositioning and encouraging his men.

He was the ideal company or battalion commander, possessing a rare set of qualities greatly admired by those who have seen combat but ill-suited to the challenges of his later life.

Around this time, he spent two months at parachute school, culminating with night jumps laden with heavy equipment. Equipment jumps are difficult on a black night because the equipment must be released seconds before landing. Over half a century later, old and nearly deaf, he remembered gauging the ground's approach by the growing sound of insects and the smell of the earth.

His instructors were Americans—his first contact with them—but he retains no particular memories of that.

***

In the fall of 1961, after a rocky start to his presidency in foreign affairs, John F. Kennedy turned with hardened resolve to stop the spread of Communism in Southeast Asia, choosing Special Forces as the tip of his spear.[17] With his initial blessing, they would proceed to involve Montagnards far more deeply in the coming war than the French had in theirs.

Six-man teams from Okinawa began training Rhadé highlanders to defend their villages against the VC. The idea was that hamlets would dig ditches and build palisades, thus signaling they were allied with the government; defenders armed with light carbines could then hold off the VC until a "strike force" of better-trained highlanders arrived, summoned by radio.

Underlying this was the belief the VC were terrorizing villagers. However, the VC—at this stage—were paying for supplies and recruiting by persuasion. Executions were still targeted at individuals who were, or were thought to be, government informants.[18] Thus, for most Montagnard hamlets, a nocturnal visit by Vietnamese guerrillas may have been very unwelcome, but not terrifying.

Yet, by the end of the Green Berets' first week, would-be Rhadé recruits were lining up at the front gate. At first, only hamlets near Ban Me Thuot signed up, but soon remote ones were doing so too. This was all the more remarkable because remote villagers knew perfectly well that forces sent overland to relieve them would be ambushed.

Three years before, the Vietnamese authorities had confiscated all Montagnard crossbows, sabers, and iron-tipped spears, leaving them only with bamboo spears. For all Montagnard males, but especially those who had followed their warrior tradition and served in French military or paramilitary units, this must have felt like a *coup de grâce* in the decades-long, slow, stripping away of Montagnard agency. Suddenly, here were American soldiers handing out M1 carbines to take home and keep. Choosing to ally with these new foreigners was risky, especially in remote villages, but it would have been a risk most proud Rhadé were willing to take, armed with a decent weapon.[19]

And, for a good while, the VC kept their distance.

By the end of the 1962, more than six thousand carbines had been handed out. The South Vietnam Government, never happy with the program to begin with, was becoming increasingly nervous. One Vietnamese general complained of having "an army at [his] back." The government eventually took back 4,000 carbines from hamlet defenders—though not from the growing number of full-time strike-force soldiers.

With time and mission creep, the strike forces, now called CIDG (Civilian Irregular Defense Group), were moved to isolated, fortified Special Forces camps astride infiltration routes used by VC and North Vietnamese. The soldiers' wives and children moved as well.

Eventually, the CIDG would become very important to FULRO, and FULRO to the CIDG.

***

Y-Bham Enuol was sentenced to a year in prison but ended up serving six. He spent the first nine months in *cachots noirs* (black dungeons), then transferred to the same prison in Ban Me Thuot that had been assaulted by the French in 1945. (It is still there today, a minor tourist attraction, mossy and quiet, with butterflies.) He was kept there until the rumors of impending jailbreak grew too strong. Highlanders were bad at keeping secrets.

If highlanders had a common dread, it seems to have been fear of confinement: a frequent miracle in their hero stories is that the Hero was thrown in jail "and, the next morning, was standing outside." You might think the failure of a flesh-and-blood hero, like Y-Bham Enuol, to accomplish this might have diminished him in their eyes, but the opposite occurred. They assumed he had chosen not to.

He grew in stature over time. Some of this was attributable to who he was, some of it to who the highlanders wanted him to be. Bad change was in the wind. Prophets had been arising almost every generation in response to some threat from the outside world, but this threat was much worse.

Unlike those prophets, Y-Bham Enuol made no claims to supernatural powers. But his people, especially the simpler ones, ascribed such powers to him anyway. Over time, he became cloaked in myth and rumor. Elders pointed out he was a firstborn son in a clan known for bravery because, when the world was created, the Enuol clan had emerged first out of the Hole of the World. When he came home to sleep, it was said, large snakes came to coil beneath his bed, and he conversed at night with the spirit of The Old Man on a White Horse (his guards had heard his murmurs through the walls, and the sound of hoof beats). These specific rumors echoed a messianic movement in the 1930s, but the rumors updated, too. Because he carried a small pouch of spirit pebbles, he could escape a police escort at will or hold a helicopter on the ground until he willed it to rise. And once, when he was meeting with the president of South Vietnam—itself a myth—a piece of paper fluttered down between them, from the sky, with writing on it. A plangent detail, no one knows what it said.

Notes

1 Rhadé troops became a go-to for French trying to suppress Vietnamese communists and nationalists in the early forties. We can assume Bhan picked up at least some secondhand anti-communism—and possibly anti-Vietnamese sentiment—from his father, though the relationship between father and son was cold at best. Then Bhan himself served, aged 17–21, under the French, fighting the Viet Minh. These influences no doubt made him anticommunist. However, his ethnonationalism appears homegrown because, as a teenager, he and some companions considered attacking Vietnamese plantation workers. Jonathan Padwe, *Disturbed Forests, Fragmented Memories: Jarai and Other Lives in the Cambodian Highlands* (University of Washington Press, 2020), 97.

2 He had not played one for 40 years when I asked him if he thought he still could. "No", he replied, "there must be somebody to play with. There's no meaning to play alone."

3 Ban Don pops up repeatedly in this story and in early history of the highlands, because it was located at a good place to ford the great Sre Pok river, in turn a spot easy to find because it was indicated by a knife-like mountain visible from considerable distance. But, mostly, it was in elephant country, savannah-like, known far and wide as the source of captured and/or trained elephants—rather like the Detroit of ancient Indochina.

4 The last French troops left Vietnam in April 1956 but Ban Don earlier.

5 This is termed paedonymy or teknonymy, calling parents by the names of their children. Bhan's own father was called "Ma K'ju" (Father of Blackie) because of Bhan's dark skin, which, incidentally, had no negative connotations, presumably being relatively common (a surge of Dravidian genes?).

6 Two of the groups were religious sects with their own armies, the Cao Dai and the Hoa Hao. The third was the Binh Xuyen, a Saigon criminal gang grown political. France cultivated all three to help in its battle against the Viet Minh, developing personal loyalties. The SDECE (French Secret Service) never forgot the defeat of their clients, the Binh Xuyen, at the hands of Diem's CIA-advised forces. One Frenchman in particular, about whom we will hear more, was Charles Meyer, an "advisor" to the Binh Xuyen, who never forgot the CIA trashed his personal library during all this. Three years later, in Cambodia, the SDECE paid the CIA back, foiling one of their proxy operations to unseat Sihanouk.

7 The expansionary Han were still at it, moving into Tibet after 1949. In a small irony, Bhan remembered being asked by Americans if he wanted to go fight in Tibet. This had to be between 1957 and 1960, when the CIA ran paramilitary operations into Tibet to harass the communist Chinese. (Bhan was popular, invited to Algeria too—see next note.)

8 One of the last to leave was Lieutenant Guy Simon, who smuggled 109 Rhadé/Jarai soldiers (plus some ninety others, including Cambodians and Nung) out at night on a ship from Vung Tau. They spent the next four years in Algeria, fighting against the FLN (nationalist/communist rebels), as the Dam San Commando (after a Rhadé hero who died trying to catch the sun).

There they would infiltrate at night deep into rebel territory, in groups of 3–5 men with a radio, set up as trail watchers, then call in airstrikes or reaction forces (tactics previously developed by the French to combat the Viet Minh and later copied by the US, adding helicopters, to combat the Viet Cong.) Forty out of 200 were killed in action. General Guy Simon, interview with author, March 7, 2018. Simon talked as if the ship's stop in Algeria had been unplanned. However, Bhan was asked by the French if he wanted to go fight in Algeria in 1955–56. In any case, Simon made sure that the 160 survivors became French citizens and integrated into French life.

9 Françoise Demeure remembered one donation of massive amounts of unnecessary cooking oil.

10 Jonathan Neale, *A People's History of the Vietnam War* (New York: The New Press, 2003), 38. Neale's point of view on the war is Trotskyite, so the figures may be exaggerated.

11 Bernard Fall, *The Two Vietnams: A Political and Military Analysis* (London: Pall Mall Press, 1967), 156.

12 Either February 1958 or February 1957. If the latter, it was contemporaneous with an assassination attempt on Diem in the highlands.

13 Y-Thih Eban (via Bhan).

14 CIA, *The Highlanders of South Vietnam: A Review of Political Developments and Forces*, CIA-RDP80T01719R000300010003-8 (Washington, D.C., 1966), 19–22. Dhon is not named in this document that looks back at Bajaraka, but its few references to a militant and/or French-aligned leader in 1956–58 can only mean him.

15 Ken Swain, interview with author, April 1973.

16 Nay Luett, interview with author, April 1973. My notes read "Water put in his face," referring to Dhon.

17 The CIA had originated the Montagnard training program, called Buon Enao, and President Kennedy could have left them in charge, but the Cuban Bay of Pigs fiasco in April 1961 had angered him against the CIA.

18 Roger Hilsman, "Foreign Relations of the US (FRUS) 1961–63, Vol II, Vietnam 1962," #42 (February 2).

19 Francis X. Kelly, *Vietnam Studies: U.S. Army Special Forces 1961–1971* (CMH Publication 90-23, Washington, D.C.: Department of the Army, 1973), 24. Kelly said "part of [the program's] popularity was getting their weapons back." But I think that was by far the largest part.

CHAPTER 5

Witness

1966–67

I arrived in South Vietnam in September 1966—a 21-year-old lieutenant in Special Forces—to spend the next four months at the Gia Vuc camp in the mist-bound northern reaches of the country.

Some of the Montagnards there, in the Hre ethnic group, still wore their hair long and patrolled barefoot. A few had pearls sewn under their skin to protect them from bullets. The year before, some of the Hre CIDG had shot up the Americans' team house, though this was thought to have been the result of a drunken misunderstanding between an American and a proud Hre out in the *ville*.[1]

The climate was dark. My memories are sodden: the moon like a bruise in the night; bellying down into wet mulch to fire at unseen enemies; and trying to torch a thatch roof in the rain. (This was to force outliers to move in under government control, which made sense to me at the time but was part of the many forced relocations of highlanders that unquestionably created more Montagnard Viet Cong.)

However, my interpreter, Dinh-Nieu, was a sunny soul, one of those people, often marginal to begin with, who joyously embrace a new and different world. He was a partial cripple, unusually short, swiveling as he walked. He taught me the Hre dialect, I taught him English. Together, we built a one-room schoolhouse. Above all, his presence was a comfort in the jungle.

On one five-day patrol with him, 30 Hre soldiers, and an American sergeant[2] as young and green as I, we clambered and slipped up and down unnamed mountains through forests dripping with cloud mist. We met no enemy. In retrospect, those wastes were too wild. But for us the jungle, especially at night, was ghastly, with its creature calls, its phosphor glow of rot, and the drips and the drops, the latter like shots in the silence after midnight. Daylight, 100 feet below the canopy, was grayish green, like being on the sea floor.

When we finally broke into a clearing, it was as though we had passed through a membrane. A small stilt house stood at the center of an expanse of grass

The author and Dinh-Nieu. (Author's collection)

cropped to baize. Though far from the valleys, its owner was related to one of our soldiers and invited us in. We had no idea if the enemy might strike that night, and we were not completely sure of the loyalty of the highlanders themselves. The sergeant felt better sleeping outside. But I had been trying to learn the local dialect, which seemed to please the younger soldiers enormously. I felt we could trust them. Nieu and I spent the night inside.

Our host, a small, wiry man with front teeth filed to nubs, gave me a wilted salute, palm forward, and dragged some French words bouncing down from his mental attic. We three sat cross-legged at his hearth and shared rice wine through a bamboo straw. In the cathedral forests beyond, requiem roared in the heart. Here, bamboo glowed like organ pipes, as pigs snuffled quietly beneath the house. He brought out a gourd violin strung to a disk in his mouth. Words wavered in his notes like distant radio.

His family, huddled at the rear, chins on knees, was equally enthralled—except for an old woman whose eyes were like black pebbles, wet side up.

Death was about. To her, it was me.

I got pulled away to another assignment after four months. I never saw Nieu again but learned decades later that, after 1975, he had spent years in a "re-education camp," dying shortly after his return home.

***

I first heard of FULRO during my next assignment, now early 1967, commanding a battalion of Rhadé and Jarai firebrands (the B-50 [Omega] Mike Force). We guarded the bases of a recon unit and did recon in force along the Cambodian border. However, from my highland soldiers' point of view, our battalion was a training camp and supply dump for FULRO. They would announce when one company was leaving; I would look the other way as fit young men staggered onto helicopters, bulging with pilfered ammo, grenades, and Claymores. Their replacements would arrive light.

General Westmoreland, commander of all American forces in Vietnam, had made it clear we were not in Vietnam to support rebellion against our ally, South Vietnam. But most Green Berets favored FULRO anyway. The highlanders were our more proximate ally. Equally, they were our protectors. Casually, we stoked enmity between them and the Vietnamese because our enemy was Vietnamese. Beyond this, FULRO's cause seemed just, echoing the Civil Rights Movement back home.

Some of us were becoming uneasy with our mission. Special Forces had been created in the 1950s to support guerilla resistance behind the Iron Curtain. At Fort Bragg, we had trained to parachute behind enemy lines and link up with partisans on the run from oppressors. In Vietnam, however, our mission was the mirror opposite. Still isolated deep in enemy territory, we operated from easily observable camps. Still matched with irregular soldiers, we fought against a surrounding enemy that was experienced, invisible, and claimed the mantle of liberator. It seemed our enemy, even regiment-sized units of North Vietnamese regulars, was now the doughty underdog. This made for dissonance until it came to us that, in the long view, our Montagnard troops themselves were the underdogs.

At one hilltop base, time and space seemed to balloon. The rivers on the plain all ran west, glinting far into the haze, as did the broken French road below our hill, the ancient route to Angkor. At night under the stars, I drank beers with my interpreters and heard about FULRO, its name spoken with a nod to the west. From excited, proud whispers, I learned that thousands, including families, had followed a fabled character named Y-Bham Enuol to Cambodia and were now camped in its forests. They kept mentioning something "to go." I finally realized "to go" was "de Gaulle." They were talking about the president of France who had recently visited Phnom Penh. Y-Bham Enuol was rumored to have met with him.

Cambodia and FULRO were pulling me, via Phnom Penh.

But first I had to make it back to civilian life. On patrol in an area known to be booby trapped, I told the point man to follow a tunnel made by wild pigs, reasoning the animals should have tripped any wires. I was flat wrong—an explosion behind us wounded my interpreter and me. The young man who had been behind my interpreter was reclining on a fan of elephant grass. He looked asleep but was trickling blood from a hundred stings. I recorded his name—Y-Djhap Eban.

The old woman had been right.

***

1973

It took me six years. In the spring of 1973, I went back to Southeast Asia to find FULRO.

I stopped first in Vietnam, where the war had been on hold since January's signing of the Paris Peace Accords. Very few Americans were still working in-country. Visitors like me usually fell in two categories: penitents or scavengers. I did not think I qualified as either.

Travelling in the highlands felt strangely levitated. At first a feeling of release, the absence of danger, it soon became a twilight sense of floating above the earthbound and the doomed, from a vague height with guilt, not only for having survived but for politically having turned against the war. By the end of my tour in Vietnam in 1967, I had come to see the war as unwinnable against an enemy who would never, ever quit. The human cost had become too great, largely because of my country's resort to ever more firepower in its frustration. I spent the next six years pursuing political solutions, first clutching at an impossible idea for Balkanizing South Vietnam,[3] then working as an advance man in the 1968 presidential campaign of Senator Eugene McCarthy—a one-time seminarian whom I found eloquent, humorous, and moderate. When the movement turned too radical for me, I switched to organizing for Cesar Chavez's labor strike in the northeast. The Grape Boycott was ultimately successful, but by then I was slipping into quietism, first as a taxi driver in New Orleans, then as a seeker in the cleanliness of deserts, with a whiff of patchouli and the dirt-grit taste of mushrooms. In Oaxaca, I had an epiphany of sorts about the futility of politics and hitchhiked home to begin pre-med studies on the GI Bill, knowing I would one day practice medicine in what was then called the Third World (now Global South). But Vietnam was proscenium to my dreams at night, and the Montagnards were often there.

In 1973, Y-Bham Enuol's photo hung in every longhouse, but none of his partisans had heard from him since early 1969. They were politically eviscerated. Having outgrown the world they had struggled to preserve, many were jug huggers. At the top of a slide into alcoholism myself, I spent a memorably forgotten evening with a number of his old comrades. A last, scrawled note to myself, dribbling off the page—"Nothing's gonna change my world"—brings it partly back: John Lennon on the radio, turquoise sky outside, purple faces under fluorescent light, and "*Nous avons versé le sang pour rien*" (We spilled our blood for nothing).

I found Father Bianchetti saying mass in his tiny church with its roof of corrugated tin, windows of broken blue-and-white glass, and walls faded yellow except for a patch of exposed concrete where a glass crucifix had been shot up by "the communists" five years before. It had wooden benches in two rows, on the left for Montagnard men and boys, on the right (behind the planters' wives) for women and girls, whence gurgles and stifled wails. With a greying goatee, Bianchetti was in his early fifties, but close-cropped hair and sinewy forearms gave him the look of a legionnaire. The racket of helicopters drowned out all but his repeated "*Yesu!*" as he lifted the chalice.

Afterward, I spoke with him, in my could-be-better French. "The Protestants taught [the Rhadé] to be afraid of God," he said, pithy but arguable. And "Montagnards prefer old men as leaders." And, speaking of the young men who signed up as soldiers with the CIDG, "Their poverty killed them [meaning they did so for American money]."[4]

My notes say he called Dhon "a communist."

Two ex-interpreters took me home to their villages, where the tropical climate had been busy. Halloween-orange barbed wire was flaking toward oblivion. Plastic sandbags had burst into confetti, a reptilian, shiny gray-green.

The sky seemed cleaner to me. If there had been bright-yellow days with birdsong when I was here before, they did not register.

One of the Montagnards expressed contentment with the simple life again, having "learned not to trust any Americans except missionaries." He guessed that "40 or 50" young men from his village had been killed as CIDG. By rough extrapolation, this was about one out of two. Even if exaggerated, this proportion was clearly far worse than the death toll from attacks on that village by the communists, in which one man was killed in 20 years.[5]

The other was more modern—a development worker who bemoaned his people's lack of progress yet had chosen proudly to revert to animism from Christianity. In his village of 600 people, 50 young men had served as CIDG; "five or six" had been killed. Some had joined for the money, he said, but others had done so for a "higher purpose."[6]

Back in Saigon, I stopped in to see anthropologist Gerald C. Hickey, the single-most knowledgeable American about highlanders. Having been the Montagnards' most-effective proponent with Vietnamese and American officialdom for over 16 years, he knew many mid-level FULRO leaders within South Vietnam. Three years before, he had met briefly with its higher leaders in Phnom Penh, though he had not seen the highest, Y-Bham Enuol, apparently because he was under house arrest to prevent his selling out. There were three young Turks, all now in the army of the Khmer Republic[7] as officers. Two were Paul Y-Bun Sur, a Mnong colonel and Mondulkiri province chief, and Kpa Doh, a Jarai major. A third was a Rhadé colonel named Bhan.

(For narrative clarity I have already described the early lives of Bhan, Dhon, and Y-Bham Enuol, using information I learned decades later. In reality, at this point I still knew nothing about them except what Hickey was telling me.)

He had also met the mysterious Colonel Les Kosem, a Cambodian Cham widely assumed to be pulling FULRO's strings as Sihanouk's representative and thought to be a military intelligence officer. Hickey had found him urbane and charming though with a jarring habit of referring to Montagnards as his "little brothers."

Hickey was a generous man and encouraging. Perhaps I could find out what really happened to FULRO. Had Kosem stifled it, intentionally or otherwise? Was Y-Bham Enuol still alive? And what, exactly, had happened to Dhon, one of FULRO's founders, who was known to have died, possibly murdered?

In the short-hop flight to Phnom Penh, I came up with a title for my article, imagining it on the cover of *Harper's*: "Mercenaries, Missionaries." Catchy, but I knew better.

***

Three years before, Cambodia's thousand-year-old monarchy came to an abrupt end when a group of Army officers and leading citizens deposed Prince Sihanouk, angry at his having let the communist Vietnamese use their country as sanctuary for too long. Immediately tagged as a right-wing coup because everything at that time was seen through the left–right lens, it may in fact have been as much visceral/racial as ideological, spurred by Cambodians' age-old fear and hatred of the Vietnamese. This was particularly true of Lon Nol, who, on becoming president of the new Khmer Republic, immediately ordered the North Vietnamese Army out of his country and later failed to stop a vicious anti-Vietnamese pogrom.

The North Vietnamese, in order to hold on to their longtime bases in Cambodia, quickly overran the eastern provinces, then surrounded Phnom Penh, besieging it for the next two years. Over the course of 1972, they gradually withdrew to be replaced by homegrown Cambodian communists, the Khmer Rouge. American airpower was the single most important element in holding them at bay, but it pulverized peasants as well as attackers. Bombing was often close enough to the city that windows rattled and glasses jittered across tables.

I checked into the city's elephantine colonial hotel, found some journalists by the pool, and inquired about FULRO, expecting blank stares. Several spoke at once.

Kpa Doh (Author's collection)

"You gotta meet Kpa Doh," said one, "with Special Forces in Vietnam. He'll tip you to where there's fighting—but watch out travelling with him." He chuckled, "He's a character. A while back he took me out to their camp, and we blew a tire," adding, as the others leaned forward, "We're way out in nowhere, backlit on a paddy dike. He has me get down while he changes it. Takes about three minutes. As we drive away, he grins and says in that raspy voice of his, 'Not bad for a man who didn't see tires until he was grown, huh?'"[8]

They told me FULRO's troops were defending one approach to the city about 15 miles out, at the neck of a peninsula across the river. Its top officers lived in town with their families, except Y-Bham Enuol who was rumored to be out by the airport where he could be better guarded. The journalists had little awareness of FULRO's previous incarnations, either in Mondulkiri or Vietnam.

Kpa Doh came to get me in his jeep. As he cranked through the gears, we ticked off who we knew in Special Forces. He was jokey from the start, gravel-voiced, emphasizing points by punching my leg. He had just gotten back from six months at Fort Benning, Georgia. It was as though I had known him for years. Over time I got the impression he mirrored Americans, sometimes with a hint of amusement.

Explaining I only had a five-day visa, I asked to meet Y-Bham Enuol and Les Kosem as well as his comrades. "May take a few days," he replied. "Kosem's still sick from an operation. With Y-Bham Enuol, you never know. But, sure."

We stopped first by his villa. As with Phnom Penh's nickname, "Paris of the Orient," tropical grime and clutter took "villa" down a few notches. Inside it seemed more like a barracks, with radio blaring, soldiers lounging about in undershirts. One was ironing. (I never did meet Kpa Doh's wife, whom a friend of mine described as the most beautiful woman he had ever seen.)[9]

"Next stop," he said, "the governor of Mondulkiri."

An old black Dodge with curtained rear window sat outside the governor's villa, kept shiny by a Montagnard chauffeur. In the cool of a parlor loomed a piano, an expensive stereo, and a color TV though no stations here broadcast in color (in fact, decades later, Cambodia would be the last country in the world to have color TV). On a lacquer sideboard was a row of cheap jelly glasses and liquor. The only sign of the governor's ethnicity were some children's play crossbows.

The governor was taller and younger than I expected, and slightly plump. With him was a sturdy, scowling fellow with a US Master Parachutist Badge on his chest. Kpa Doh introduced them to me. The governor was Monsieur Paul Y-Bun Sur. The fellow with the jump wings was a colonel and FULRO's chief of staff, Bhan.

Paul spoke little English, Bhan not much more.

They answered my questions in sessions spaced out over the next four days, tag teaming me in ones or twos, sometimes at restaurants. We got by on a combination of English and, when Kpa Doh was not there, my French.

They were candid about their struggle being stalled. Since March 1970's removal of Sihanouk, Cambodia had been allied with South Vietnam and could no longer be used as a platform for anti-Saigon activity. FULRO's only course was to help Cambodia survive against the communists so it could be used again another day.

They preferred to talk about their struggle in the present. It was difficult to cadge pieces of FULRO's history.

In contrast to Kpa Doh's six years, Bhan had only spent six months with Americans. We shared jump stories instead of who-do-you-know. Present at the birth of Montagnard ethnonationalism, he was the repository of FULRO's early history, from about 1955–58, back when it was Bajaraka. He also possessed an unusual perspective on the period from 1958–62, when Vietnam was largely out of the world's eye, and Saigon had exiled him to remote military postings.

Bhan, Paul (Y-Bun Sur). (Photo on left in author's collection, on right courtesy of Meidine Natchear)

Paul was often busy elsewhere. In the evenings, he brought out drinks. We took Biere Larue, he took Johnny Walker. He said he had married a half-Vietnamese in France. (In fact—I learned later—he had married a Frenchwoman and brought her to Cambodia, then taken up with a Cambodian bargirl. Perhaps the fib was intended to cover either, should one or the other appear.) I noted photos of children in the room. He drank more than the rest of us but seemed to regulate it. After his third whisky, I asked what had happened to Dhon, guessing this might be an edgy topic. He began with the same adjectives everyone else used for Dhon—"*energique*" (vigorous), "fiery" and "strong," as though the lexicon for describing the man was trapped in amber.

He said Y-Bham Enuol had ordered Dhon killed.

Startled, it took me a second or two before hearing him again, now saying, "Or maybe he wished it and was overheard." In any case, it was still Shakespearean: Dhon was second-in-command but too ambitious; the king-like leader was jealous and given to rages; one day he expressed a wish to be rid of Dhon, and unnamed minions took it literally.[10] More startling still, Dhon was "buried up to the chest." This awful phrase sits alone, without elaboration, in the margin of my notes.

Kpa Doh was the group's folklorist, filling me in on the meager list of Montagnard heroes, including the man who had killed Henri Maître in 1914. French sources portray the man as a treacherous savage. In Kpa Doh's version, however, "Maître came with a hundred men, armed with rifles, and demanded that the Montagnards sign a piece of paper [signaling their submission]. The Montagnards only had crossbows ..."

To Kpa Doh, the man was a Trickster Hero, not a murderer.

About Americans, he said, "They are good, as individuals. They had good intentions. But they got replaced every year. They gave us the material to make revolution," the last word striking me as a bit grandiose, "but now—no more *cartouches* (bullets) ..." He went on, "Montagnards are open and sincere. For them, one is one, two is two. Not like the Vietnamese. They are easily misled, by the French, by the Americans—attracted by material things ..." And then, as a swipe at Y-Bham Enuol: "Our old people understand very little, the opposite of in your culture ..."

I tried to feel out how much he was driven by hatred of Vietnamese, as opposed to ideology. Surprisingly, like Dhon, he had attended the Lycée Yersin, where he said he had fought constantly against Vietnamese boys "*pour la dignité*" against racial slurs. But he had also "begun to dream at age 17" of a country of the Montagnards' own, for which he used a phrase that could have been uttered by 1960s youth worldwide, "We were excited, not afraid."

From him I got a few glimpses of recent years in Phnom Penh. By April 1970, North Vietnamese forces had approached to within 15 miles of the city in several directions, loosely surrounding it. Then the Americans' Cambodian incursion 100 miles to the east temporarily took pressure off the capital but, by June or July, small enemy units were probing Phnom Penh's defenses, coming in at night. FULRO was charged with blocking these probes on the peninsula. Its early combats were frenetic, almost hallucinatory, with meager forces. Nightly, a skeleton crew sallied forth—ordered out "in battalion strength" by clueless headquarters—to meet the enemy, finding themselves in firefights by the swaying light of flares, once memorably against a thudding machine gun. It was rainy season. Slowly, the marshy country swelled, driving snakes onto the road and rats into the trees. (They would shoot the latter for food.) "Captains with no men" is how Kpa Doh described this period.

All three men spoke of Y-Bham Enuol with apparent warmth but made clear he was now only *chef symbolique* (symbolic leader, or figurehead), though a potent symbol that needed protection against kidnapping or assassination. Both Hanoi and Saigon wanted to get their hands on him. Kpa Doh let slip comments about his being *sous la table* (under the table, or drunk).

I had heard he was also their prisoner. Five years before, they had participated in his abduction from Mondulkiri following a schism at the heart of FULRO. They were open about this.

In 1968, Y-Bham Enuol returned to Vietnamese soil, for the first time since the 1964 rebellion, to negotiate with Saigon. They expected him to drive a hard bargain because Saigon and the Americans were flailing and needed Montagnard help. Instead, they said, he was seduced by offers of rank and privilege. To block this, Kpa Doh enticed him to come back across the border to get his wife and children, where a company of Cambodian Army Chams sent by Les Kosem materialized to surround his bungalow. A standoff ensued. A handful of militant leaders, mostly Jarai, faced off against thousands of Y-Bham Enuol's armed followers, who were mostly Rhadé. Whether this was a literal or figurative face off was unclear. What was clear was that Y-Bham Enuol averted bloodshed by telling his followers to stand down. The majority of the Rhadé then trekked back to South Vietnam,[11] and Y-Bham Enuol and his family were brought to Phnom Penh.

This seemed to be what had really happened to FULRO. As I would hear decades later from the Rhadé soldiers who returned to Vietnam and eventually constituted the core of the Montagnard refugee community in North Carolina, this was the moment their music died.

Efforts to fill in the schism's backstory were less successful. It sounded as if little had happened in the four years between the 1964 rebellion and the 1968 split. There had been a second uprising in 1965, but it had quickly failed due to unexpectedly heavy rains. Four Jarai had been publicly executed by firing squad.

Bhan was my main source about FULRO's doings at its jungle base during those four years because Paul was in Paris and Kpa Doh was mostly in South Vietnam. However, Bhan was opaque; "We walked, we fished," he said.

Towards the end of my visit, Kpa Doh became fatalistic. "We don't need great hope, we don't need to believe in final victory, in order to keep fighting, to go into the jungle and the mountains to carry on *une lutte silencieuse, sans avenir, malgré le manque de moyens* [a silent struggle, without future, despite lack of means] ..."

This seemed at least a partial pose, political smoke aimed at generating sympathy from the American public. But the American public had no sympathy left. Vietnam had become an embarrassment to almost every segment of the political spectrum and most Americans considered the war in Cambodia to be part of the Vietnam War. In the American mind's eye, Montagnards were sad wretches. The only way I could imagine re-awakening American interest would be to tell a story with hope, with heroes. And, look as I might, I could not see any.

The morning of my last day, I was delivered to Les Kosem's doorstep in a compound near the center of town, its cloister-like stillness contrasting with the frenzy outside of jeeps, deuce-and-a-halfs, Citroens, and vendors dodging and calling midst the flow of *cyclo-pousses*.[12] Inside, red-tiled bungalows were aligned along paths bordered with white stones, their walls a faded, serene saffron. Tropical riot was tamed. Even the bougainvillea cascaded just so. Like military posts everywhere, and some missionary ones, it was also a temporal cloister, its order and serenity muting terrors past while bracing psyches against future ones—an atmosphere that strikes most people as noble, if melancholy. But here, with the future literally crowding in closer every day, the pathos was beginning to show.

Two little girls were playing in the dirt near steps in front. Kosem came out, chided them gently in French, and turned to me, with large, red-rimmed eyes and broken complexion in a long face. Tall for a Cambodian, his handshake, like many non-Westerners', was limp. Despite a waiting jeep and driver, he gestured for us to sit on chairs on the low verandah, crossing his legs, very erect, hands clasped on a knee, and asked about me. His half smile and floating demeanor made me wonder about opium until he mentioned he had just returned from surgery in Paris for a deviated septum,[13] a strange thing to volunteer until I realized Kpa Doh must have told him I was heading to medical school. In Kosem's eyes, I was no journalist. He called to his young wife to meet me, we exchanged more pleasantries, then his jeep started up. I took a stab, asking if he had visited a well-known Paris museum to see its Champa collection. He brightened, "Many times!" But this only made his regret more sincere as he continued down the steps. "Y-Bham Enuol will be here soon."

And that was it with the mysterious Colonel Les Kosem.

Kpa Doh had chipped away at my expectations of Y-Bham Enuol, but the man's myth still preceded him. Inevitably, I was disappointed. When he arrived with the three younger men, he seemed shrunken, his face frog-like. His responses to my biographical questions were too practiced.

My final impression of him was of sorrow. Dignity was all that was left of his reputed magnetism. Even that wobbled when, as we were saying goodbye, he muttered to me in French, "I hope very much that you can help me come to America."

We gathered for a photo.

On the way back to Saigon, I wrote that "he was asking me to help save his life," a bit too thrilled by the drama of it all as I returned to my comfortable life. Cambodia's eventual defeat was almost certain, but its subsequent horrors were still unimaginable to all but a few.[14] Exits still existed in 1973.[15] I could

(From left to right) Bhan, the author with Kpa Doh behind, Y-Bham Enuol, and Paul. (Author's collection/Photo by E. Cavanaugh)

not have guessed that, exactly two years later, Y-Bham Enuol would disappear into the maw of the Khmer Rouge.

I also wrote, in a determined hand:

> Still to be answered:
> Who is Les Kosem? What is his story?
> What really happened to Dhon?
> What happened during the 1968 abduction?

I crossed the last one out. No, I had nailed that one; FULRO had been destroyed by conflict between militants and moderates.

I was so imprinted on the FULRO of yore, imagined from a border hilltop six years before, that I discounted the men in front of me. I was least interested in Kpa Doh because he was too American.

1975

America was preoccupied with Watergate by the time I got home in 1973. One way to cleanse the stain of Vietnam was to cast out Richard Nixon. Another was simply to strike tents and leave Southeast Asia. In August 1973, Congress forbade any further military action by Americans in Southeast Asia, which in practice meant cease bombing because ground troops were long gone.

American readers did not want to hear another Vietnam story, much less one that did not jibe neatly with opinions on either the left or right. I shelved the FULRO story and entered the all-consuming apprenticeship of medicine.

In one final twist, however, I returned briefly to Phnom Penh—on break from my sophomore year at med school. This was in February 1975, two-and-a-half months before the city's fall. A pediatrician friend was investigating a strange kind of pneumonia in orphanages in Saigon and asked me to accompany him to Vietnam. He then sent me onward to check out an orphanage in Phnom Penh, which I did, though the babies there faced worse threats than *Pneumocystis carinii*.[16] I found myself trying to hydrate dying infants with enormous shots of saline injected into what little subcutaneous fat they had left above their buttocks. Some 10–20 rockets per day were landing in the city.

I took no notes this time. Only images remain: the vulnerability of infants' backs with washboard ribs, tiny shoulder blades meant to fly; Hôtel Manolis across from the post office, with dark wood paneling and sweeping balustrade and the owner's daughter in a peach-colored satin dress; riding a motorbike down the riverfront and glimpsing a partially built luxury hotel, its open concrete structure like roosts fluttering with refugees, an image I would later conflate with Ridley Scott's *Blade Runner*; a shower of white-hot fragments, like a thousand fireflies, when a 107-mm rocket struck at night.

I did not contact Kpa Doh or FULRO. A layer of unease obscures my reasons now. I was forced to leave suddenly, on learning that civilian flights to destinations outside the country were temporarily suspended, but this does not explain my inaction before. There were the babies, of course, but my efforts felt futile, with an aura of displacement activity, like a nervous pigeon. Evidently, I thought Cambodia would survive because, on return home, I submitted long-range suggestions to the orphanage's board. In a note to myself at the time, I maintained that "I had nothing to offer Kpa Doh, thus did not want to give him false hope."

And yet.

The only flight available was up-country to Battambang near the Thai border on a Khmer Airlines DC-3. I was waiting in the sandbagged terminal with a young man and several turbaned old women chewing betel nut when a rocket exploded nearby. I bellyflopped behind my purple, blessedly thick *Robbins' Textbook of Pathology,* while the young man only crouched and ducked. A typical Cambodian, he smiled at the same time.

From Battambang, I took a combi taxi 100 kilometers (60 miles) to the Thai border. The dry, alluvial flood plain felt like the ancient invasion corridor that it was. In the heat, tree lines always seemed to be on the horizon, which suited me fine—less likely to hide Khmer Rouge. The risk I was taking was very small, but its consequence was almost certainly execution. (Ironically, execution would have been merciful compared to the fate of other young Westerners trusting blithely in their luck and whiteness only a few months later, after Khmer Rouge paranoia went into high gear: being subjected to months of unimaginable horror, their agonies coming to an end only when they were trucked at night to a site south of Phnom Penh and executed while kneeling trussed, looking down at worms in a freshly dug pit.)

***

From Saigon, I returned to the US and Cincinnati Med School. A river town, Cincinnati had one thing in common with Phnom Penh, the feeling that the sea was very far away.

I was a hoplite in a new war in which I was a Good Guy and our technology was effective against microscopic enemies visible as gayly pink dashes and purple dots. Against a more-malignant enemy visible as eerie disorder in cell nuclei, I understood there was light at the end of the tunnel.

Before heading to school every morning, I searched for news of Phnom Penh in *The Cincinnati Enquirer.*

"Cambodia Kindergarten Hit by Red Rockets, 8 Tots Die" was a heading on page 12 my first day back. That night, on TV, I spotted a close-up of wailing parents, followed by a pull-back shot of the French lycée with its orange-tiled roofs, then the *Cercle Sportif,* a tennis and swim club, and finally the cathedral glowering down a boulevard of flame trees.

All roads to the capital were in Khmer Rouge hands, Now, supply convoys on the Mekong could no longer get past a gauntlet downriver. Ship captains refused to sail anymore after one of them lost both legs to a mine.

America stepped up its airlift. As many as 100 aircraft per day were landing with fuel and ammunition for the army and rice for a population swollen with refugees, edging close to three million.

Defense Secretary Schlesinger said Cambodia's fall was inevitable without an additional $222 million in aid. But Sihanouk worked to block it by telling selected anti-war congressmen that the Khmer Rouge were not communists—ironic because he himself had named them "Red Cambodians." The goal, he claimed, was only a socialist monarchy, like Sweden's.

Cambodia's and South Vietnam's death struggles dominated the news, taking place in parallel. Few Americans realized Phnom Penh was only 280 kilometers (175 miles) upriver from Saigon. The news was like a twin drive-in—where Saigon's fate was the movie they came to see, while Cambodia's agonies were soundless on the screen next door, visible over the fence. For me, however, I was sitting in my '47 Mercury, rivetted on that other screen.

Newspaper columnists on the left said it was time to stop shoring up past mistakes.[17] Those on the right warned of a bloodbath.[18]

If Lon Nol's government could survive a few more months until next rainy season, then maybe the communists would forswear reprisals in return for surrender. But 78 percent of the American people said forget it, and Congress killed the Cambodian appropriation.[19]

The airport became the focus of daily battles to keep the Khmer Rouge from shelling it. Paratroopers were sent out to push them back. Villages lost or recaptured were identified by name for readers, probably to make their agony seem more real, though these could have been on Mars.

On April 1, Lon Nol left Phnom Penh for exile in Hawaii. He was thought to be an obstacle to "the orderly transfer of power," a euphemism for surrender with minimal heads rolling.[20] This led to a dance with Sihanouk, but it soon became obvious he did not have any influence over the Khmer Rouge and that, being a merciful modern monarch, if he could have exterminated his opponents' families, he would have stopped after the third generation instead of the seventh.

On April 5, Australia and Britain closed their Phnom Penh embassies like the first two pops of microwave popcorn; then came a staccato of closures, leaving only the French and the Americans.

At dawn on April 12, thirty-six Marine helicopters clattered down onto a soccer field near the American Embassy in Phnom Penh while warplanes growled overhead. Codenamed *Eagle Pull*, faintly oxymoronic, the operation plucked 159 Cambodians and 82 Americans to safety.[21] The last person out was the ambassador, a tall man in a suit and tie carrying a folded American flag. Each chopper carried eight people, meaning they had gone out half-empty.

Events picked up speed. Headlines told the story: "Americans Abandon Cambodia," "Rebels in Sight of Phnom Penh," and "Rebel Forces Slice Deeply into Phnom Penh." By the 15th, the northwestern outskirts had fallen.

Sources in Paris said foreigners in the capital had sought refuge in the French Embassy. Communication with the outside world was flickering out.

April 17: "Cambodian Appeal for Peace Fails." This was a last sigh of direct news, coming from Geneva. (The International Red Cross had telegrammed Sihanouk in Beijing, asking for a ceasefire on behalf of Cambodia's leaders. The prince's answer: the leaders better run or face hanging.)

The government radio kept broadcasting right up till the end. "We will fight on to the last drop of blood even though a certain superpower has left us on the spot."

Then a silence fell, so total that it belonged—like the concept of a city "falling"—to a different era.

On April 24, a French Government spokesman revealed that over a thousand people had taken refuge in the embassy but that the Khmer Rouge had demanded all Cambodians be expelled. Now only foreigners were left in the compound.

On the 25th, Sihanouk in Beijing announced the "liberation" of Cambodia, in the same breath foreshadowing the paranoid hellhole his country would become: "Our forces must track down hostile and pro-American Cambodians," elaborating that "networks remain which must be dismantled … One must know who is who, put labels on people to be watched, and ferret out [enemies]."

Sometime before the 29th, the Khmer Rouge found the embassy's morse-code transmitter and shut it off.

On April 30, Saigon fell too.

On May 3, hundreds of the foreigners from the embassy arrived by overland convoy at the Thai border, trucked there by the Khmer Rouge, including *New York Times* reporter Sydney Schanberg.

Cambodia was now a tomb. Intercepted radio traffic was handed to favored reporters, becoming "reports reaching Bangkok." On May 4, these generated a small headline, "Massive Bloodbath Beginning in Cambodia." Orders were being carried out to execute all officers in the defeated army down to the rank of second lieutenant and—with an atavistic touch—their wives.

On May 9, *The New York Times* finally revealed what had happened since April 17, a scoop for which Schanberg would win a deserved Pulitzer. I rushed to a downtown hotel to buy a copy, certain that, if Kpa Doh had ended up in the embassy, he would have made himself known to Schanberg.

But there was nothing in four front-page articles about what had happened to FULRO or the Montagnards.

Schanberg did elaborate on the Cambodians' expulsion. Out of 1,300 people who had taken refuge in the large compound, about 500 were forced to leave—any Cambodian "without foreign passports or papers." On these "days of deep sorrow … sobbing could be heard in every corner of the compound."

The morning of the day of the fall, April 17, the first Khmer Rouge arrived, looking like "peasant boys, pure and simple—darker skinned than their city brethren, with gold in their front teeth."

People were told to leave their homes and evacuate the city. A sense of menace and dread replaced the morning's hope, spreading through the defeated population like the murmuration of a flock of birds. For a terrifying two hours, Schanberg and two other journalists were held by the Khmer Rouge as though about to be taken to execution.[22] Two Cambodian officers with them, desperately trying to look civilian, were taken away, one kissing his Buddha amulet and praying.

Later, Schanberg watched as a Khmer Rouge general assured a group of 50 high-ranking Cambodian prisoners that there would be no reprisals—which no one believed—then turned to the newsmen to send his "thanks to the American people who have helped us and supported us from the beginning, and to all people of the world who love Peace and Justice."

That evening, Schanberg and other foreigners took refuge in the French Embassy, expecting the victors to respect it as sanctuary.

The next morning, through the gates of the compound, they saw:

> [an] astonishing spectacle … [of] two million people suddenly moved out of [Phnom Penh] en masse in stunned silence—walking, bicycling, pushing cars that had run out of fuel, covering the roads like a human carpet, bent under sacks of belongings hastily thrown together when the heavily armed peasant soldiers came and told them to leave immediately … Hospitals jammed with wounded were emptied, right down to the last patient. They went—limping, crawling, on crutches, carried on relatives' backs, wheeled on their hospital beds … Everyone—Cambodians and foreigners alike—[had] … looked ahead with hopeful relief to the collapse of the city, for they felt that when the Communists came and the war finally ended, at least the suffering would largely be over. All of us were wrong …
>
> The Communists declared that they did not recognize the compound as an embassy, simply as a regroupment center for foreigners under their control. This shattered the possibility of asylum for [a handful of very] high officials who had sought sanctuary … In a gloomy drizzle, [these] figures were taken away in the back of a sanitation truck.

The fear was that high-ranking Cambodians—enemies in Khmer Rouge eyes—might compromise the safety of the other refugees in the embassy. A disturbing photograph showed two large Westerners wrestling with an obviously frantic, smaller man in an immaculate tropical worsted suit. The day after, the rest of the Cambodians were obliged to leave, walking out the gate.

Schanberg went on to recount the drama of living cheek-to-jowl on the park-like grounds of the embassy, a two-week ordeal under real threat as well as the duress of inadequate food, water, and sanitation. Some rose to the occasion, many did not. He singled out two who rose: François Bizot, a Frenchman and archeological restorer, fluent in Khmer, who became the foreigners' intermediary with the Khmer Rouge, and Douglas A. Sapper III, "an American with Special Forces background … [whose] Ranger-training—and his colorful language, none of which can be reproduced here—kept us eating regularly."

In the cool early hours of April 30, Schanberg boarded the first convoy out, "looking into the dawn sky and seeing airplanes streaking west, carrying Vietnamese pilots and their families on their own evacuation to safety."

In the same issue of the *Times*,[23] a tiny blurb mentioned the nationality of those who had come out on the second convoy, mostly French and Pakistanis, then Indonesians and Chinese, then a handful of others.[24] I looked in vain for a similar enumeration by nationality of those who had been on the first convoy. Could there have been Montagnards, perhaps listed as something else, say, Vietnamese?

Notes

1 James (Mac) McNamara, interview with author, February 23, 2022.
2 Frank Dailey, eventually Sergeant-Major.
3 Floated by the centrist Republican Ripon Society, it proposed granting autonomy to South Vietnam's Montagnards as well as other fractious groups like the Hoa Hao and Cao Dai in hopes they would better resist Communism if doing so on their own behalf. This was essentially what the French had done without making it explicit.
4 Roger Bianchetti, interview with author, May 1973.
5 Y-Ton (Tony) Hwing, interview with author, April 1973. Ex-Project *Delta* interpreter, from Buon Ea Khit where there were (probably) 211 families.
6 R'Com Ali, interview with author, May 1973. From Plei Pa, where my notes are more certain that the denominator was 600 people in the village.
7 The Cambodians' word for themselves and their language is "Khmer." I use it here for the language only.
8 Haney Howell, interview with author, February 25, 2015.
9 Jim Morris, interview with author, July 8, 2016.
10 Dhon was almost always mentioned together with Y-Nhuinh Hmok, who was his faithful follower and friend and who suffered exactly the same fate. Y-Nhuinh's photo is on p. 119. I know too little about him, thus, I am leaving him out.
11 Where the CIA kept its identity and recent provenance hidden, even from the Green Berets in border camps that they passed. This sort of secrecy kept the FULRO mystique alive, among GIs at least, even though FULRO had long ceased being an important player. Larry Kerr, interview with author, June 7, 2017. He told me about hundreds materializing outside Bu Prang, some of them apparently Mnong.
12 Literally, "push cycle," or bicycle rickshaw, where the passenger sits in a canopied seat in front of the driver.
13 It was cancer, either of the nasopharynx or liver, that would kill him within three years.

14 Only one young US Foreign Service officer, Kenneth Quinn, foresaw the genocidal plans and programs of the radical Khmer Rouge communists and submitted a report to his State Department superiors in February 1974.
15 They existed as late as early 1975. Kosem offered Y-Bham Enuol an escape to Indonesia or Malaysia around January 1975, but he refused. As early as 1971, inquiries were made into getting a visa for him.
16 A microbe that would become notorious a decade later for its association with AIDS.
17 Tom Wicker, "More Aid Only Means More War," *The New York Times*, March 25, 1975.
18 Rowland Evans and Robert Novak, "The Guilt for Cambodia," *Cincinnati Enquirer,* March 17, 1975.
19 Gallup Poll, March 9, 1975.
20 William Safire, *The New York Times*, March 15, 1975. Safire also took issue with the media's persistent use of "regime" for Lon Nol's government, which was certainly no less legitimate than the medieval monarchy preceding it or the ideological monstrosity succeeding it.
21 "D-Day in reverse" is how a French photographer described it. Roland Neveu, *The Fall of Phnom Penh, 17 April 1975* (Bangkok: Asia Horizons Book Co., 2015).
22 The other two journalists were Jon Swain and Al Rockoff.
23 Sydney Schanberg, "Cambodia Reds Are Uprooting Millions As They Impose a 'Peasant Revolution,'" *The New York Times,* May 9, 1975.
24 David A. Andelman, "More Foreign Refugees Leave Cambodia." *The New York Times*, May 9, 1975, who was covering the story from Aranyaprathet in Thailand.

CHAPTER 6

Ishmael

1975

In May 1975, I received a collect call from Columbus, Georgia. I did not recognize the name garbled by the operator, even when the caller himself barked it. But when he addressed me as "willchickering," all one word, I knew it was Bhan.

In English and French, I gleaned he had been at Fort Benning when Cambodia fell and was now a refugee. He needed my help finding out what had happened to his family back in Phnom Penh. No one else could help him the way I might.

After finishing exams, I drove down to Columbus, where he was living in a small house on the grounds of his sponsor, a wealthy ex-GI, earning his keep by driving a lawnmower tractor. The one thing we had shared, up to that point, was parachuting, so I took him to Benning's three jump towers, idle on a Sunday, and we talked as we wandered beneath them, scuffing the woodchips.

At the end of April, he and the 20 other Cambodian officers training at Benning had been called in to their quarters' common room where an American major told them they no longer had a country. He had no other information. Literally, zero. They had a choice: they could stay in the US or be given a one-way ticket to any country they wished, except Cambodia. About half elected to stay. The other half—those with families back in Cambodia—either chose France or reluctantly stayed in the US.

Bhan chose Thailand. Everybody else left.[1] Three days later, the infantry school commander himself, a bird colonel, called him in and said, "You can't go to Thailand, Bhan. We know you. You're going to sneak across the border, and you're going to eat leaves, and the Khmer Rouge will catch you and you'll die."

His only interest was his family. Before he had left in December, the FULRO leaders had discussed what to do if Phnom Penh were about to fall. Les Kosem had told the Montagnards to seek asylum in the French Embassy, but Bhan had told his 15-year-old son to take his mother, two sisters, and baby brother to the American Embassy, where he should make it clear to the Americans that his father was a guest of the United States at Fort Benning, Green Card number such-and-such, residing at Bachelor Officer Quarters 4, Room 9. I cringed at this, picturing the boy's despair in the heavy silence following the flurry of helicopters on April 12, the soundlessness of the abyss. Even if he had gone earlier, I could imagine the distracted reaction of a lowly, Cambodian employee to his confusing story: "What country are you from? You need to go to their embassy."

His wife had written him in early April of frantic troop movements within the capital, mentioning she had twice turned down offers from one of the Cham women to bring them along to a town near the Thai border "in case the Khmer Rouge turned out to be worse than they thought."[2] The Chams always seemed to know more about what was going on than anyone else.

"Why wasn't I there? Why did I come here now?" he asked in a half moan.

His wife had wanted him to be more ambitious. Other top officers like Kpa Doh had already been to the US for training. She pushed him to do what another officer had done, to bribe someone—bribery being so common by that time in Phnom Penh that its slang name was *bonjour* (hello)—but he insisted on earning it, patiently studying English for a whole year in order to get a high grade on the test. This made him the last to go.

"Maybe God told me to," he concluded—an unusual phrase from a Montagnard. I probed. He meant Fate. Still a believer in spirits with an overlay of polytheism, his words might have come from an ancient Greek.

He had no idea how his tortured tale had only just begun, how he would be so jerked about in coming decades that onlookers like me would lean in with disbelief to see if they could glimpse the pale flash of hands. And I had no idea that one day I would come to know so much about his life, including its secrets, that I can give a name—if not to his Fate—to his Fate's lieutenant—Les Kosem—and see how much Bhan resembled Ishmael, bobbing up alone in the flotsam.

***

Douglas A. Sapper III, the ex-Green Beret in the French Embassy, was one of those people everybody knows.[3] I located him at the Trocadero Hotel in Bangkok and finally reached him by phone on a Cincinnati midsummer night rich with the smell of honeysuckle and winking with fireflies. We were both drinking. Soon it was as though we were side-by-side on barstools, easy, but raising a question of veracity.

"Shit, yeah, I knew the Yards," he said, confirming that they had been expelled along with the other Asians without papers. One of them, a woman who had just given birth, tried to give him her baby. "We're going to die," she said. She ended up giving it to a childless French couple.

He did not know Bhan's wife or children, thus could not say for sure they were there.

The Montagnards had buried their weapons in the compound and changed into civilian clothes, but Sapper was sure they had been killed by now. Since arriving in Bangkok, he had heard about the execution in Cambodia of officers and their wives, whose "graves had already been dug." (Most of the FULRO men were officers in Lon Nol's army. The question was whether the Khmer Rouge were aware.)

"They are racially different, speak a different language. They would've stood out," he said.

I was not so sure. Physically, Montagnards are indistinguishable from Cambodians, and Bhan had told me his son was fluent in the Cambodian tongue. Perhaps his son sensed that survival hung on his doing all the speaking for his mother. I was imagining that he could have remained invisible to the Khmer Rouge; then, with a wince, I remembered that, genetically, he was Vietnamese. The idea of such a burden on still-narrow shoulders was heartbreaking.

Sapper said he had wanted to go out the gate with the Montagnards but had been dissuaded. "You'll make it worse for us."

***

We assumed Bhan's family had been present in the embassy. If they had not been executed, they would have been part of the exodus from Phnom Penh. Bhan guessed his wife would have tried first to take their children overland to the Vietnam highlands, but, if blocked, would have headed to Thailand.

He and I needed a clearer idea as to what was happening inside Cambodia. The news media knew next to nothing, so we turned to the CIA and State Department.

The only person I knew in the CIA was semi-retired, a one-time Office of Strategic Services (the CIA's predecessor) operative now a recruiter at my old college. He checked with his ex-colleagues but learned nothing. I assumed he was out of the loop—campus recruiting being the CIA's Vestibule of the Futile in the 1970s—but, with time, we would learn the entire US intelligence apparatus was without a clue.

In September, we walked in cold to the State Department and asked to speak to someone about Cambodia, expecting to start with an intern. Instead, the head of desk received us, a measure of how far Indochina had fallen in importance. He was sympathetic and apologetic. Cambodia's curtain of silence was impenetrable. Sources of human intelligence were feared dead. He put us on a phone with his Vietnam counterpart, who said that Vietnamese living in Cambodia had flooded back across the border in June and July but nothing else was known. Bhan immediately wanted to return to Ban Me Thuot, but the Vietnam expert advised against it, not for a few years at least, not unless he wanted to find himself in a labor battalion cleaning up unexploded bombs. If his goal was to learn whether his family had showed up in Ban Me Thuot, he might do better trying to communicate with people there through longtime leftist groups in the US, or through communist Montagnards. He could even send a letter if he got someone to put it in a Paris mailbox.[4]

***

Bhan took a job in a carpet mill in Columbus, where he was the second man in a night-shift assembly line, applying latex for $3.15 an hour. Soon he moved up to shipping, where he wrapped carpets for $3.40. He had his own apartment, first deciding against buying a TV, then doing so to watch the news. For enjoyment, he would go to a supermarket and simply walk around.

When he had amassed $600, he bought a small car to get to work, scoring 97 percent on his driver's license test. In keeping with the pattern of his life, the car was a red Pinto (pronounced by Bhan with a very hard T and accent on last syllable), a model later recalled by Ford. However, he was not one of the unfortunates who died in fiery rear-end collisions, perhaps because he was cautious, driving only short distances.

He felt no racism in Georgia. Some of this was because Columbus was a military town, with many Vietnam vets grateful to Montagnards, but some was seeing what he chose to see. Caution, and selective vision, were features of his endurance mode. Unable to fight, he could only endure. As the years stretched on, this would become the only exercise of a warrior's courage left to him.

***

I had tried to reach Sidney Schanberg in May, right after Bhan popped up, but so did lots of people. *The New York Times* had given him leave to write a book. I could only send him a letter.

In mid-November, he graciously replied, unnecessarily apologizing for not having answered earlier, explaining that his life had been in a state of upheaval, writing a book and himself searching for news of Cambodian friends still inside the country:

> About the Montagnards who were expelled from the French Embassy, I regret that I have no specific information on their plans. Of the 100 to 150 in the Embassy, the only Montagnard I knew personally and fairly well was Major Kpa Doh, the group's leader, another brave but gentle man after years of fighting.
>
> He embraced me and was crying like a child. "I could have got us out of this country ten days ago … but I believed that the US would come and help. If you get out, please write about this. Tell the world what is happening here."
>
> They were so distraught as they left the Embassy on the morning of Monday, April 21—most of them weeping—that I'm afraid that the idea of asking them their escape plans never entered my mind. We were all crying together. They buried whatever valuables they had in the Embassy gardens, knowing they would be confiscated if they took them on the march into the countryside. One Montagnard woman had given birth to a baby the day before the Khmer Rouge took Phnom Penh; the father, after entering the Embassy with his family, went berserk from his anguish on April 20 and fled alone over the Embassy wall. On April 21, his wife was in frenzy and close to breaking. But, despite the chaos and tears, the Montagnards still maintained their dignity, and some their hope.
>
> If I were to guess what border they would head for, I would say Thailand, because they knew Vietnam was falling, and also because those who left the Embassy were pointed to the Northwest by the Khmer Rouge. But all this is speculation …
>
> I myself am groping with the same problem and have no answers. I think Thailand is the best, and maybe only, starting point because there are Cambodian refugees there in border camps who can be interviewed …
>
> It goes without saying that if I should come across some news about the Montagnards, I would notify you immediately. I would greatly appreciate your doing the same if by some chance you or [Bhan] should learn something about my close friend, Dith Pran, who was the New York Times stringer in Cambodia.[5]
>
> You mention you were a "failed journalist." I'm sure you realize by now that that was probably a benevolent turn of fate in your life. Good luck at medical school. (Incidentally, I am a failed law-school student, having fled Harvard Law School in 1951 after only three months.)
>
> Sincerely,
> Sydney H. Schanberg[6]

I started calling contacts at refugee staging areas like Camp Pendleton, Travis Air Force Base, Eglin Air Force Base, Fort Chaffee, and Indian Town Gap, looking for other Montagnards. Here and there I located one. For such a phlegmatic soul, Bhan was surprisingly connected; he usually knew who they were, some personally. All had come out from South Vietnam in its frenzied last days and knew nothing about Cambodia, but they did give Bhan the names of several Rhadé in Paris, through whom he sent letters home.

Many months later, amazingly, he got an answer from his mother. She had been forced to sell the family's elephant (actually two now, the first gave birth) and 500 goats (!). She needed the money for rice. Also, there was no one left to tend them.

***

In April 1976, a year after Cambodia's fall, *Time Magazine* reported an estimated 500,000 to 600,000 people had already died in Cambodia from political reprisals, disease, or starvation and that whole families—and sometimes entire villages—had been massacred, clubbed to death "to save ammunition."[7] But *Time* was a conservative publication. Those who saw the Khmer Rouge as utopian liberators—and there were many—discounted this as right-wing propaganda. I was somewhat open to their thinking, chronically able to see both sides, but I remembered hearing a rumor in Phnom Penh that the Khmer Rouge killed with hammers to save bullets. The journalists made light of it at the time with spooky noises, pretending to conjure a bogeyman named Old Hammerhead. The word used by the Khmer Rouge for killing enemies, "to smash," was beginning to sound sickeningly literal.

***

By early 1977, 25,000 refugees had made it out to those camps. With each escapee, word of atrocities within Cambodia mounted. Khmer Rouge supporters in the West were increasingly reduced to whack-a-moleing the emerging evidence. "Refugee accounts are often extremely unreliable," intoned one, adding, as though judiciously, "they must be taken seriously but with care and caution."[8] Then, in March 1977, French journalist, Jean Lacouture—to what must have been some teeth gnashing by editors at the *New York Review of Books*—published a review of *Cambodge: Année Zero* (*Cambodia: Year Zero*) by French priest and missionary François Ponchaud, calling it "by far the best informed report to appear on the new Cambodia" and a "book [that] can only be read with shame by those of us who supported the Khmer Rouge cause."[9]

Ponchaud had been in the embassy, and spoke of the same scene as Schanberg:

> Around 10:00 am, a pitiful column of about 800 people walked quietly through the embassy gates to an unknown future … I can still see one hundred and fifty FULRO [Montagnards], men and women who had fought the Saigon regime [and] the Vietcong in Vietnam … to defend their territory. They had counted on France, and she had let them down. They marched away sorrowfully but with their heads high. [Y-Bham Enuol], founder of the movement, and Colonel [Y-Bun Sur], their chief, led the way.

No mention of Kpa Doh.

Ponchaud went on to describe the Orwellian horror of the new Cambodia. Fluent in Khmer, having spent a decade there, he had gleaned his information from hundreds of interviews conducted in refugee camps in Thailand. It detailed the Khmer Rouge's "very intelligent, very enlightened, and very just" leadership, which had "eyes like a pineapple that see everything"—often meaning children between 6 and 12 years old, culled away from their parents and taught to stand listening at night beneath the floor of stilt houses, reporting on anyone with a bad attitude, even their parents.

In the beginning, The Organization killed by category. First up were officials in the previous government and ex-military, especially officers. Years of negative reportage on the Lon Nol "regime" made this seem almost deserved—even to me—as though all authority had been corrupt and all troops either cowards or war criminals.

A common denominator of early massacres—in fact a denominator of The Organization's entire approach—was a slyness approaching sadism. Functionaries and technocrats were often lulled to their execution by an invitation to "help rebuild the country." On one occasion, officers were brought in by an "invitation to meet Prince Sihanouk," then sent back home to return in their dress uniforms and medals before being trucked out of town to a rice paddy and machine-gunned. (As an exception proving the rule, the sergeants and common soldiers were simply tied with their arms behind their backs "the way you tie a parrot's wings," then trucked out of town and brained with Cambodia's version of a baseball bat, the pick handle.) "Sharing two meters of rice paddy," or simply "making fertilizer," became euphemisms for being executed.

Next up were present and future enemies, whose detection and execution dovetailed with The Organization's desire to elicit maximum labor out of the populace. The disappearance at night of individuals who complained or even seemed to balk, to say nothing of broke a rule, was as good as a lash to others and simplified the revolution's task, which was to create a completely self-reliant, agrarian-communist society in record time.

The Organization's social planners thought it best to regulate how, when, and with whom people ate, worked, and had sex. The first infraction brought a reprimand, the second a punishment, and the third—proof of counter-revolutionary spirit—death.

Apologists for the Khmer Rouge held that centuries of oppression and feudalism—and especially American bombing—had led to this, but most Cambodian peasants owned their own land and were fond of their feudal monarch, while the radical policies of the Khmer Rouge had sprouted in areas under their control before there had been any bombing.[10] The Khmer Rouge saying, "Better to kill an innocent person than leave an enemy alive," was the giveaway, the kind of thinking peculiar to those who are certain they are on the side of the angels.

In 1978, Khmer Rouge insanity in Cambodia reached full boil, spilling across the border to Vietnamese villages in murderous xenophobia. In response, Vietnam invaded Cambodia, taking Phnom Penh in January 1979 and driving the Khmer Rouge and their leader, Pol Pot, back into the forests to take up their old role as guerillas. This brought the Khmer Rouge horror to an end but no resolution to conflict and confusion. Cambodia's new government, basically an extension of Vietnam and backed by Russia, was opposed by the US and China.

It is hard not to see the US position as petulant and vindictive, not unlike Sihanouk's a decade before. Also like Sihanouk, the US then contorted itself into supporting the Khmer Rouge, now in the *maquis* as a "resistance" force, but no less evil than before.

***

Sometime in the early 1980s, Bhan found one of his grade-school teachers in Tulsa, a Montagnard kinsman[11]—the kind of fellow guaranteed to end up on high ground in tsunamis—and moved from Georgia to live with him, first taking a job washing dishes, then bottling Coca Cola. His supervisor at the plant was a Vietnam vet who asked him what he did in Cambodia.

"I was military," Bhan replied.

"Me too," the man said. "You're the boss now."

Bhan became foreman over 25 other workers. After a year, he was promoted to a higher position but "just walked around, with nothing to do," so he quit, though with an excellent recommendation, and moved onward to Firestone Tire where he became a member of the United Rubber, Cork, Linoleum, and Plastic Workers of America, making $10.00 an hour and eventually amassing a nest egg of $6,000 (over $15,000 today).

***

I called him one last time during this period, to suggest he could come live with me in Texas and support himself as a hospital orderly while taking courses to certify as a paramedic (I was still thinking job skills to make him attractive to Vietnam). But he had other ideas, about finding people who had come out of Vietnam or Cambodia more recently, thus possibly knowing something new.

Last I heard, around 1986—I do not remember how—he had moved to Los Angeles.

2008

Twenty-two years later, I got an email out of the blue from an American anthropologist[12] in the Cambodian highlands asking if I was the same person who had met FULRO's leaders in Phnom Penh in 1973. Someone there wanted to get in touch with me but did not want his name used yet.

It had to be Bhan, though for a second I wondered about Kpa Doh.

***

I was working at an ER in Beijing so flew down to Cambodia at my next break, accompanied by my French wife and our two children. We landed in Phnom Penh, then caught a flight into the highlands on a missionary Cessna. Being batted about in a light aircraft brought back memories of overflights with FACs (forward air controllers), as did wallowing down onto a red-dust airstrip.

I could make out distant mountains across the border in Vietnam, crenellations on the horizon. From a foothill there, long ago, I had gazed this direction into a blue haze, wondering what terrible spawns it hid. Today, from the same hill, the haze would be orange because the rolling red-dirt terrain of Cambodia had been stripped of jungle, its nakedness emphasized by pinstripes of sapling rubber trees. There were no more North Vietnamese soldiers to worry about, only Vietnamese state-capitalist-agro-industrialists with 99-year leases granted by a government installed by the Vietnamese.

Bhan was no longer mahogany dark but bald with white eyebrows and slightly milky eyes. However, he was still erect and sturdy, still with his Polynesian scowl, still with energy when he pointed out a table in our Vietnamese-owned hotel—the varnished cross section of a giant tree—and spit, "Stolen Montagnard wood!"

His English was surprisingly good except for double negatives and "d" for "th"—as in, "I don' know dat," which he said a lot. My wife said his French was good, too. He was still crisp, chopping with his hands when he explained things, the back of his fingers forward, pulling towards himself like a croupier. He had a way of saying, "Ohhhhh" that must have been common in Rhadé speech because the first time I heard it brought a jolt of memory the way a smell can. Though apparently not a sound of regret, I could see in my mind's eye the chorus's commentary in Sophocles, "O-o-o-o."

He had never found his family.

Out of that wound had grown a burl of paranoia. He had come to believe the Vietnamese—not the Cambodian communists—were behind the horrors of the Khmer Rouge and that he was still targeted by Vietnamese agents, hence the secrecy about his name.

It had taken him 18 years to get back to Cambodia, hopping along an archipelago of refugee communities, pausing for long periods to listen for any hint of what happened to the Phnom Penh Montagnards. He moved from Tulsa in 1986 to an industrial corridor of Los Angeles that had become a magnet for Southeast Asian refugees, asking questions even of Vietnamese ("All the good Vietnamese are in California," he explained), but anything he heard was stale. After that, Paris, to contact Rhadé comrades from his youth who had fought in Algeria. It was like a Space Fleet reunion after lives spent in different galaxies.

He located Paul Y-Bun Sur's wife in Brittany. A Frenchwoman of humble background, she had integrated enthusiastically with the Montagnards in Phnom Penh and had known Bhan's wife, lunching with her in the shade of corner brasseries. From her, he learned his wife and children arrived late at the embassy, two or three days after the others. Someone in the FULRO group had noticed her absence, asking "Where's Bhan's wife?" and someone else went back to the FULRO villa to get her. This was a hugely fateful twist, probably not good, though we never said that out loud.

Next stop, Singapore. From the grapevine, he heard Malaysia had been quietly accepting Cham refugees because Chams were their Muslim brothers.[13] But his initial reception was not what he had hoped—prison in a cramped cell with many others, where he got skinnier and skinnier from dysentery until he learned from an Indian to eat only *chapatti*. Then, one day many months later, they handcuffed him behind his back, told him he had a very important visitor, and sat him down facing an empty room through bars.

In came the wife of Les Kosem, tall and elegant in a silk kaftan. Though Muslim, she wore no head covering.

They knew each other well. There had been a time, in 1970–71, when he had been FULRO's quartermaster, obtaining supplies in Phnom Penh, and had lived for long periods with the Les Kosems, sleeping outside in a hammock but dining with them at night, mostly in silence except the cry of the gecko.

She had been looking for him. Having stepped into her husband's shoes and playing a large role in keeping Malaysia's doors open to Cham refugees, she had connections.[14] She felt obligation to Bhan as well as fondness for him. Because she had lost her mother and a sister to the Khmer Rouge, she was pessimistic about his finding his family. Not a hint had emerged from Chams in Cambodia as to the fate of the FULRO Montagnards. The Cham community itself had been specifically punished by the Khmer Rouge, she assumed partly because of her husband. She half-believed a story about three of Kosem's kin being speared together on sharp bamboo and then plunged into the Mekong. (One could discern the imagination behind this kind of hallucinatory detail—Chams were a riverine people who ate beef on skewers—and hope that such grim poetry meant it was false.) She urged him to accept relocation to the United States, even arranging for an American consul to come see him in prison. But, of course, she could not say for sure that Bhan's family was dead. He declined the offer to go back to the US.

Shortly thereafter, he was transferred to a true refugee camp for some thousand Chams, where he had a room of his own. Ever dutiful, he studied Malay to take an exam necessary to be released from the camp. He also converted to Islam, taking the name Ibrahim. Twenty years later, he could still recite the *al-Fatihah* prayer in ululant Arabic, explaining to me that it meant "guide us to be among the blessed, not the cursed."

Eventually he went to live with a Cambodian Cham couple who made a living peddling clothes from baskets on their heads, during which Bhan babysat their four children and watched TV. At one point, he saw a German documentary about the Cambodian genocide, with many photos of the dead, at another point a Japanese documentary about the Khmer Rouge torture center—each time lunging toward the screen to look for his wife, not seeing her, then waiting months for a re-run.

In 1989, the Iron Curtain fell, and Russian support for the Cambodian Government melted away, as did North Vietnamese soldiers. A fluid, lawless period followed. Eventually, it became evident peace could come to Cambodia only with outside help. From 1992–93, United Nations forces helped prepare the country for elections.

In 1992, he met with Madame Les Kosem and Son Sann, her favored candidate for president of Cambodia (see photo, overleaf). She urged him to accept a job managing the man's campaign in a highland town where, she assured him, the Vietnamese were long gone. He finally accepted, though not because he thought he could find his family—he had given up hope they were still alive—but because he wanted to learn how they had died.

When Bhan arrived in 1993, there were too many people with guns. "There was shooting everywhere," he said, explaining why he waited a month before

1992 meeting, probably in Malaysia: Meidine Natchear (Mme Les Kosem) on left, Bhan on far right, Son Sann in the dark suit. (Courtesy of Meidine Natchear)

going out, "because a Cambodian will look you down and up, starting with the face, and shoot you if he doesn't like what he sees." From his life's arc—from actor to pawn to state of suspended animation in Malaysia—we might think this was timidity, but it was hard-earned prudence. Whatever Bhan was, whatever he would become, however old and weak, he was not a timid man.

***

He joined the legions sifting Cambodia's ruins for the missing. "I wanted to see with my own eyes where they killed her."

He went straight to the flimsy hovels surrounding the French Embassy. Though no one from 18 years ago could still be there—not after total social devastation—the place had meant something to him from before, from the mornings he had walked his son to school past its walls. Like any parent, even decades later, he could still feel his child's hand in his. Perhaps stories had lingered too.

Most chillingly, someone had told him a Khmer Rouge asked his wife if she were Rhadé. "Yes," she replied. "Where is your husband?" the soldier asked. She told him. "So, sing to us in Rhadé," he said, then killed her.

Perhaps the entire population was like someone who recovers from a psychotic break but ever after remains convinced their delusions were true. Or maybe people were paying their suffering forward with idle, idiot malice—especially the "sing to us" story, which seemed too intimate to become known. On the other hand, who is to say that, over 18 years, his wife's executioner had not told it over and over in drunken confessionals?

Almost as painful—because crystalline, therefore certainly true—was what he learned from Chams about his childhood friend and fellow commander, Y-Nam (whose friendship had drawn Bhan to Cambodia in 1965). Y-Nam and his 200 troops had held out for three days at the FULRO caserne across the river before its defenses finally broke and Y-Nam escaped with a Cham comrade. Arriving at a Cham house, they were told, "Hide here, they'll catch you if you run." Then they had been betrayed and captured. Y-Nam was last seen being led away, hands on his head.

***

If Mme Les Kosem had been hoping to revivify Bhan by finding him a job in the highlands, she succeeded, but not exactly as expected. The red earth was balm to his soul, but he only lasted two months in politics before he soured, spotting what he thought was corruption.

However, the office cook was a Lao widow in her late forties who flirted with him, asking him if he could learn to like Lao food. She had a small farm of rubber trees, inherited from her husband. When Bhan resigned, he went to work for her, and eventually they married. "We could help each other," is how he put it, but he knew this was it for him. On a trip to Phnom Penh, he turned in his Green Card to the US Embassy. A year later, he bought a house on stilts and its piece of land for $1,000, then added on to the house to make room for her five children.

After nine years together, she died in her sleep. He was working at the farm at the time. As with his first wife, he was not there with her when Death came.

Notes

1 Many of these went to Philadelphia where they were housed in a YMCA. With time, most of these came to believe their country and/or families needed them and returned to Cambodia, either via Paris or Beijing. They were all subsequently executed. Joel Brinkley, *Cambodia's Curse* (New York: Public Affairs Books, 2011), 201.

2 Pailin, though this was very likely unreachable in any case (Steve Heder, email answer to query, October 4, 2020).

3 My brother, Sherman Chickering, publisher and journalist, had met Peter Arnett of the Associated Press in Vietnam, who located Sapper for us.

4 Mr. Kirkpatrick at the Cambodia Desk, interview with author, September 1975; Mr. Peters at the Vietnam Desk, interview with author, September 1975. My notes do not distinguish who told me what.
5 The story of Sydney Schanberg and Dith Pran became the 1984 movie, *The Killing Fields*, with Sam Waterston and Haing S. Ngor. Directed by Roland Joffé, it also starred John Malkovitch as photographer Al Rockoff.
6 Letter, November 18, 1975, author's collection.
7 *Time Magazine* (April 19, 1976), 57.
8 Torben Retboll, "Kampuchea and the Reader's Digest," *Bulletin of Concerned Asian Scholars* 11, no. 3 (1979): 26.
9 Jean Lacouture, "The Bloodiest Revolution," *New York Review* (March 31, 1977).
10 Kenneth M. Quinn, "Explaining the Terror," in *Cambodia 1975–1978: Rendezvous with Death,* edited by Karl Jackson (Princeton University Press, 1989), 215–40. Quinn was the young foreign service officer who foresaw as early as 1974 what the Khmer Rouge would do in power. The subject of American bombing will remain a contentious topic until someone finally looks at all the data from the United States Air Force, plotting it over time and in relation to known population densities on the ground. My guess is that, though the Air Force will have enough to answer for, it will in no way resemble the infamous "carpet bombing" that has become a trope. I also suspect that extremely low population densities in certain areas of the highlands, combined with very high tonnage dropped on the North Vietnamese Army bases in precisely those areas, will show that the oft-repeated statistic about "total tonnage dropped on Cambodia being in excess of World War II's total" is considerably less damning than it sounds.
11 Y-Bling Buon Krang Pang.
12 Jonathan Padwe, whose research focusses on the Jarai of Andoung Meas District in Cambodia which abuts Vietnam at the level of the Plei Trap Valley.
13 Rie Nakamura, "Becoming Malay: The Politics of the Cham Migration to Malaysia," *Studies in Ethnicity and Nationalism,* 19(3) (2019): 290.
14 Meidine Natchear, multiple interviews with author over span of seven years, 2011–2018.

CHAPTER 7

Searching for Bhan's Family

Bhan said he had given up looking for his family, yet, in almost the next breath, he would wonder out loud if his youngest child "might be somewhere in the US"—which was not entirely impossible.

On one trip down with my family from China to Cambodia, we four rode overland on motorcycles, each of us behind a motocross driver on sandy, swiveling tracks that had been part of the Ho Chi Minh Trail (photo, p. 135). Bhan himself had once taken this exact route, on elephant back with his wife and son. My far-happier life was starting to overlap on his.

Possessing tools Bhan did not, I aimed to help him resume his search for his family, but some of that would close the circle for me, too.

Actually, I had two circles to close. Forty years before I had shelved my notes on FULRO. The anthropologist who connected me to Bhan, now a friend, suggested the *Journal of Southeast Asian History* might be interested in a piece of Vietnam War history that would be unusual, if not unique, in having a Montagnard as its subject, not an American or Vietnamese.

I pictured a short biography of Bhan but knew it would not stop there. Half-jokingly, I told my wife this was as close as I would ever get to writing *Lord Jim.*

This took us both to places we did not expect.

***

Bhan was not very introspective. To hear him tell it, the most significant decision of his life—to cross the border from Vietnam into Cambodia to join FULRO at its jungle base—was motivated simply by loyalty to his friends. He rarely said anything overtly political. As for Communism, he hated the Khmer Rouge, of course, but he had only positive things to say about the leader of the Montagnard Viet Cong, Y-Bih Aleo.

His attitude toward the Great Ideas presented to him over the course of his life was like that of a busy adult asked to pick a card, any card, from a deck held up by a 10-year-old. He had been exposed at an early age to American

Protestantism but "didn't have time for it." In the South Vietnamese Army, some higher officers urged him to sample Buddhism, so he did. Much later came Islam in Malaysia. And now, he announced, "I believe in the *yang* again," meaning spirits. Animism is said to be a religion that does not travel well, being tied to specific boulders, trees, springs, etc. However, Bhan was/is the classic reed in the wind. Perhaps he found an itinerant solution.

***

I took a part-time position in a Phnom Penh charity hospital, commuting back to China to work two weeks out of every six in the emergency room of Beijing's American hospital.

We enrolled our children in the city's only lycée, René Descartes, because it was time for them to grapple with written French. Only after we began the process did I realize this was the same school Bhan called "De-Kat," where his oldest boy had gone. My first reaction was to suggest to my children they downplay mention of it around him. Such a call to evasiveness led immediately to my having to explain Bhan's full story to them and thus the outlines of Cambodia's dark history. That night, my eight-year-old son had nightmares.

I would take them to school, my wife would pick them up. They were small enough to sit behind me on a 125 cc Kawasaki. Exhilarated by the tropical mornings despite the traffic and fumes, we would weave in the blue air, swooping like a swallow to nest in a frenzy of motorcycles outside the school. They would disappear under the same, orange-tiled roofs I had seen on TV news in 1975, when 10 children had been killed and 30 mangled by a rocket that struck an attached nursery school (Bhan's son had been in the high school next door, thus spared).

To one side of the school, where the sports club had been, the entire block was now taken up by the American Embassy, slung low with a row of square windows that give it the look of a gunboat. In the other direction was open sky, where the cathedral had stood before the Khmer Rouge tore it down.[1] Squinting, I tried to summon memories from 1975, but such flashes only came unbidden, mostly while driving the city very late at night, when trash set outside for collection seemed rubble again and pale concrete turned ghastly, with tropical vents suddenly appearing like shark gills out of the gloom.

But, in Phnom Penh, the past bleeds into the present, even at a school. On the sidelines at soccer games or at PTA meetings or around playdates, sooner or later my wife or I heard from Cambodian parents about how someone they loved had been swallowed into the throngs driven out of Phnom Penh in April 1975 and never seen again. My daughter had an otherwise normal classmate who spoke to ghosts. My son played rugby on Sunday mornings in the same stadium where the FULRO Montagnards may have been sorted by the Khmer Rouge after being expelled from the embassy.

Our fortyish housekeeper confided to us that the dead were visiting her at night and sitting on her chest, suffocating her. She had nothing to suggest sleep apnea, nothing on physical exam or chest x-ray to explain shortness of breath. My Cambodian colleagues at the hospital said this was common and sometimes responded to anti-psychotic medication. I started her on one and got her into the medical system before we left Cambodia, and she held off the demons for eight more years, but she hung herself in 2023.

Backdrop to all this were Phnom Penh's two shocking tourist sites, the Khmer Rouge "killing field" outside of town and their main torture center, Tuol Sleng—a school in a quiet suburb whose structure echoed the lycée's but was a cadaverous grey concrete marbled with black mildew. Two ground-floor classrooms were empty but for an iron bedframe in each to which victims had been shackled while "confessions" were extracted, one of the horrors being that a confession's desired content was so unguessable that victims might never stop the pain, no matter what they could conjure between screams. Upstairs, the classrooms had been partitioned into cubicles where the victims were shackled in slave-ship rows, with American ammo cans for urine and feces, listening at night to the horror below. My wife and I had visited only once, three years before, but the images were indelible, often affecting our most simple perceptions now. The two light towers at my son's rugby stadium[2] were exceedingly tall, perhaps meant to evoke triumphant arms thrown skyward, but, because these were of brick, even on cloudless blue days they seemed to whisper "Auschwitz." A similar phenomenon may have been behind the belief—reported as fact by The *Lonely Planet* guidebook—that the top officials loaded onto a sanitation truck outside the embassy by the Khmer Rouge had been taken to the elite *Cercle Sportif* next door to the lycée and executed. Though this was most unlikely, it seemed as if it should be true. The sports club had functioned almost to the end, using precious fuel to run generators late into the night while the rest of the city sweated in the dark. You could almost see the bright, white-clad tennis players cavorting Nero-style.

The cordite smell of hallucination could be had at any time. One day, I was talking with a Cambodian nurse at the hospital about a group of young, leftist Cambodians who had eagerly returned home from Paris after the fall of Phnom Penh to join the revolution. They had been set to tearing down the hated French cathedral, which they accomplished with zeal. But then, being educated and thus potential counterrevolutionaries, they were imprisoned, tortured for many months, and killed. The nurse had heard from someone—like a silent scream bubbling up from the depths—that their shackles at the torture center had been rebar from the cathedral.

***

As with any missing-persons case, first step was to learn everything possible about the victims' last moments. A mountain of books had been written about the last days of Phnom Penh. I started reading, confident that I would find mention of the Montagnards. But the forced evacuation of Phnom Penh had been like a natural disaster, suffered by hundreds of thousands of people—possibly a million, or two—within a relatively short time and small space, where its density seemed to suck the oxygen from its telling. The stories seemed all the same.

It was still mesmerizing.

The beginning of the fall, like the first puffs in a building-demolition video, can be timed and dated exactly to 11:30 am on April 12 when the last Marine helicopter, carrying the American ambassador and flag, disappeared into a painfully bright southern sky. Small-arms fire from the city below indicated angry realization that this was not an 11th-hour rescue by the United States.

Predictably, military morale collapsed. But the people remained surprisingly calm, expecting that the Khmer Rouge could not be all that bad, that peace had to be better than war, and *Papa* Sihanouk—assumed to be coming back, soon—would only scold them and treat them like errant children. They knew he would be harsh, even medieval, toward those who deposed him, but the Lon Nol government had largely lost their support through corruption. They were unaware that Sihanouk, Lear-like in his rage and injured vanity, had become a Khmer Rouge stooge.

The French were only mildly apprehensive. Some of the old hands, licorice-flavored pastis at hand, tracked the enemy's progress through binoculars from a terrace atop one of the few buildings above the trees. Their government had just recognized the Khmer Rouge, and they could hope this had bought them goodwill. At the very least, they expected to be allowed an orderly departure.

Like the demolition video, there was a moment, almost lilting, when the enemy's progress stalled, blocked in the north and west by masses of refugees sludging inward with all-they-own bundles, pigs and chickens in tow—and in the south at a bridge where government troops fought either for their lives or because they knew they would die.

Then, on the peninsula to the east, 400 meters across a river, tiny black-clad figures appeared on its shimmering swampland. A doughty commander on the palace grounds lowered his howitzers' barrels to fire directly at them, scattering them across a mirror of sky that roiled with black smoke from fires on the city's rim.

On April 16, the day before the fall, some Swiss took over the old colonial hotel and draped it with white sheets and a large red cross, stolidly declaring it a neutral zone. They also put up a shortwave antenna aimed at Geneva. Scottish doctors set up a surgical suite in back and never emerged, operating continually as the number of wounded increased inversely to the distance to the front. Gradually, refugees surged inward to occupy every patch of the hotel's grounds, then the lobby, then corridors, as Western volunteers tried to bar entry to anyone in military uniform or carrying weapons, hoping to keep the "neutral" fiction alive.

That night, fires coruscated the horizon and green tracers hatched an orange sky as a few helicopter pilots rocketed the enemy before fleeing with their families. Sometime after midnight, the now-familiar noise of war—occasional explosions against a low-level background of thumps, pops, rips, and snarls—quieted, ceasing altogether at 4:00 am. With no more distant blasts buffeting faintly in the chest, it felt like a vacuum.

By daylight on April 17, strips of white bedsheets had sprouted everywhere, and the French flag hung from some windows.

The first Khmer Rouge arrived from the north around 8:00 am, passing the embassy where the French consul emerged to embrace one of their leaders, then moving on down the main boulevard in single or double file, teenagers with weapons on their shoulders but fingers near the trigger, most wearing sandals and the red-checked Cambodian scarves, some with puffy Mao hats, all festooned with pouches and grenades. A few young boys ran out to meet them, drawing smiles from some of the frowning soldiers, then onlookers pressed in from the sidewalks. Soon, small celebrations broke out, as though the citizens were welcoming long-lost brothers instead of lying prostrate before victors who could kill them at will. This fed back into a delirium of mistaken relief as some of the youngest Khmer Rouge grinned shyly, even letting mortal class enemies drape arms around their shoulders.

Some Western print journalists seeing this interpreted it as joy at liberation, but photographers, venturing out first and farthest, got darker glimpses. The Khmer Rouge approaching from the south were tired and dirty from the battle at the bridge, fresh from killing. Government soldiers who tossed their rifles almost gaily onto a growing black nest at a principal street intersection found themselves in formation under guard, marching west, bootless. A few raised their hands without being told.

By late morning, the mood had changed. The Khmer Rouge began circulating with bullhorns, telling everyone to leave the city immediately because the Americans were expected to bomb anytime. People were told to take supplies for only a few days. Those in the western part of the city were told to head out the airport highway, those in the northern part up the road past the French Embassy, and those in the south across a bridge toward Vietnam. Enforcement was pitiless, and families separated by only a few blocks could be separated forever. A poke in the ribs with a rifle or a shot in the air was usually enough to get people moving, the message amplified in the growing crowds by murmurs and wails at every gunshot. Despite this, some people hunkered down inside shuttered homes, more fearful of being looted than killed by the Khmer Rouge. These were rousted the next day, only a few shot dead in their doorways.

The crowd crossing the southern bridge was packed so tight it took a person 12 hours to shuffle 200 yards. The first few people stepping out of the crush to relieve themselves without permission got shot. People also learned that something dropped or lost, like a sandal, was gone for good. Stories circulated of children who got lost that way.

It was the height of dry season, with a mustard sky. The trees lining the streets of this one-time French colonial city would normally have been in brilliant bloom, some lavender and white, others yellow, but refugees camped on every open space had stripped them of branches for firewood. Despite this, here and there was a cascade of yellow so pure it belonged on a paschal altar.

Cambodians with some sort of connection with France—mostly upper class, though some bargirls too—had begun seeking refuge at the French Embassy as early as April 16. The first ones felt safe, even welcome, in a garden that must have felt like a piece of France, magisterial in size and groomed lushness. But, as the sense of safety dissipated on April 17, the compound filled with frightened people. Any sense of welcome vanished as the crowd got divided, or divided itself, into Europeans and Asians, the Europeans with roofs overhead (in embassy buildings or in cars driven onto the grounds), the Asians outdoors.

As early as that evening, a rumor swept the 1,000–2,000 people in the compound that Asians would be expelled. By the next night, word got around that this was a Khmer Rouge demand, though its details were not yet clear.

***

There was no mention of Montagnards in the mountain of books. Their Cambodian authors' agony was just beginning.

So Bhan and I went to see the one individual who knew the most about who died, and where, under the Khmer Rouge. For 15 years, Youk Chhang, founder of the Documentation Center of Cambodia, had been locating "smash sites" and, if possible, putting names to the dead.

He was gracious but had no specific knowledge of FULRO Montagnards among the flood of evacuees from Phnom Penh. Like the Cambodian authors, his perspective was too broad. Plus, only 14 years old when the city fell, he had been separated from his family and swept alone into the maelstrom. His attitude toward the drama at the embassy was faint irritation: it was a preoccupation of Westerners, especially the French, focused on only two weeks in Phnom Penh at the very beginning—nothing compared to the subsequent sufferings of millions of Khmers.[3]

However, his investigation of the fall of Phnom Penh had been no less meticulous than his investigation of the following three and a half years. He had interviewed scores of Khmer Rouge troops who had entered the city first. Surprisingly, many of them had been Jarai Montagnards from Ratanakiri, the northeastern Cambodian province right across the border from Vietnam—the same people French explorer Cupet had encountered in 1890. This fit with Schanberg's description of dark-skinned peasant boys with gold in their front teeth. (Pol Pot had developed an almost sentimental attachment to the Jarai because they had been among his first converts during his years in the wilderness; plus, the Montagnards' moneyless and supposedly egalitarian society appealed to the anarchist core of his radical vision.)

The impression Youk Chhang got from these interviews was that the Khmer Rouge were too busy in the first days carrying out specific plans to be able to gather groups for execution, and certainly not at the *Cercle Sportif* (which even the simplest peasants would have remembered), though rumors among the soldiers suggested that truckload(s) of bodies of important people had been dumped in a creek on the northern outskirts. The place had a name, "Kilometer Nine."

Bhan was disappointed to learn nothing about the FULRO Montagnards, but I was intrigued by the strange coincidence their immediate fate had been in the hands of fellow Montagnards—Jarai, like some of them—and wondered if this might have made a crucial difference. Might it have given Kpa Doh a slight edge in guessing what to do? I could imagine his hearing Jarai being spoken and, knowing all avenues of escape would close within hours, intensely trying to overhear something that might point to a way out. Interestingly, according to Bhan, Kpa Doh had been specifically tasked months before with planning for FULRO's escape should the situation go bad.

Youk Chhang had investigated scores of mass executions, and at that time may have been the world's foremost authority on the subject, so it carried considerable weight when he said *someone* almost always survives a massacre.

He offered to make a nationwide appeal to see if any of the FULRO group had survived, publishing their names and estimated current ages in newspapers and a bulletin widely circulated by his organization

Overnight, Bhan produced a detailed list, 86 people, of whom half were children. He had spent years with this group, and no doubt Rhadé teknonymy (see note 5, p. 59) accounted for his knowing the names of firstborns—but knowing the names of a third or fourth child seemed a feat no 80-year-old in Western society could perform.

Despite eventually being published twice nationwide, the list never got any response, not a peep. (It did find its way onto Google, cruelly raising hopes among members of the Montagnard diaspora.) This reduced the possibility of survivors but did not rule it out, because the four Khmer Rouge years, followed by another 13 years of strife, had created an entire generation of semi-literates. People did not read. If they wanted the news, they gathered at street-corner cafés with TVs.[4]

***

The National Library was across the street from our children's school. The Khmer Rouge had tried to burn its books. Only 20 percent of its materials had survived and, of those, little in French. But my wife and I stopped by to give it a look.

A marble plaque inside read, "*La force lie un temps, l'idée enchaine pour toujours*" (force binds for a time, ideas forever)—ironic near the start of a century in which ideas would rise, kill millions, then fall away.

The only collection we found was a sampling of the papers of Sihanouk's main French advisor, Charles Meyer—no doubt secret agent of France, possible agent of China, and bitterly anti-American.[5] Among them was a copy of the January 1965 issue of *National Geographic,* with an article about the 1964 Montagnard rebellion. It had a single phrase underlined in pencil about Y-Bham Enuol's threatening to join the Viet Cong if Saigon did not meet FULRO's demands. Meyer probably did not read *Geographic* to enliven a dull life, so this seemed meaningful, but trying to ascribe meaning to underlinings felt pathetic. Filed along with it was a copy of FULRO's manifesto from September 20, 1964, possibly the version Dhon had read out loud by lantern light.

But we could find no smoking gun about French involvement in FULRO.

We did find a 1967 letter referring to an escape route for American deserters via Phnom Penh to Paris, with France having "already accorded [them] 'de facto' right to asylum."[6]

On our next vacation, we headed as a family to Ban Me Thuot, then beelined to the Rhadé ghetto where Y-Bham Enuol's house had been, and, from there, asked our puzzled taxi driver to slowly drive one kilometer due west, following Captain Chuck Darnell's memories. At 900 meters, we came on a large church under construction. A young Vietnamese priest showed us a bald spot in the garden where Roger Bianchetti's chapel had been.

So, the three Caucasians were French.

***

Bhan gave me the idea, obliquely, that he was poor and could use a little financial help. I was disappointed, not so much in him but because of the problem this posed for a would-be journalist: I could not pay a source (I was less sure about historical journalist). I thought I saw a solution in helping him get a pension. He remembered having a chunk taken out of his paychecks for years, so US Social Security benefits were possible.

Also, France—far more serious about honor than the US—might give him something for his military service from 1950–54. The Rhadé in Paris had advised him to apply for a pension, but the process came to a sharp halt when he could not produce his service number. However, he had memories of specific events and French officers during those years, and I hoped to find records of them in France's military archives at Château de Vincennes, possibly mentioning Bhan by name.

Vincennes is the last stop on a Parisian Metro line. From the subway's exit, the chateau is a long, black wall of stone, entered by crossing a moat on a drawbridge through a gatehouse. Intense light awaits at the end of a short tunnel, reflected from a huge, empty parade ground and sky. A castle-keep juts upward in the distance to the right front, unchanged from its depiction in a famous parchment painting from 1400.[7] In the distance to the left is a royal chapel whose size and stained glass befits a cathedral. And in the far distance are 17th-century buildings housing the library.

Ho Ch Minh himself might have had second thoughts about the merits of French colonialism upon stepping out into that glare—but certainly not about its demerits, not about how poorly that reach toward God and Beauty travelled, how that greatness of spirit stepped off the boat in Saigon or Haiphong as *petits blancs* (low-life whites), haughty and thieving. Because, ultimately, one of the engines of colonialism was covetousness, the opportunity to take what you want—often things crafted with a sensibility higher than your own—at gunpoint. (I winced at my own memory of a more explicit form of the colonial exchange—war booty—and the thrill I felt on opening a bag of someone else's treasures, brought to me after a firefight in which we had driven some wretched Montagnard Viet Cong out of a tiny forest hamlet. It was filled with 19th-century silver coins and trinkets, now all mine because I had won a fair, if uneven, fight for it. In a pathetic coda, my storage locker in Nha Trang burned down later, and it all melted into the white sand.)

I spent six days at Vincennes, going through one musty carton after another of original Army documents, looking for Bhan's all-day firefight in 1954. I finally found it, summarized in faded serif type on a page with faintly sunken splotches from drops of sweat:

> April 8, 1954. Air sought against Viet-Minh Buon To Ke 10 km north of Poste Bac.

This was just 15 kilometers (9 miles) southeast of Cheo Reo and right where he had put his finger on the map, and he did call in air support that day. But that was it. Nothing else. Nothing that would get him a pension.

Then, one afternoon in Phnom Penh, my 12-year-old daughter had a friend over from school for a playdate. I asked the girl's parents to pick her up; her father came and he turned out to be the senior French military attaché.[8] We sparked, and I peppered him with questions about April 1975. Only as an afterthought did I mention Bhan, wondering if the French military kept detailed pay records some place other than Vincennes; if so, perhaps I could find his service number there.

"I've got a better idea," he replied.

Three weeks later, 60 years to the month from his all-day battle with the Viet Minh, Bhan had a pension from France, around $300 per year for the rest of his life—fortunate because, as for American Social Security, he had "only" worked 38 out of the necessary 40 quarters to qualify.

***

We kept meeting parents at the lycée who knew someone who had been in the embassy in 1975. Many of these were Cambodians who had been able to prove to the Khmer Rouge that they had a connection with France, thus had been trucked out with the Europeans.

They had then returned years later to Cambodia. Some had hair-raising stories of almost missing their chance. The mother of one of my daughter's teachers, also a teacher, had been blocked from reaching the embassy until a Khmer Rouge officer who had been one of her students rescued her.[9] The Khmer Rouge troops blocking her had been Jarai.

Another had been able to pass as the daughter of a Franco–Khmer couple when their own daughter failed to make it to the embassy.[10] A pharmacist, she connected me with the widow of another pharmacist crucial to this story.

***

We found Father Ponchaud in his tiny, spare apartment in a poorer section of Phnom Penh.[11] He was friendly and open. Still muscular, with ears and nose close to his head and close-cropped hair, he looked as if age had only streamlined him.

He had been at the Red Cross neutral zone the day before the fall, collecting weapons from refugees who wished to enter. Some Montagnards had shown up with "big knives" that he confiscated in addition to rifles and pistols. This did not sound like the FULRO contingent, and for the first time I wondered if there had been other Montagnards in Phnom Penh.

In the embassy itself, the Montagnards camped as a group beneath two tall tamarind trees. He brought them sacks of rice and dried fish, but they were partially self-sufficient, climbing trees to eat caterpillars and other insects. They showed Europeans how to dig latrines, crucial in a campground for 2,000 people, and, when someone started digging a well, they stopped him, patiently explaining, "There is no water here." In general, he found their dignity to be impressive.

When he first heard Asians might be expelled from the embassy, Ponchaud advised the Montagnards to leave before that happened, to go over the wall and slip into the stream of evacuees from the city, but he did not know if any had done so. He did not know any individuals other than Paul and Y-Bham Enuol.

He suggested we contact Father Berger in Paris, who was in the embassy too and knew the Montagnards. Ponchaud and Berger had ridden out to Thailand together, sitting on the cab of the truck, feet on the windshield.

***

I found Father Berger in Paris. He was still ministering to Cambodians but now they were refugees in France.[12]

He said there had been two groups of Montagnards in the embassy, the one beneath the tamarinds mentioned by Ponchaud, and the other a group that had shown up armed, with *obus* (rockets). The consul had tried to deny them entry, then relented. They only stayed about 24 hours, long enough to bury their weapons, then melted away again. Thus, the question remained: who were the other 60–70 Montagnards who walked out the gate with FULRO?

Berger had a personal connection. A Montagnard woman from the FULRO group had given birth the morning of their expulsion and had tearfully given her baby away to a childless French couple. Three days later he had baptized "Baby FULRO." Some 14 years later, Berger received a call. He knew it was a teenage boy because the boy's voice was changing; the boy began to ask about the baptism but then hung up, never to call back.

His other personal memory was of smuggling a high-ranking Cambodian—one of the "Seven Traitors" Sihanouk had marked for death—into the embassy under a blanket in the back of his Citroen. A leader admired by both French and Americans, he was subsequently rooted out by the Khmer Rouge and executed.[13]

***

Al Rockoff was a Phnom Penh institution, usually found at one of the riverside cafes or bars, but I was told not to approach him unbidden. An unwilling celebrity ever since John Malkovich portrayed him in *The Killing Fields*, a 1984 movie about the fall of Phnom Penh, he was said to be prickly. If so, he had earned the right long ago as a notably risk-taking combat photographer.

I got his phone number from another parent. He agreed to meet upstairs in the Foreign Correspondents Club, where many of his photos from 1975 still hang. Easy to recognize, with walrus mustache and large blue eyes, he was gracious when I joined him but then launched into a long, too-oft-repeated speech about the fall, bristling if I interrupted. Any question cost me a measure of his patience.

Rockoff knew Kpa Doh from before and was surprised to encounter him on the 16th, the day before the fall, at the Red Cross hotel, when Kpa Doh came up to him "covered with thousands of scratches and bug bites," to ask if he knew the whereabouts of a specific individual (assumed by Rockoff to be CIA), unaware the Americans had all flown out four days before. With Kpa Doh were his wife and two other Montagnards. Evidently, they had escaped through brambles and swamps out on the peninsula. Their caserne, encircled for weeks by Khmer Rouge bypassing it, had finally been attacked.

Within the embassy, he remembered Kpa Doh and his wife gathering their gold jewelry and placing it in the freshly dug grave of a soldier, but beneath the body with a grenade as a booby trap. (This does not make a lot of sense unless they were planning to come back for it, thus only pretended to leave a grenade—to deter onlookers from coming back, too.)

Rockoff had not witnessed the Montagnards' exit from the embassy because photographers had been kept away. He did hear shooting from the direction of the Old Stadium shortly after the Asians were expelled but thought it could have been Khmer Rouge soldiers firing into the sky to drive away rain. However, some other witnesses had said it was sunny. I should have left it alone. By the time Rockoff and I finished batting this back and forth, he was almost apoplectic, and my interview was over. (This set me off on a months-long quest to find out the weather that day. The problem resolved itself when I learned that Asians had been expelled from the embassy on two successive days, one rainy, one sunny.)

***

I found Doug Sapper by phone in Oklahoma, wary to the point of paranoia, having been "burned by journalists" in the past.[14] He did not remember my telephoning him in Bangkok in 1975, but when I told him his hotel's name and room number, it was like a hit on a bong.

Years of telling had dug a centripetal rut in his tale: the Montagnards had come into the embassy because he was there, in the belief he could get them out.

I doubted this. But he had been ground manager of a CIA airline and an ex-Green Beret. Kpa Doh would have seen him as potential help in escaping, if an extreme long shot. Despite the whiff of bombast now, Sapper had been the real thing. Three books paint him admiringly as one of the more proactive, even hyperactive, people in the embassy.[15]

He hatched at least two escape plans. One involved landing an airplane on a street converted into an unexpected landing strip by blowing down light poles with explosive (Street 108). He even started work on a roster of people to be given an orange patch, to distinguish them from those who would mob the airplane ("We're playing for all the marbles here.") He also buried "a radio, map, and bugout equipment" in the swamp out back of the embassy.

These plans required nightly forays into the city, of which he was justifiably proud. Foreigners had been stopped by hostile Khmer Rouge to know if any of them were American; so far, no one knew what would happen if they finally found one, especially alone at night. In retrospect, Sapper's plans sounded bizarre, but during the first 4–5 days after the fall of Phnom Penh, no one knew how bad things might become or how fast.

***

The father of one of my son's friends worked at Cambodia's toothless version of the Nuremburg Trial and gave me copies of some cables between the consul at the embassy and the Quai d'Orsay (French Ministry of Foreign Affairs) during the period of April 16–22, 1975.[16]

The consul had spent the previous three years in Cambodia. Before that, he had been at the French Embassy in Saigon, but no amount of diplomatic experience could have prepared him for a host country turning hostile and denying protected status to his embassy.[17] He seems to have been a solid individual, but one who nevertheless would have been overwhelmed had he not sought advice from a small group of experienced Frenchmen who knew Cambodia well.

April 17

The morning of the 17th, the consul reported by cable that, during the night of the 16th, a number of people had come into the embassy over the compound's long back wall. At almost thirteen acres, the embassy was dotted with thick shrubbery, bamboo groves, and great overarching trees.

The evening of the 17th, he reported that panic had driven "about 1000 [more] people [to seek] refuge in the embassy compound by climbing over the metal fence."[18]

These had been frontal entries in daylight.

The chaos out front demanded triage criteria. "Whites only" would have been easiest to enforce but a large number of the remaining French citizens were either Eurasian or full-blooded Asian citizens of French colonies like Pondicherry in India. For a day or so, the consul blocked the full-blooded Asians. During that crucial time, the criterion became, in effect, Whites and Eurasians only.[19]

I wondered how 150 Montagnards got in. The 86 or so who were FULRO were eligible for asylum, having rebelled against Vietnam, thus unable to seek refuge in the Vietnamese Embassy (which was closed anyway). Probably more important was their long history of close association with French military attachés. They must have come in early, through the front gate.

April 18

Early on the 18th, the consul reported a shocking sight: patients from the hospital next door being evacuated in their beds on rollers. This made him and many others fear the worst.

At noon on the 18th, he met with Khmer Rouge leaders who expressed "profound satisfaction [at France's recognition of their government but who also] expressed suspicion that the nearby hospital's wounded included government soldiers."

This sounded ominous. To forestall their visiting either the hospital or the grounds of the embassy, the consul and his counsellors promised to make up two lists within 72 hours, one list of the hospital's patients, the other of people in the embassy.

The idea was to anticipate anything that might give the Khmer Rouge an excuse to enter the embassy, which made sense as a measure to reduce the likelihood of violence. Thus, the French policed themselves behind walls that became powerfully symbolic, and it fell to a coterie of old Cambodia hands to make and enforce the rules. With time, the idea gained an intensity that became a sort of proactive Stockholm Syndrome. After it was all over, the French leaders were justifiably proud that armed Khmer Rouge had never set foot in the embassy, but critics back in France wondered at what cost. Who had not been saved that might have been saved by filling in a few more blank French passports? Some even grumbled—from their armchairs—that it might have been possible to resist the Khmer Rouge demands.

At the noon meeting on the 18th, the victors also delivered a veiled warning. They hoped news coming from the embassy would not lead to "a regrettable interpretation" around the world of what was happening in Phnom Penh.[20] The consul allowed a chosen correspondent to send a cable to *Le Monde* about the "liberation" of the city, which included a description of the surrender of one top official as voluntary and cordial when, in fact, the man had been incoherent with grief, knowing he was one of the "Seven Traitors" marked for death.[21]

April 19

At noon on the 19th, the consul reported the Khmer Rouge were now preventing the entry or departure of anyone unless authorized by them.[22] However, there was a low opening on a side wall, covered with a mat—the compound's one-time servants' entrance—that apparently was not guarded, and daring souls made repeated night-time forays to better understand the situation rather than passively await their fate. One was Doug Sapper. One or more of the Montagnards did, as well, because someone had gone back to retrieve Bhan's wife and children.

April 20

The afternoon of the 20th, the consul reported back to the Quai d'Orsay that the Khmer Rouge had "authorized Cambodian nationals who had taken refuge in our embassy to leave it freely."

This is a howler. Who was the consul kidding in painting the expulsion as voluntary? His superiors? The French public? Posterity?

He went on to describe a first contingent of "a hundred or so Cambodians of humble origin [as leaving the embassy and] being directed by the Khmer Rouge to the northern exit point of the city"—which made the Khmer Rouge sound almost gracious.

In the same vein, he added, as if surprised:

> Following a new check, we noted the presence of 155 FULRO members (Montagnard minority) under the direction of Y Ben Suok [meaning Paul Y-Bun Sur], ex-Governor of the Province of Tattanakiri [meaning Mondulkiri]. The latter expressed their determination not to leave the Embassy whatever happens to them. Not considering themselves [Cambodian], they demand to be evacuated if possible to a destination in [the South Pacific French territory of] New Caledonia ...[23]

But without doubt the consul had been aware of FULRO's presence from the beginning.

April 21

A cable on the 21st, contains the terse report:

> This morning ... 155 members of FULRO ... along with 450+ people of Khmer, Chinese, and Vietnamese nationality, left the Embassy [and] were directed by our guards to the north exit of the city ... They all departed apparently without being worried [*sans apparemment être inquietées*].[24]

This explained Ponchaud's figure of 150. It was also contrary to Schanberg's description of the Montagnards as "distraught ... most of them weeping."

And, again, why say "directed by" the French [gendarmes], when it was entirely under Khmer Rouge control?

Clearly, the consul was painting the expulsion of the Asians as an almost happy event, which was so far from the truth as to be clearly, indubitably, deliberate.

The best explanation is that he knew the Khmer Rouge would learn the cables' contents, either by intercepting them or, more likely, through a Quai d'Orsay sympathizer.

***

Father Ponchaud's book, *Cambodge: Annee Zero* (see p. 86), tells what happened after the Montagnards and other Asians walked out the embassy gate, quoting a Khmer pharmacist among those expelled (he had escaped to Vietnam in June 1975, thus was the sole known survivor of hundreds):

> We were taken to [a stadium] two hundred meters [north of] the embassy. There we went through a preliminary "processing": the Khmer Rouge asked us to state our identities and write our names on one of three lists: military, civil servants, [and] people. Then the officers like … Colonel Y Bun Sur … and high-ranking officials … were taken away in trucks. The rest of us moved into the huts built around the edge of the stadium by officers' families and spent the night with the rats …
>
> The next morning the Khmer Rouge came back and called out some more names from a list they had ready and took them away. Then they told us to go north and set to work building the country. We pointed out that the people of Phnom Penh already had a [2–3-day] head start on us, and they provided trucks to drive us [10 miles north] where we joined the bulk of the capital's population. The attitudes of the Khmer Rouge varied enormously from one to the next, and we got the impression that their orders were not very specific.[25]

"Some more names from a list" sounded way too selective for a simple Montagnard woman and her four children. Bhan and I had accepted this as proof his family had at least made it into the crowd flowing north out of Phnom Penh.

But then our friend at Cambodia's own "Nuremburg Trial" dug up a verbatim transcript of the original interview with the pharmacist, presumably by Ponchaud himself. It had a small but very disturbing difference from Ponchaud's book:

> [The Pharmacist was] taken to the [Old Stadium just north of the Embassy] with all the Cambodians expelled from the Embassy, where an initial triage took place … high officials and military officers … Paul Y Bun Sur *and his Cambodian Montagnards (one hundred or so FULRO members with Y-Bham Enuol)* were taken away by truck [author's emphasis]. The rest moved into huts on the benches for the night.[26]

So, which was it? Were only Paul and Y-Bham Enuol taken away by truck, as Ponchaud's book says? Or were some 100 members of the FULRO group taken away with them?

***

Ponchaud remembered interviewing the pharmacist sometime in 1976. And he would never forget the time before that, when the pharmacist was about to go out the gate on April 21, 1975, and his last words to Ponchaud were a jaunty, "*L'année prochaine sur les Champs Elysées!* (Next year on the Champs Elysées!)."

But he could not help with the discrepancy between his book and the recorded interview. All his notes were back in Paris at Rue de Bac, at the Society of Foreign Missions.

***

The pharmacist had died only a few years before—but I learned from another pharmacist (p. 105) that his widow was still alive and in Phnom Penh.

I expected little from her.[27] She had been in Saigon when Phnom Penh fell. He had taken their two toddlers to the embassy and asked the Belgian consul and his wife, old friends of theirs, to take them to France. So, she had not been with him during his ordeal, and, even if he had told her everything a hundred times over, it was unlikely he knew who the Montagnards were, much less noticed them. Memories etched with adrenaline's acid can be remarkably clear but are often so focused that context is anyone's guess.

So much for expectations.

It turned out her husband had been one-half Cambodian, one-quarter Chinese, and one-quarter Laotian, the latter giving him an affinity with Montagnards (she used the word *assimilé*, with the idea of similarity, equation). He had been very much aware of them. They were on the trucks, then, like him, got back off. They stayed with him for a few days, then separated.

I probed, not quite believing her memory could be that good about things she was told. At one point, I commented that no Chams had sought refuge in the French Embassy. "No," she interjected, "there must have been one. A woman there heard our children crying from hunger and gave them her pork ration [being Muslim]." This was so quick and the detail so arcane, that there was no longer any question in my mind: the simple Montagnards had made it out onto the highways.

This was the end of the line for our search, one that began in June 1975. Or, more exactly, it was the end of my search.

Bhan had no reaction when I told him. He had returned to endurance mode sometime after the second nationwide notice produced no response.

Notes

1 They demolished only three structures: the cathedral, the National Bank, and a too-triumphal World War I monument that faced the French Embassy.

2 Called ether Lambert Stadium or The Old Stadium (*Stade Cha*), to distinguish it from "Olympic" Stadium built in the 1960s, it has a 1950s modesty, along with hopefulness.

3 Youk Chhang, interview with author, September 17, 2014.

4 Michael Hayes, interview with author, May 12, 2012.

5 Milton Osborne, *Sihanouk, Prince of Light, Prince of Darkness* (Honolulu: University of Hawaii Press, 1994), 147–8.

6 Jacques Beaumont letter to Sihanouk dated October 26, 1967, requesting Sihanouk's permission for this, warning of potential international repercussions should word get out, and identifying the ubiquitous Wilfred Burchett, a well-known Australian communist, as a prime mover behind the project.

7 December in the *Très Riches Heures du Duc de Berry* illuminated *Book of Hours*.

8 Patrick Cabanes, who no doubt helped Bhan out of personal sympathy as well as a sense of French honor. Perhaps the records of his long-ago predecessors' support for FULRO were available to him as well.

9 Saorun Tchou, interview with author, November 23, 2014.

10 Duong Nguon Hoa (aka Mai), interview with author, November 20, 2013. Her Chinese–Cambodian husband, who spoke Mandarin, was certain some of the first Khmer Rouge officers in Phnom Penh were Chinese military (not Chinese–Cambodian like himself). I ran across other suggestions of the same thing. If true, the Chinese have since wiped all their fingerprints.

11 François Ponchaud, who died in 2025. Interview with author, September 24, 2013.

12 Bernard Berger, interview with author, July 2, 2014.

13 Sirik Matak, one-time prime minister, cousin and bitter rival of Sihanouk, had stood out as an honest and capable leader. His last official words are notable. On the 12th, when the departing Americans offered him a helicopter ride to safety, he declined, decrying in a letter to President Ford "the policy of abandonment of a poor country, decided brutally without warning or preparation, [that] puts us in a position of heartbreaking betrayal. We will struggle alone now without your support. We will die on our soil achieving our last desire, to die in freedom. I lay on the American conscience all Khmer deaths, past and future." His last known personal words, on the 20th, as he was being led out the gate to a garbage truck, erect and head high, were to the Khmer Rouge, "I am not afraid. I am ready to account for my actions," as though he thought they might put him on trial instead of gunning him down.

14 Douglas A. Sapper III, interview with author, February 7, 2009.

15 Sydney Schanberg, *Beyond the Killing Fields* (Washington, D.C.: Potomac Books, 2010); Jon Swain, *River of Time* (London: William Heinemann Ltd, 1995); and Roland Neveu, *The Fall of Phnom Penh, 17 April 1975* (Bangkok: Asia Horizons Book Co., 2015).

16 ECCC—Extraordinary Chambers in the Courts of Cambodia. On trial were the number two and number three leaders of the Khmer Rouge (Pol Pot had died in his sleep in 1998). At the time, the court was looking at whether the rapid and brutal evacuation of Phnom Penh was itself a war crime. The tribunal was toothless because Cambodia's longtime dictator, Hun Sen—a one-time Khmer Rouge himself—preferred it that way. The cables are no longer in my possession, and I do not know where, or if, they can be accessed in 2024, but my transcriptions are 100 percent accurate.

17 Jean Dyrac was 55 years old. The reason he was in charge rather than someone of ambassador rank was that the ambassador had been withdrawn to France a month before to signal France's imminent recognition of the Khmer Rouge.

18 Cable #589. This was a copy of a cable from the Consul to the Quai d'Orsay, from the files of the ECCC.

19 Jean Morice, *Cambodge: Du Sourire à L'Horreur* (Paris: France-Empire, 1977), 278. At one point, the consul tried to restrict entry to "citizens of Metropolitan France" but anything that required inspecting papers was impossible when dealing with a frightened mob.

20 This cable's number is no longer available to me, but it is between 589 and 596. See note 16, above.

21 Schanberg, *Beyond the Killing Fields*, 80.

22 Cable #596, See note 16, above.

23 Cable #609, See note 16, above.

24 Cable #614, dated April 21 but apparently not sent until the morning of the 22nd. See note 16, above.

25 François Ponchaud, *Cambodge Année Zéro* (Paris: Éditions René Julliard, 1977), 15.

26 Document #00410372 ECCC."*Emmené au Stade Lambert avec tous les Khmers expulsés de l'ambassade. Là a lieu un premier tri … les haut fonctionnaires et militaires … Paul Y Bun Sur et ses Khmers Loeus (une centaine de members du FULRO avec Y-Bham Enuol). Ils sont emmenés en camion … Les autres s'installent dans les cabanes, sur les bancs, dans la nuit …*"

27 Yvette Truong, interview with author, November 25, 2014. Her husband was Kyheng Savang (very definitely the pharmacist called S… in the ECCC document #00410372-376). He had died in 2010 (?), playing tennis.

CHAPTER 8

Paul

Browsing in a bookstore, I came across a book called *The Gate,* about the fall of Phnom Penh in 1975, its title a reference to the gate of the French Embassy.

Leafing through it, I felt my neck prickle.

Leaning forward, I saw the name, Paul Y-Bun Sur. It was like finding a note left by someone long ago, someone you thought had left without goodbye.

It was moments before the Montagnards were to leave the embassy. Paul was facing execution. The rest of the 150 men and women and children were heading out towards the unknown but—from what they saw of the crowds trudging past the embassy's gate with an occasional hospital bed, IV bottle clanking and waving—they could guess the unknown held terrible things for them too, if not as certainly as for Paul.

The following is what the author said about Paul:

> There were still some 150 FULRO commando troops left on the premises ... These toughened men never wavered for a moment ... yet Colonel Y Bun Sur, alias Paul, who commanded them, could not conceal his chattering teeth, for fear had paralyzed him and taken away all movement from his arms.
>
> Married to a Frenchwoman, the war had turned him into a playboy, handsomely paid by the Americans ... As far as his temperament was concerned, he was a pure product of the Catholic schools in [Ban Me Thuot]: an unhappy creature, well-educated but artificial.
>
> It is the first time that I have witnessed such a pitiful collapse. [Sitting in the grass], he lost control of everything, his mind as well as his intestines.
>
> And now this cowardly glamour-seeker ... was the only fulcrum for more than a hundred fighting men who were ... ready to do anything for him and nothing without him ...

Several people approach Paul to convince him to get up and move. One is a priest who seemed to have known him well, whispering, "[*Mon petit*] Paul ... it's what you have to do." Paul then comes back to himself enough to stand and ask for a glass of brandy, after which he is finally able to call out "in a steady voice, 'Come on, boys! Let's go!'"

Here the author adds, "Of all the emotional moments we experienced during that period, Paul's exemplary courage certainly provoked the most tears."[1]

Even if I had not known Paul slightly, I would have found the mention of soiling himself totally unnecessary. If he pulled himself together at the end, why mention it? Why speak such gratuitous ill of the dead?

The man who wrote it—a Frenchman of great sensitivity, a scholar of popular Buddhism—was fluent in Khmer and a classic example of a man rising to his moment, becoming pivotal in the embassy drama. He also wrote beautifully. I was both envious and angry.

I was irritated by his retraction at the end—the false magnanimity of praising the exemplary courage of someone you've just painted forever as a coward.

I wondered how, if Paul was such a coward, he could have inspired such devotion from hardened troops.

The phrase, "handsomely paid by the Americans," was irritating as well, in part because it was a dog whistle to his French readers, and in part because I suspected it was untrue.

If any outside power was responsible for Paul and his rise, it was France.

***

I found one of Paul's sons, Louis, by phone in Florida. He had a complicated story.[2]

Louis had never really known his father, who left to join FULRO in Cambodia when he was three. Then he lost his mother, killed by the Viet Cong during fighting in 1970, and he and his older brother were taken in by the French nun.

Meanwhile, his father had remarried, to a Frenchwoman, and had three more children, bringing them all to Phnom Penh in 1970. Once settled in as a high-ranking official, Paul sent his French wife to Ban Me Thuot to check on Louis and his brother, taking them a letter from him in Rhadé. In it, he urged them to study hard, maybe go to university in France, and one day to be a better man than he, signed "I will always love you." And perhaps he did in a way: the photo I saw in his parlor in Phnom Penh in 1973 must have been of Louis and his brother.

In two rare twists of good fortune, Paul never succeeded in bringing the boys to Cambodia, and his emissary, the Frenchwoman, became good friends with the nun. Eventually she, too, became like a mother to Louis and his brother.

When the nun was expelled from Vietnam in 1975, the two boys were sent to live with their Montagnard maternal grandparents, who were very poor. However, Louis took his father's letter to heart and graduated from university nine years later as an engineer (which, it must be said, would have been less likely for a Montagnard to do under the system before 1975).

Three years later, working as a forestry expert in Laos, Louis escaped to Thailand. After a year's detention there, he got into France, thence the United States, and was now a sushi chef in Miami.

The letter, the only words he had ever had from his father, had been lost somewhere along the way.

Both his "adopted mother," the nun, and his "stepmother," the Frenchwoman, were still alive and in France. Every year, he went back to see them and now had close relations with his three half-siblings, too. They had created a family. He asked if I would like to meet his two mothers.

I certainly would.

***

I found the nun, Françoise, at a cloistered convent in Paris, where I was led to a room for meeting outsiders, where speaking was allowed. Energetic despite her 90 years, she glowed with enthusiasm. Her favorite word seemed to be "joy." At age 30, in 1954, she had been sent to the Central Highlands of Vietnam to set up a school for Rhadé girls and stayed until the communists kicked her out 21 years later.

She knew of the ugly description of Paul's last hours in the embassy. She had been childhood friends with the goateed priest who encouraged Paul to face reality at the end, and she had met him years later. He recounted shuttling between Paul and the consul, bearing Paul's arguments for asylum for the Montagnards in New Caledonia until it became hopeless.[3]

She had known Paul especially well, as he had been 14 when she arrived in the highlands, the age when some adolescents imprint on great ideas, and he had seized on Catholicism.

He was Mnong, but from an advanced subgroup that spoke both Mnong and Rhadé (Mnong Rlam) enabling him to communicate across the principal language divide between Montagnards.

He was *métis,* with one-quarter French blood.[4] His grandmother, said to have been tall and beautiful, was thought to have taken an anonymous Frenchman as a lover—"an officer," or the governor's cook, or possibly the governor himself—while her husband was away on tiger hunts as chief mahout to the Emperor of Vietnam. Neither Paul nor anybody else saw this in a particularly negative light. Less acceptable to him was the fact a great-grandmother had been a slave and that this was evident in the name Y-Bun Sur.

He had a traditional Montagnard boyhood except that he grew up with sky and water instead of forest, on the shores of a broad lake surrounded by

At school in Ban Me Thuot at age 12 (1952), Paul Y-Bun Sur is the tall boy in a loincloth at the center, front row. (Photo courtesy of Françoise Demeure)

mountains. One of the most beautiful spots in the highlands, the emperor had a chalet nearby. Like all boys in his hamlet, he became one with a pirogue and could pole it standing on its rear gunwales, as though floating inches above the water like a mirage. His first nine years were timeless because the world stayed beyond the mountains.

In 1946, the French reopened their schools in Indochina. One of their policies, simultaneously enlightened and exploitative, was to require that every Montagnard family send one child to school for three years. The next year, Paul left for beyond the mountains, beginning 1st grade in Ban Me Thuot as a boarder.[5] His father got a job as a *boy* in the French Army, a servant, which was actually a position of some prestige in the eyes of other Montagnards.

At school, he was influenced by a fervently Catholic teacher. As the French began to withdraw, Catholicism and its durable connection with France must have seemed like an overhanging branch as the current of history gathered speed.

Over the summer of 1955, the school in Ban Me Thuot changed to a curriculum taught only in Vietnamese. Many Montagnard children had to quit. However, Paul won a scholarship to the Lycée Yersin, still taught by French holding tightly to their cultural influence in Vietnam.

Paul Y-Bun Sur (on the left) with the Bishop of Kontum, Paul Seitz (the other two boys are Pierre K'Briuh and Y-Nhuinh Hmok). (Photo courtesy of Françoise Demeure)

Vietnamese settlers were flowing into the highlands. In case anyone missed the cosmic significance of that, in June there was a total eclipse of the sun, the longest since the 11th century. Montagnard villages erupted in a terrible din to break up the coupling between the beautiful maiden in the sun and the handsome young man in the moon who eternally chases her, because otherwise the world would end.

Paul arrived at the lycée in October by chicken-bus, like Dhon before him. The Vietnamese arrived in cars. For the boy in the pirogue, the colonnaded halls must have been terrifying even without knowing this would be a one-way leap and that, with time, he would come to see his parents as *des pauvres Montagnards* (poor Montagnards, in both senses). Indeed, his father's job evaporated that year when the French soldiers pulled out.

His new faith helped get him through the year. On Saturdays, with the other Montagnard boys, he practiced choir and, on brilliant, tropical Sunday mornings they walked together across town to sing in the cathedral. He wrote to Françoise back in Ban Me Thuot, "My heart smiles thinking of God and how He is always with me," but of course belief's armor could not be 100 percent. He also wrote, "You know my heart, how it wants to be like a lion but is still so weak."

During that first year, the monsoon back home was unusually heavy and prolonged. Rivers overflowed their banks, famine ensued. Without the French, no DDT was sprayed, health posts had no quinine or transport. Malaria and dengue surged. Meanwhile Diem's dictatorial tendencies were growing, with censorship, then surveillance.

The summer of 1956, upon returning home, Paul ran into social pressure against Catholicism from his friends' traditional parents. His solution was for him and his friends to show respect for tradition six days a week by throwing themselves into community farm work, then, on Sunday, meet in their best clothes, study scripture and sing together, then parade joyously through their hamlets.

Paul had been betrothed at birth, to a girl named H'Kruk. Initially, he described her as the only girl he had ever loved. He began teaching her to read and included her in his Sunday group, though simply bringing her across the lake was like ripping out a root. Through effort, he was hoping to satisfy both Catholicism and Montagnard tradition, but a tipping pirogue cannot be steadied by more exertion.

That same summer, Paul attended the bishop's conclave (see photo on p. 46). The next year at the lycée, he was more confident, mature. He still attended mass and sang with the other boys, but he was also drawn to the excitement of the *foyer*, the common room where every evening after supper boys and girls would congregate in their 30 minutes' free time before studying. There was music, the latest, on 45 rpm records, already some Elvis (there is a hint of Elvis in Paul's appearance in the photo on p. 119). And there was dancing. Somehow, Paul learned to dance, and he was the best at be-bop, the cha-cha, even the waltz. This was an "in," with boys as well as girls, even with the louche kids, who smoked and smirked. He also discovered, if he had not suspected it before, that he was extremely attractive to women, which sailed over differences of class, wealth, even ethnicity. Looking back across 70 years, the boy next to Paul in the photo, himself still a fervent Catholic, explains that "the flame faded, and Paul found the World."

Unlike most Montagnards, Paul got along well with Vietnamese, becoming secretary general of the student council.[6] One Vietnamese classmate today has fond memories of passing holidays with him at school, both of them too poor to travel home during the school year. A decade after graduation, the same classmate met Paul again and sensed no change in him, unaware that at the time Paul was leader of a violently anti-Vietnamese movement.[7]

Sometime in here, when H'Kruk was finally baptized, he married her. During his third year at the lycée, they had their first child, a boy. He also impregnated a Vietnamese classmate who had to drop out of school.[8]

In September 1958, Paul was the youngest of 45 Montagnards to sign the Bajaraka letters to foreign embassies. His youth spared him punishment, as he spent only one day in jail.

He obtained his final baccalaureate in 1961, only one of a handful of Montagnards to have done so up to that time, then went to Saigon to work at the *Banque Franco–Chinoise*, living in a small apartment with H'Kruk and their now two little boys.

In August 1964, he told an old friend that he would soon have to leave, hinting it would be to Cambodia. Shortly thereafter, he rolled up some food and documents in a blanket and left for the border. His wife and sons, aged six and three, never saw him again. She would be killed by the Viet Cong in 1970. The boys were adopted by Françoise, the nun, until 1975 when she was expelled from Vietnam; thereafter, a high-ranking Rhadé communist oversaw their care, apparently out of a childhood friendship with Paul.

A few days after the September rebellion, he was among the seven Montagnard signers of the Flag Decree in Mondulkiri.

***

Louis's other "mother," Paul's widow, Maud, was in eastern France. I took a train through countryside that was unusually empty, as though devastation from past wars were now an epigenetic trait. I imagined groans weaving fugue-like into the hum and clack of the rails.

She lived on the ground floor of a drab high rise. Her mailbox read "Maud Y-Bun Sur," even though she had been married and widowed a second time after Paul.

She looked unwell on opening the door—gray face, gray hair, and ponderous. But she became animated, with lively dark eyes, on the central subject of her life.

She made clear she had not kept Paul's name out of love. He had married her because he "wanted a French wife," and one year before the fall of Phnom Penh, he had peremptorily replaced her with a new wife, a Cambodian bargirl. When she refused to share a house with her replacement, he threw her out and kept their three children, allowing her visits.

But her small, clean apartment was a shrine, with a prominent but blurry photo of her and Paul, both in Montagnard dress. On the coffee table was a book about the Mnong by a French anthropologist.[9] She had embraced the identity of a Montagnard's wife and mother of three half-Montagnard children, which made her fiercely defiant of racism.

Her father had been an alcoholic, deserting his family when she was six. At age 13, she started a pen-pal relationship with a schoolboy in faraway Vietnam. The next year, she left school to work as a chambermaid. She was 19 when her pen pal, Paul, showed up at her doorstep with the figurative glass slipper. For the first five years, it fit poorly. She had moments of Parisian high life on the arm of a handsome, charming, and intermittently rich young man, but, between bearing him three children and being ignored, the main Cinderella parallel was a mother and sisters who screeched at her, "Go back to your *Chinetoc* (perjorative for Chinese)."

However, the next five years—in Phnom Penh—were a dream, the best years of her life. Paul was a provincial governor. She made it her job to care for refugees from his province (Mnong from Mondulkiri), visiting their camps in Montagnard dress with food for the children, even calling on Lon Nol, the president of the country, in his palace to intercede on their behalf.[10] Even after Paul threw her over, she found dignity in teaching French at the Phnom Penh *Alliance Française,* considering it a good year like the others. Then, with the fall of the city, it was all over, and she returned to France and to cleaning hotel rooms for the rest of her working life.

***

Shortly before the fall of Phnom Penh, the French Consul had summoned her to the embassy to meet with him, ostensibly to tell her of a meeting she had missed for all French citizens and their spouses.

But instead, he harped on the fact that her non-French husband, Paul, had shown up in her place and, worse, had brought his new wife, the bargirl. The consul let Maud know in the crudest terms that "there were people there who found the Cambodian woman's presence objectionable." In an aside, she explained it had been common knowledge among French wives of Cambodian men that they—the wives—were not welcome in the embassy. Though himself married to a Laotian woman, the consul manifested the usual double standard.

Maud swallowed her anger and pushed for asylum in France for Paul and his Montagnard followers. (This was several days before anyone knew the Khmer Rouge would demand expulsion of all non-French.) But the consul replied, "It's out of the question, I don't want him entering France," adding, "There are enough bad elements in France without my letting in those of others."

The consul died in 2013 and cannot defend himself. A number of people have testified to his character, humanity, and *education* (upbringing)—evidence that runs counter to what Maud told me. Plus, Maud surely was aware this was her chance to settle scores. But the consul would not be the first man with these particular feet of clay, and the testaments were all by white men.

I would not include her version here except that it explains the cringe-inducing picture of Paul painted by François Bizot, author of *The Gate*; the consul was the likely source of most of what Bizot knew about Paul. Bizot had been elsewhere during Paul's nightclub years and, as an outsider, was unlikely to have heard about him from other French expats. Bizot was the consul's closest confidant during the embassy ordeal, and they remained close for years afterward, including the period in which Bizot wrote the book.

***

On the morning of April 17, Maud went out into the streets "with everybody else to cheer the arrival of the Khmer Rouge." That night she put the children to bed early but could not sleep herself. (Several days earlier, Paul had brought her children back to her.) The next morning, three "twelve-year-old Khmer Rouge soldiers" burst in on them, shoving her hard with their rifle barrels to make them leave. She grabbed her children and little else, one photo, no papers, and hurried to the embassy.

The FULRO group was already there. Someone told her that her husband was with the Montagnards in the far back. She saw him but did not speak with him, instead settling in with some French on the lawn outside the embassy buildings—which meant she knew nothing about the FULRO group during their embassy stay.

Her eldest son did go over to hang out with the Montagnards, learning to eat fat red ants by crushing them with his fingers and popping them in his mouth. His real motive in going must have been to see his father, despite Paul's neglect. In later years, he turned to hating Paul, but it takes a lot more than neglect to make an eight-year-old hate his father.

Maud surprised me by saying she had seen individual Montagnards she knew from her visits to refugee camps across the river, which meant the unaccounted-for 65 or so were from those camps (or stay behinds from the armed group). In either case, they were Mnong—a group that would have passed more easily as guiltless peasants in Khmer Rouge eyes because they were, or could pretend to be, primitives from Mondulkiri.

Kpa Doh's wife was Mnong. Perhaps she could have passed too.

***

Maud met Paul to say goodbye, on the last day.

The first thing he said was, "Why can't we go to France?" by now a rhetorical plaint but indicative of how much hope he had held out for it.

Both of them were *angoissés* (anguished). He was standing in front of her and said "*On ne se reverra jamais certainement* (For certain, we'll never see each other again)," but then added, "If you still haven't heard from me after five years, go ahead and remarry." She did hope he would survive but thought to herself that 10 years with him had been enough.

I asked for her visual memories of his departure (she was aware of the extremely harsh picture painted by Bizot).

She was to the side, watching them.

Paul was standing the whole time, she said, trembling of course, but not "*accroupi* (squatting)." "He was afraid, but we were all afraid." He did not soil himself.

Paul gave an order and his men formed up behind him military fashion, in two long files, with their families alongside them, followed by a larger group of Mnong refugees. Everyone, including the women, walked with their head high. Everyone was impressively calm, unlike the Cambodians who sometimes showed their anguish.

"It was as if they were saying, 'Look at us,'" she said. "'This is how to behave.'"

The Khmer Rouge were waiting with two trucks, picking out the important people as they passed and making them climb into the open backs, where they remained standing. She saw about 12 men—Cambodians—already in Paul's truck. One of them was a colonel married to a Frenchwoman at Maud's side, who had five children with her.

The Khmer Rouge knew exactly who they were taking. Maud's eight-year-old, who spoke Khmer, had seen a Khmer Rouge point at her and say, "That's Y-Bun Sur's wife."

The trucks pulled away. Only a short time later, everyone heard what sounded like a fusillade from the direction the trucks had gone. Someone said, "*Oh-la-la-la,* that's the guys in the trucks." She later went out through the hole in the wall, with someone else, to the boulevard to see if bodies were visible in the distance but saw none.

When the Khmer Rouge were finally secure in power, they revealed they had executed high officials and officers in the first days. There is no reason to think Paul and Y-Bham Enuol were not included. The exact execution site has never been identified, but the site at which bodies were dumped has been identified with near certainty, corroborated by Bhan's having heard "from many people" that the bodies had "been thrown in the water."

This was "Kilometer 9," a muddy slough on the northern outskirts of the city, in which their bodies must have moldered a long time, drifting like smoke to a larger stream, then to the Mekong, and finally to the sea.

***

So Bizot's statement that Paul "was a pure product of the Catholic schools in [Ban Me Thuot]" was partly true. The rest was slander, either careless or conscious. Yet his depiction of Paul could not have been made up out of whole cloth. There had to be another explanation.

My first glimpse of one came from learning that an American airplane mechanic in the embassy had had a seizure.

My second came from reading about Paul's "determination not to leave the Embassy whatever happens" in the consul's cables, with his demand for evacuation to New Caledonia.

The timing of the airplane mechanic's brief convulsion, on his second day in the embassy was—as any good ER doc knows—consistent with alcohol withdrawal. A fair number of people, including Paul, must have been heavy drinkers who had been forced to take refuge in the embassy with little or no time to take any alcohol with them. In Paul's case, he probably did succeed in taking a flask or two, but when these ran out, his situation became even more hellish, afflicting him with both the shakes and clouded thinking.

Then, fixated on the idea that the Montagnards qualified for diplomatic asylum at the French Embassy, which was correct, and on the possibility the Khmer Rouge would care, which by then was a pipe dream—he succumbed to a combination of agitation, denial, and terror and attempted a one-man sit-down strike, a huge misjudgment.

Some may find this picture of Paul pathetic, though certainly better than Bizot's picture of cowardice.

To me, however, it says that Paul, whatever his failings, met his end well. If he got to his feet, cleared his head with brandy, and then led his men out the gate with dignity—straight into the leering face of Death, waiting just for him—none of us can say we would have done better.

Notes

1 François Bizot, *The Gate*, translated by Euan Cameron (London: Vintage, 2004), 203–05.
2 Louis Y-Pen Bing, interview with author, May 22, 2014.
3 This was Father Hidulph (aka Félix) of the Kep Benedictine Monastery
4 This brief bio of Paul is about half from Françoise, one third from Pierre K'Briuh (his good friend), and one sixth from what he told me himself in 1973.
5 He probably attended a local school on the Lake for grades 1–3, then transferred to Ban Me Thuot in 1952 as a 4th grader.
6 Thanks to Roih Kra. Though not particularly athletic, he did throw the javelin.
7 Dr. Pham Van Song, "Le DVD: 'Je me souviens'," (2010), www.vietthuc.org.
8 When I googled her name (remembered by K'Briuh), I found an obituary with the picture of a lovely young woman. Though born the same year as Paul, she had graduated from the Lycée Yersin three years after him, most likely because of the pregnancy. She had eventually married an American, had children in the US, and died at age 75 in a small midwestern town. The obituary made no mention of a child born in Vietnam.
9 *Nous Avons Mangé La Forêt,* by Georges Condominas (Paris: Mercure de France, 1957), who had mentored Paul in Paris.
10 The detail about Montagnard dress came 40 years later from Catherine Scheer's interviews with Mnong survivors.

CHAPTER 9

The Mystery of FULRO

Compared to tracking down what happened to Paul and to Bhan's family in 1975, finding out what happened to FULRO after the September 1964 rebellion should have been easy. Bhan had been one of FULRO's three top leaders. We had a long history together. We were friends. He had no apparent reservations about being the subject of research, even contributing a footnoted autobiography in his own hand.

But, since the beginning, he had been stonewalling me about FULRO's forest years 1965–69, and especially about 1965–66. I suspected it had something to do with the Montagnards in North Carolina, his peers.[1]

In 1973, the other two young leaders—Paul, and Kpa Doh—had not been any more forthcoming about those years, either. Since the beginning, much of FULRO's power had lain in bluff and camouflage, looking stronger than it was, looking capable to outsiders of tilting the balance of the war, looking capable to fellow Montagnards of defending them against the Vietnamese—in other words, in keeping its mystery alive.

A few Google searches told me FULRO's mystery had never been penetrated. Despite hints that something dealt it a crippling blow in 1965–66, its mystique kept growing. By 1967, it even fascinated GIs in infantry units with no direct contact with Montagnards, startled by encounters with naked, pot-bellied three-year-olds in remote hamlets who would chirp, "I am FULRO."

I expected the CIA would have learned its secrets and that I would find these at the National Archives in Columbia, Maryland. Indeed, CIA documents with references to FULRO or Y-Bham Enuol were now computerized. At first glance, these were a startling find, like access to someone's psychiatrist's notes. On closer examination, however, they were disappointing. While knowledgeable about FULRO's activities within South Vietnam, they could only guess at what was happening at its heart, in the forest, across the border in Cambodia.

***

After the First Rebellion in September 1964, the challenge facing FULRO was to keep up the pressure on Saigon, especially after an unproductive parley with government representatives in October. Some wanted another rebellion in December, but Saigon was still on alert.

In January 1965, FULRO began crossing back across the border to tax vehicles on the main north–south road, a demonstration of sovereignty. But one unit stopped a bus, pulled nine Vietnamese down and murdered them. A few days later, another group did the same, executing 12 more, and then a third killed the crew of a logging truck. It is unclear if these were the out-of-control acts of angry young men, or under orders. If the latter, it was terrorism, to sow terror among the Vietnamese in the highlands. The logging truck incident came closest to a concise statement as to what FULRO was really fighting for: land and resources.[2]

A larger challenge was to build a FULRO army. For this they needed Bhan, who was now at his second posting with the Americans, commanding the Montagnard Civilian Irregular Defense Group (CIDG) Training Center at Kan Nak, which had caused him to miss both the rebellion and the cross-border raids.

He was one of the two most-qualified Rhadé officers. The other was his oldest friend, Y-Nam Eban, commanding the force in Cambodia, who recognized that Bhan was now better qualified than he to train FULRO's young recruits, being up to date with American arms, equipment, and tactics. Plus, he considered Bhan a better disciplinarian with more command presence. Y-Nam began pleading with Bhan to come, sending him urgent secret messages.

Meanwhile, at Kan Nak—an isolated camp in the coastal mountains—Bhan was increasingly certain an attack was coming. Patrols he sent out were picking up rumors. One patrol found signs from the night before that the enemy had reconnoitered right up to the camp's wire, in a blind spot.

But the messages from Y-Nam left him with no choice. He had to go to Cambodia. Before leaving, he analyzed the camp's weaknesses. A creek could be used as an approach, so he cleared fields of fire overlooking it with a bulldozer and put in wire to chest level. The 81 mm mortar was vulnerable, so he built a pit for it inside the camp's inner perimeter, right outside the team house.

He left at the end of February 1965. A week later, two main-force Viet Cong battalions attacked at night, using the creek, killing 34 Montagnard soldiers and wounding 32, getting inside the camp at a cost of 131 dead of their own. But the inner perimeter had held, and the mortar had been crucial.[3]

***

In the late 1950s, having cadged independence for his country from France, Sihanouk faced two major problems, the first centuries old—how to avoid being swallowed by his historically hungry neighbors, Vietnam and Thailand—and the second brand new—how to avoid being pulled into the growing Cold War conflict next door.

His solutions over time were to appease the Vietnamese communists in hopes of getting their guarantee of Cambodia's borders while they still needed his help, and to wholeheartedly embrace China as Cambodia's long-range patron.[4]

That his neutralism was always left-leaning was based on his conviction that Vietnamese nationalism was irresistible and the communists would win. Unlike the Americans, he could never underestimate the Vietnamese. No next-door neighbor could.[5]

By secret agreement in 1955, Sihanouk allowed the Viet Cong to use Cambodian territory for transit and temporary sanctuary. As the conflict intensified, this became increasingly galling to both Saigon and Washington, who responded by supporting several operations to dislodge or kill Sihanouk. One involved Cambodian anti-monarchists operating from sanctuaries in Thailand and South Vietnam, who became an obsession to Sihanouk because the survival of the monarchy was as important to him as that of Cambodia itself.[6]

In 1959–60, he authorized the creation of two irredentist groups to clamor for return of lands "stolen" by the Vietnamese, presumably to pay Diem back and to inhibit border operations by those anti-monarchist rebels. As a plus, they might serve as leverage in future border negotiations with South Vietnam.

One group was the Khmer Krom ("Southern Cambodians"), whose lands in the Mekong Delta had been occupied over centuries by the Vietnamese, then officially granted to Vietnam by the French in 1949. To oversee this group, Sihanouk chose a colonel in the Cambodian Army who was himself from the Delta: Um Savuth.

The other group consisted of Chams from both Cambodia and Vietnam who dreamed of clawing back lands that had once constituted the fabled kingdom of Champa. Stretching the definition of Cham, this group included Vietnam's Chamic-speaking Montagnards, the Rhadé, and the Jarai. To lead this group, he chose Colonel Les Kosem, good friends with Um Savuth but, more importantly, a true believer in the Cham irredentist cause. In early 1962, the newly arrived Americans began arming Rhadé villagers in South Vietnam. It seems likely Sihanouk saw this growing military force on his border as a threat, much as Diem did, and ordered Les Kosem to co-opt it.

***

In October 1964, Sihanouk met with North Vietnamese and Viet Cong leaders and invited them to attend a conference in Phnom Penh four months hence, grandly billed as the Indochina Peoples' Conference. They agreed, probably seeing it as a minor platform for condemning American imperialism.

However, Sihanouk intended to show the world true neutralists existed in Indochina and that, while angry at America, he was not in the pocket of the communist Vietnamese. The conference would also showcase the irredentist fronts he had created, which demanded the return of large chunks of Vietnam. Whether or not he saw this as an ambush, that was how the Vietnamese would see it.

In 1964, true neutralists still existed, though they were fast dwindling, especially among South Vietnamese for whom holding such views was dangerous unless they were in exile. Like rare orchids, one group of Vietnamese neutralists was being nurtured almost hydroponically in Phnom Penh; another would need to be flown in from Paris.

A born publicist, Sihanouk set out to pack the house. The communists would produce bogus groups; he needed to produce bogus groups. He would use FULRO as an authentic nucleus because it had real soldiers who had just participated in a real uprising. From it, nine other front groups would appear as though by mitosis, balancing the communists. The larger idea was to create the impression of diversity of non-aligned peoples in Indochina.[7]

Beyond that, though, Sihanouk seemed to have had a special affinity for Montagnards.[8] This was true as well of his chief minister, Lon Nol, especially so, who was rumored to have Montagnard blood due to his dark complexion (as a teenager at boarding school in Saigon, his nickname was Black Chinese, perhaps explaining—as these things can do—some of his later actions toward the Vietnamese, thus a small degree of his people's fate).[9]

***

In November 1964, Paul Y-Bun Sur was seated at a typewriter in Les Kosem's bungalow in Phnom Penh, writing speeches to be delivered by the various front groups at the upcoming conference. At the time, Paul was among the most-educated highlanders in the movement and had mastered its rhetoric. Kosem lent him his cherished personal copies of *The History of Tchampa* by E. Aymonier (1893) and *The Champa Kingdom* by G. Maspero (1910) so he could understand and explain the historical connection between Cham and

Montagnards that justified FULRO's claim over two-thirds of the land area of South Vietnam.

A speech already written by someone else was peppered with references to America's crimes and imperialism. Having little experience with Americans, Paul asked one of the other speechwriters about this. The man, a Rhadé, had an opposite take on Americans: during the FULRO rebellion two months before, the Americans had allowed the Montagnards to spirit weapons away and take them to Cambodia. "They even gave us the keys to the arsenal," the Rhadé said, "then told us to tie them up so the Vietnamese wouldn't suspect."

Later, Paul asked Kosem about why they were blaming Americans.

"Because we're in Cambodia," Kosem replied, "It's government policy. And because this conference is essential to getting our movement recognized. Everyone coming to the conference is against the United States—if we didn't condemn American aggression, we wouldn't be able to attend."[10]

Being Mnong was fateful for Paul. His feeling of ethnic connection to Chams may not have been as strong as that of a Rhadé or Jarai, but being Mnong must have influenced Lon Nol's picking him out as a long-range prospect for leadership of FULRO. Lon Nol himself felt closer ethnically to the Mnong than to Rhadé or Jarai. It helped that Paul could communicate with both Montagnard language groups, and that he spoke fluent French and understood Khmer, and that he was a young man of charm and presence, but the core reason for his selection was likely one of blood: Lon Nol—who would one day depose Sihanouk and lead the country—had intense feelings about race and ethnicity.

All Paul needed now was a university degree, in France.

Lon Nol proceeded to adopt him, which affected him little in Paris other than bringing him occasional visits by Lon Nol and probably a larger stipend. But afterwards, once back in Cambodia, it lent him a life of velvet and license that cannot have done his character any good. And, one day, it would be among the things marking him for death.[11]

***

In February 1965, when the Indochina Peoples' Conference opened in an airy Polynesian-styled conference hall on the Mekong, Phnom Penh's boulevards were heavenly with trees blooming lavender and brilliant yellow against a large blue sky.

It was a time of great hope but, over the next 10 years, exactly, Cambodia would slowly sink into hell on earth.

Y-Bham Enuol, Prince Sihanouk of Cambodia. (Photo courtesy of Meidine Natchear)

The conference was FULRO's political debut, giving it credibility on a regional stage, perhaps even on the world stage when its doors opened to the international press. Kosem arranged a meeting between Y-Bham Enuol and Prince Sihanouk in which the latter seemed truly affectionate toward the Montagnard, telling him, jokingly, "You are the real Cambodian. You are more Cambodian than I am."

Sihanouk chose the Khmer Krom (FULRO's Southern Cambodians) to represent Cambodia at the preparatory session with the North Vietnamese and Viet Cong. Though the session was closed to outsiders, this was a poke in the eye of the Vietnamese because the Khmer Krom existed only to claw back the Delta from Vietnam.[12] Worse, the Khmer Krom were talking openly about the fact that the communists, too, were violating the neutrality of Laos and Cambodia. They skirmished over the definition of "peace." The Vietnamese wanted it defined as what would follow the Americans' expulsion from Indochina. The Khmer Krom retorted, "No—a negotiated peace, not your peace of the cemeteries."

Sihanouk hoped to convince the United States to leave South Vietnam by getting North Vietnam to truly and verifiably withdraw its troops from Laos and Cambodia.[13] We know now that would never have happened, but at the time it was not unreasonable. Sihanouk prepared an opening speech that vibrated with belief that this was the key to peace.

However, history had just lurched hard beneath his feet. The week before, the Americans began their air war against inland North Vietnam.[14] It took the communist delegations several days' back and forth with Hanoi and Beijing to stiffen; when they did, they swept the neutralist solution off the table, enraged.

When the main conference opened on March 1, it was a pure-tone denunciation of American aggression. Sihanouk rewrote his speech to agree, as did the FULRO delegations: yes, the South Vietnamese were the prime colonialists, but they could not do it without the imperialist Americans. A few speakers dared to drop "South" from in front of "Vietnamese," but all put blame on the Americans.

If FULRO had been hoping for instant visibility, the American bombing, called Operation *Rolling Thunder*,[15] took everyone's attention away. If anyone was left listening, Y-Bham Enuol's proud and inflated reference to FULRO's "stunning general victory of September 20, 1964"[16] must have seemed puny and irrelevant.

This was the Montagnards' political high point, much as their September rebellion was their military high point. But someone had made a poor public-relations decision:[17] at the conference's finale, a few of the FULRO delegations dressed in their native attire in order to illustrate diversity, but this attracted only "skepticism—and often hilarity" from the sophisticates of the international press.[18]

That was it. The Montagnard ethnonationalists were a joke. Dhon was seething.

***

At Kan Nak, Bhan agonized over telling his Montagnard troops he was leaving for Cambodia to join FULRO. He finally decided not to tell them because they would have wanted to come. He concocted some excuse for the Americans and quietly caught a ride out on a Caribou aircraft to Ban Me Thuot.

He tried to dissuade his wife from coming to Cambodia, pointing out that joining the FULRO rebels would make him a wanted man in Vietnam, a target.

"If I go, I can't come back," he said.

"No," she replied, echoing her words when they had met 10 years before, "I will follow you." She meant their four-year-old too.

This was the most fateful decision of their lives.

Her motive may have been partly social. Some of her friends were already in Cambodia. Her two younger brothers were going as well, to protect their sister but excited by FULRO as well.

As to Bhan's motives, despite his ideology and militancy, he was drawn most powerfully by friendship. His childhood friend, Y-Nam Eban, the commander in Cambodia, needed him. They had been together since 1st grade, kicked oranges as soccer balls going to school, had joined the French Army together at 17, spending their first three years at the same caserne. He was loyal as well to other friends who had taken this fateful step, like Dhon and Y-Bham Enuol.[19]

In late February 1965, Bhan, his wife and little boy, and her two teenage brothers, walked 40 kilometers (25 miles) northwest from Ban Me Thuot to Ban Don (instead of southwest to the FULRO base). He was in a loincloth, she in a wraparound black cloth, like simple Montagnards. The route was intentionally roundabout because the Vietnamese were watching the border closely further south. At Ban Don, he hired an elephant and its Laotian mahout, who would know the route back down through Cambodia's savannah country and speak Khmer. Bhan had heard the route was flat and semi-desert much of the way, with no villages. The less people they met the better, and the faster they moved the better, because they would be travelling alone, armed only with the mahout's 1886 French rifle.

The men walked. The woman and boy rode in an open box, swaying on the elephant's shoulders, clutching the inconspicuous bundles that hid the remnants of a disappearing life. They travelled all day and reached the border, a naked river, after dark. After letting the elephant take a bath—its last for several days—the mahout disappeared to find the local Viet Cong. At that time of year, full dry season, nights are crushing. Bright stars rest right on the horizon, trembling through spindly trees. This was their last night in their homeland.

Early the next morning, the mahout came back with a Viet Cong cadre, who was pleasant and helped them reload the elephant. Bhan's four-year-old, who must have heard his parents talking the night before, asked if Bhan was going to kill the Viet Cong. Fortunately, the Vietnamese did not speak Rhadé.

They were on the route taken at the same time of year by the unlucky Henri Maître who recorded passing through:

> … dreary solitudes [where] the atmosphere is gauzy with heat-haze rising from the cooked soil. Distant hills and clouds are the same violet blue, metallic. Grass is dry or burnt. The trees, wide-spaced, seem painted cardboard, their rare leaves like cut-out zinc … At first sight [the forest] seems like a ghost forest … [because one moves] through it with ease, as does sunlight and the air. Yet its mass keeps sight from reaching very far and erases the entire horizon.[20]

The way was easy at first, heading generally south on skeins of wild-elephant trails through knee-high bamboo grass (see photo, opposite) but the simultaneous opacity and depth of the forest noted by Maître were threatening

Clear-type forest of the Sre Pok Basin on the track between Sem Monorom and Ban Lung. (Photo by author, 2011)

now.[21] Any movement at the edge of vision—a far-off fleshy leaf, turning slowly in the hot wind of winter—was startling. Anything dark in the distance, breaking the monotonous grey nimbus, had to be a structure, therefore human and dangerous, until, closer, it became natural, one of the jumbles of huge, blackened granitic blocks that dot the plain. But even these were disturbing, with their crannies and corridors, places for someone to lie back in darkness and watch and wait.

Gradually they climbed out of the basin of the Sre Pok River, crossing dried-up tributaries with black, fetid pools teeming with frogs and leeches. The forest thickened, though only sparse brush crowned low hills, some strewn with blossoms whose scent had been delicious to Maître but hardly registered, if at all, on Bhan and his wary, thirsty band. Occasionally they glimpsed blue Nam Lyr Mountain, their destination, rising out of vast flat forest. When they finally reached water again, a small river, they stopped only to let the elephant bathe, then followed it south.

They stopped again to bathe themselves and change into good clothes before arriving at the FULRO encampment. When Bhan's wife came down from the elephant, she was wearing platform shoes.[22]

Arriving in mid-March 1965, only days after the Indochina Peoples' Conference, Bhan was called to Phnom Penh.

***

From a FULRO document detailing the number of officers and NCOs in FULRO's army in July 1965, we can guess that at that early date it had some 1,200–1,800 soldiers in Cambodia. Another source corroborates 2,000. An estimate from 1–2 years later said FULRO had 5,000–6,000 troops in Cambodia with around 15,000 dependents.[23]

A US Special Forces intelligence estimate, also from July 1965, guessed FULRO had already trained 3,000 soldiers and sent them back to Vietnam.[24]

These numbers were not only large but represented a rapid, almost explosive, increase over time. Feeding such numbers by foraging, fishing, and hunting in order to supplement food trucked in by Cham soldiers ended up being a near full-time job, leaving little time for military training.

Even if there had been ample time for training, FULRO had little in the way of arms, ammunition, or equipment to train with.

Beyond that, it had no enemies within Cambodia to battle in order to gain combat experience. (The North Vietnamese and Viet Cong had been warned off by Sihanouk. Clashes occurred from time to time when FULRO crossed Base Area 740 en route to Vietnam, but these were mistakes and contact was usually broken off.)

FULRO's solution to these problems was to send its young soldiers to serve with the Americans in CIDG units where they could pilfer arms, ammunition, and equipment, and receive training in their use, and—most importantly—get modern combat experience. As Paul Y-Bun Sur wrote, "it was a good opportunity to train as real soldiers."[25]

This is important to one of the central points of this book, that many of the Montagnard soldiers who served alongside Americans in the CIDG were motivated by ethnonationalism as well as by the pay.

***

Shortly after the conference, Les Kosem arranged a tour of Cambodia to impress FULRO's leaders, now including Bhan, during which they travelled by car and plane through the rice-growing northeast, then to Cambodia's main seaport, and finally to a mountain resort.

Anger flared between Dhon and Y-Bham Enuol over how to dress. Y-Bham Enuol had mandated white shirts, ties, and polished shoes, unintentionally giving them a Mormon-missionary look (photo, opposite). Perhaps still hearing the snickers of the international press, Dhon showed up with his jacket over the arm, knowing this looked more sophisticated.[26]

Dhon (center), probably with Y-Bham Enuol (back to camera). (Photo courtesy of Meidine Natchear)

FULRO's official photo of Y-Bham Enuol (note flag with crescent for Muslim Chams). (Photo from FULRO document HISTORIQUE)

In another photo from roughly the same period (above), staged for propaganda purposes, Y-Bham Enuol's natty attire evokes Madison Avenue or Kennedy's Rat Pack. To our eyes, Fidel's army fatigues were more appropriate. But FULRO knew its people. Hungry for modernity and weary of war, they could have wondered why Fidel did not try to dress up for a photograph.

***

The western slope of the Central Highlands is gentle and long. Rivers meander toward the Mekong through skeletal forest and broom grass, with sky the only variable. Bhan's elephant trek took him across it from north to south. Even today there are wide areas with no human habitation. This makes it all the more startling to find an ancient temple in a clearing on an oxbow in the Ia Drang River. It is small, and in ruins, but of fired brick with sharp edges and, an incongruous echo, a Hindu lingam. Joss sticks suggest Jarai still worship here. This is Ta Nang. Whatever century it was built in, it is a remnant of a last external influence on the Montagnards. After this, time stopped for them.

Depending on how one frames it, the the long stretch of time since was a happy interlude of freedom from the exactions, strife, and disease of lowland states, or a dark time of fearful ignorance and intertribal predation. Either way, their world stopped changing.

One morning in November 1965, it began changing again, exponentially, only about 30 kilometers (18 miles) upstream.

A meadow at the base of a mountain on the Cambodian border began to explode, pulsing flame and smoke into a clear blue sky. Something shrieked overhead like a spall from the sun. If there were any highlanders around, they were simple woodcutters or hunters who could have imagined that Sambram's cataclysm was upon them, with three suns rising and a typhoon from the eastern sea.

In reality, the newly arrived Americans were bombing and shelling a landing zone in preparation for their first helicopter assault into enemy territory, unaware that North Vietnamese regulars happened to be on the mountain. The Battle of Ia Drang was about to begin.

But in a sense Sambram's prophecy had been right.

The world as the Montagnards knew it was about to end, with too many fireballs boiling up into the sky, too much destruction rushing up from the east like a great wind. The Americans would accelerate time. The American way of life would beckon many Montagnards. The American way of war, expending explosives instead of men, would kill many, and uproot many more. The Montagnards would side with the Americans against the Vietnamese and lose. The victorious Vietnamese would set out to eradicate the highlanders' way of life and turn them, sadly but not unreasonably, into Vietnamese.

***

The battle took place some 120 kilometers (75 miles) north of FULRO's hilltop headquarters. The Montagnard leaders would have seen a fury in distant skies that lasted days. They were probably the first, perhaps only, outsiders to hear about some of the battle's ugliest details from local Jarai who could read the signs: Americans executed with hands tied behind their backs and Vietnamese roasted by napalm.

They must have sensed, if not clearly recognized, the significance to their people of the fact this all took place in land empty and still as noon, instead of on or near roads like the battles of the French.

The Americans were clearly here to stay.

Notes

1 Surprisingly, he had made a trip back to the United States in the 1990s to meet with some of them, possibly to find out if bygones were bygones. Apparently, he learned the opposite. I never did pursue the logistics of how he did this.

2 Jonathan Neale, *A People's History of the Vietnam War* (New York: The New Press, 2003), 2. This Trotskiite analysis of the Vietnam War makes the point that the war was "more over land than over national independence," even for the Vietnamese.

3 Anonymous, "Heroic Saga in the Vast Jungle (Attack on Ka Nak Outpost, 7 March 1965)," translated by Merle Pribbenow, *Gia Lai Online*, July 24, 2009, at https://baogialai.com.vn/khuc-trang-ca-giua-dai-ngan-post95133.html. Also, Shelby Stanton, *Green Berets at War* (New York: Dell Publishing, 1985), 115. Some of the CIDG who later came to Cambodia told Bhan about the attack. He regretted not having been there, believing he would have made a difference (he would have manned the mortar himself).

4 Similarly, his grandfather, King Norodom, had signed his country over to France as a "protectorate" in 1863, saving it from being swallowed by Thailand and/or Vietnam.

5 The Vietnamese had been inexorably expansionist since the 11th century, imperialists in the slow, contiguous sense of settler colonialism, less objectionable than the arrogant imperialism of Westerners, but far more irreversible.

6 This is an assumption that cannot be proved or disproved because Sihanouk did not share his truest thoughts with anyone, but it seems obvious. The antimonarchist group was the Khmer Serei.

7 In the end, the communists ended up fielding 23 delegations, Cambodia 15 (four representing Sihanouk's party, nine sprung from FULRO, and two authentically neutralist South Vietnamese delegations). Charles Meyer, Sihanouk's principal French advisor, thinks Sihanouk packed the conference first (*Derrière Le Sourire Khmer* (Paris: Plon, 1971), p. 268). Others (Leslie Fielding, *Before the Killing Fields* (London: IB Tauris, 2008), p. 97) say the communists were first. Meyer is scathing in his description of the conference, which he considers a turning point at which Sihanouk began to "betray the Indochina resistance." His anger toward the Montagnards, which turns to derision, seems related to this.

8 Unlike Diem, Sihanouk was genuinely fond of Montagnards, but his appreciation did not extend to their culture, as he, like Diem, tried to assimilate them.

9 The lycée was Chasseloup-Laubat. Justin Corfield, *Khmers Stand Up!: A History of the Cambodian Government 1970–1975* (Melbourne, Australia: Center of Southeast Asian Studies, Monash University, 1994), 2. By my calculations, Lon Nol was in the same class as Marguerite Duras.

10 Chek Brahim, *Confession*, Catalogue #D02687 (1975–76), S-21 (Khmer Rouge torture center), Phnom Penh: Documentation Center of Cambodia (translated to English by Chenda Seang). This information was extracted over seven months prior to Brahim being "smashed" (executed) in May 1976. In 1964, Brahim was a speechwriter himself, an assistant to Les Kosem. Obviously, there is some question as to what to believe from such a source. A court of law would exclude it. On this particular point, however, it sounds right, especially with the detail about the keys.

11 On the other hand, maybe Lon Nol's adoption was nothing more than a bureaucratic move, something to qualify for a French-funded scholarship in France earmarked for Cambodians only.

12 Sihanouk had been surprisingly aggressive about the rights of Vietnam's ethnic minorities including the southern Cambodians (aka Khmer Krom). Talks with the Viet Cong in December 1964 in Beijing may have failed because of this (Fielding, *Before the Killing Fields*, p. 99).

13 Unlike neutralists like de Gaulle, he appeared to hope for a true and persisting neutralization of South Vietnam, not a disguised communist takeover. He feared the expansionism of a united Vietnam and particularly of a united communist Vietnam.

14 Three strikes just above the DMZ, in retaliation for significant Viet Cong actions, February 7, 9, and 11, called Operation *Flaming Dart*. The conference's preparatory session ran February 14–17.

15 The sustained bombing of North Vietnam, begun March 2, would last almost four years.

16 Y-Bham Enuol, speech at the Indochina Peoples' Conference, Phnom Penh, March 4, 1965. Copies of some, but not all, of the other speeches are in the Cornell Library or Charles Meyer collection in Cambodia's National Library.

17 The effort to convey authenticity was so strenuous that they all got dressed up in traditional clothing, embarked on a military airplane, circled for a while, then landed as if arriving from Vietnam. Sabu Bacha, interview with author, April 7, 2018.

18 Fielding, *Before the Killing Fields*, 99. His own choice of title for his chapter on the conference, "The Tribes Are Restless," betrays a plummy, jocular condescension that is unfortunate.

19 His exact words, on being probed about this most important decision, were repeated statements of "I had to follow Y-Nam because he had to follow me," or, "I missed him. Without me, there was no him; without him, there was no me," and one mention of "By himself, he didn't know what to do." Other friends were important too: "Dhon and Y-Bham Enuol were already there" and "Everybody was there, only I was missing."

20 Henri Maitre, *Les Jungles Moi* (Paris: Larose, 1912), 185, 188.

21 During the Vietnam War, American reconnaissance teams knew the area as The Wasteland. To them, the lines of sight were too long, potentially enabling the enemy to spot them without their being aware of it. A North Vietnamese tactic in combatting recon teams was to gather without being seen, then rush toward the unsuspecting Americans to overwhelm and kill them before any aircraft could arrive. Fortunately for everyone, the North Vietnamese only used The Wasteland for transit between its bases to the north and to the south. The Americans thus inserted very few teams.

22 Meidine Natchear, interviews with author over span of seven years, 2011–18.

23 The first estimate is based on there being three battalions, which, by French standards, would be 400–600 men/battalion. (The actual officer count, all of them named individuals, was three colonels [Bhan, Y-Nam, and one other], three majors [hence three battalions], nine captains, 20 first lieutenants, and 33 second lieutenants, with the non-commissioned officers consisting of 38 warrant officers or master sergeants, 28 sergeants first class, 40 staff sergeants, 19 sergeants, and six corporals) (document dated July 21 1965, entitled *Liste des Combatants des F.A.R.C. Promus aux Grades Superieurs,* in Les Kosem trove). The estimate of 2,000 is from Gerald C. Hickey, *Free in the Forest: Ethnohistory of the Vietnamese Central Highlands 1954–1956* (New Haven, CT: Yale University Press, 1982a), 114; the estimate of 5,000–6,000 is from the same source, 116.

24 USSF document from July 27, 1965 (Steve Sherman, FULRO I, p4) actually says they were sent back to their villages in Vietnam, but eventually they must have become RF/PF or CIDG.

25 Sur, Y-Bun (Paul). "Les Relations entre Montagnards et Vietnamiens au Vietnam Sud," *Vocation asiatique,* no. 4 (1968), Paris. ["*Pour les montagnards, c'est une bonne occasion des se former en vrais soldats.*"] A French academic introduces the article as having originally been a talk given by Paul to a group of [probably-leftist] Vietnamese in Paris. The fact that Paul does not pull his punches with such an audience, pointing out that Montagnards do not become Viet Cong because the Viet Cong are Vietnamese, plus the extreme obscurity of the journal, suggest that Paul was telling what he saw as the unslanted truth.

26 Bhan, interview with author, April 2018. The towns were Battambang, Sihanoukville, and Kirirom.

CHAPTER 10

Kpa Doh

In 1963, at a newly opened Special Forces camp near Cheo Reo, the Americans needed Jarai interpreters. At the time, few Montagnards spoke English. Those that did had chosen to take classes at one of the small satellites of the US Information Service in highland towns. This selected individuals more alert to the world beyond their plateaus, perhaps drawn to shimmering visions of America as a City upon a Hill. The earlier this was, the more unique, even marginal, they were.

One of the candidates for interpreter, a muscular 25-year-old named Kpa Doh, was from a nearby hamlet but had a very unusual resume: 10 years of French schooling followed by work for a series of American civilians—road builders, surveyors, a development worker and malaria-eradication doctor—before serving as a CIDG commander at a Special Forces camp further north.

His English was rudimentary and broken, but he clicked with the Green Berets because of his experience at the other camp and because of his quick wit and unwavering good humor.

When he and another interpreter learned PLFs (parachute landing falls) by jumping off a table a few times, then parachuted for real from a helicopter, the Americans assumed he was competing light-heartedly with the other interpreter.[1] But humorous insouciance was one of his traits. More likely, he was demonstrating courage to his fellow Jarai soldiers. In his culture, leadership had to be won.

There was much the Americans did not know about him.

From a poor family, he had waded a broad river every day as a boy to attend 1st through 3rd grade, tending water buffaloes after school. From there he boarded at primary and middle school in Pleiku, then—like Dhon one year earlier—made the enormous leap to the Lycée Yersin, where he played defense alongside Dhon on the soccer team and absorbed the older boy's politics. At first, Kpa Doh struggled academically, helped by a Jarai upperclassman,[2] but eventually he mastered the awful exigencies of written French. Far more than the other Montagnards, he was a brawler, fighting constantly with the

Vietnamese boys.[3] Though never a convert, he sang Latin hymns in the church choir because, like most Jarai, he loved singing.[4] Leaving school in 1956 after 10th grade (roughly equal to an American high school education), he took a job translating for a French engineer, but the man failed to pay him. Around this time, he began studying English. Fully committed to Montagnard militancy by 1957, he got jailed for a month for writing an anti-Diem letter. In between work with Americans, he worked part-time singing Jarai songs on Saigon radio, paired for duets with a beautiful Mnong nurse. They fell in love, and even sang pro-Diem propaganda songs.

At this point he could have profitably remained a civilian, but in November 1962 he signed up to be a soldier at the first Special Forces camp where the CIDG would be Jarai (Plei Mrong). His motive must have been related to his growing militancy as an ethnonationalist: he would need to know how to fight. He was quickly promoted to be one of Plei Mrong's three company commanders. His first significant combat was a harrowing defense three months later when the camp was attacked by the Viet Cong and almost overrun. From this battle, the Americans learned to build an inner perimeter in all their camps, a last redoubt. Plei Mrong's other weakness, almost fatal, was the presence of Montagnard Viet Cong among its defenders.

Now, a year later at a different camp (Buon Beng), the Americans saw him initially as a little brother, calling him Pardo because they had difficulty pronouncing his name.[5] Part of this was his still-poor English, part was his humorous insouciance, a characteristic that seemed boyish until they saw it under fire, part was his way of deflecting attention from himself. They did know he had sung professionally, but they had no idea that he could also write French well, operate a theolodite, help run an anti-malarial program, and name Napoleon's victories. Keeping quiet was related to his other main characteristic—an intense, purposeful curiosity. He was trying to learn the Americans' ways. Witnessing many of them emotionally naked in battle, he came to know the American character better than any other FULRO leader. Though the Green Berets' respect for him grew, he still remained one of "the indigenous," slightly blurry, describable mostly as "very effective in combat."

At Buon Beng, he began political organizing among both soldiers and civilians. In March 1964, the other interpreter revealed to the Americans that a Montagnard revolt was coming. Whether this was part of a plan or simply loose lipped, Y-Bham Enuol himself showed up in camp shortly thereafter (opposite). Despite a suit and tie in the dry season heat, the elder leader appeared relaxed, listening quietly to the American captain[6] who tried to get across that rebellion was doomed to fail. Essentially, the US military could never support it. In turn, Y-Bham Enuol laid out the Montagnard demands, knowing these would reach the ears of top-level Americans. If these demands were not met, the revolt would happen anyway.

As we have seen, the revolt did take place, five months later, in the Rhadé region further south.

Kpa Doh was not directly involved, though he did get jailed briefly for his political organizing among the Jarai.

Kpa Doh, Y-Bham Enuol, Nay Luett. (Photo courtesy of Crews McCulloch)

***

FULRO mounted a *Second* Rebellion on December 18, 1965, fifteen months after the first. One cause was anger at Saigon's unfulfilled promises, especially a promise to grant sovereignty to FULRO over slices of highland territory in return for FULRO's clearing them of enemy.

But the rebellion's timing suggests a larger purpose: to show the newly arrived American generals what Montagnards could do militarily, on their own, on their home territory—which looked to be their best shot at winning a country of their own.

Only circumstantial evidence exists for this, but it is obvious:

The First Rebellion had failed to bring any pressure to bear on Saigon. If anything, it had hurt FULRO's cause, revealing the Montagnards to be too trusting and deferential, and it had shown America and South Vietnam to be too closely allied to be easily peeled apart.

FULRO needed an outside power to force Saigon to grant autonomy to Montagnards, and that power had to be Washington. (Phnom Penh and Paris were too weak to pressure Saigon. Moscow and Beijing were only interested in deniable participation at a distance, and—because FULRO's whole reason for existence was to prevent Vietnamese domination—that power could not be Hanoi.)

The Battle of Ia Drang had just proven the Americans planned to fight the war in the highlands and that they would take it into the furthest reaches. This in turn made the Montagnard people even more key to victory than before.

Late that same month, FULRO abandoned its anti-US rhetoric, sending a letter to President Johnson and de Gaulle and the UN claiming opposition to Communism and adherence to "Free World policy," and asking that, until Montagnards could handle independence, the highlands be placed under UN trusteeship, administered jointly by the US and France.[7]

***

The Second Rebellion was far more ambitious than the first, targeting the capitals of all five highland provinces instead of two. Pleiku, Cheo Reo, and Kontum were added, which shifted the rebellion's center of gravity to the north into Jarai and Bahnar country, more rugged and remote. At last, the Jarai could weigh in to the struggle, which added a touch of the spirit captured in the Jarai's 1891 speech to Captain Cupet (see p. 22).

Because much greater distances were involved, it placed a premium on communications, but FULRO's planners stuck with primitive methods, apparently believing that only Montagnards could be trusted. Thus, instructions in invisible ink were delivered in person on Honda 90 motorbikes, and Bhan himself broadcast the start signal from a radio station in Phnom Penh, beyond Vietnamese reach. The original start date may have been in late December, deeper into dry season.

This time, fewer US Special Forces camps were involved. FULRO was more wary of Americans, remembering the Green Beret officers who spontaneously interfered last time. (As it turned out, they were not wary enough.) Instead, FULRO relied more on local militia, the so-called Regional Forces/Popular Forces (RF/PF, nicknamed "Ruff-Puffs"), which had the advantage of being pure Montagnard, with Montagnard commanders, but the disadvantage of being less well equipped, less trained, and less disciplined.

Word had been circulating since November that another rebellion was coming before the end of the year. People also said that France, Cambodia, and the United States were backing it.[8] Either this was failed secrecy, or it was a rumor planted to generate excitement for a popular uprising.

On December 16, in Pleiku, FULRO warriors began to infiltrate the town with only knives and grenades hidden beneath loincloths and tattered shirts, intending to take the unsuspecting American guards of the US motor pool hostage, then—likely with the help of Montagnard soldiers within Pleiku's ARVN (Army of the Republic of Vietnam) division—to use armored troop carriers to overwhelm the Vietnamese garrison.

But the Vietnamese police were on the lookout for them. Several were caught and induced to talk. On the 17th, the Vietnamese alerted the Americans.

This time, the American military was officially 100 percent against FULRO.

In no time, the motor pool was ringed with US troops. All CIDG units in Pleiku Province—heavily FULRO—were immediately sent out on trumped-up missions to get them away from towns. That afternoon, a Special Forces captain learned from one of the rebels that "the primary FULRO leader Y BA HAN [i.e., Bhan] was going to issue final instructions via radio transmission at 3am on frequency of 4,750 MC, SW."[9] That night, the US Army Signal Corps proceeded to jam Bhan's broadcast. (When I asked him about this, he had his customary amnesia.)

Afterward, US Army reports, which had richly described the First Rebellion, revealed little about the second. Orders from on high had been clear about not supporting FULRO. Career-minded Green Beret officers outdid themselves to paint the situation as having been copacetic and under complete control in their camps, which meant few details. Coupled with Saigon's suppression of news, this resulted in far less documentation of the Second Rebellion than the first.

In Kontum, the Bahnar leader (see note 6, Chapter 2) —no militant to begin with—doubted the authenticity of the order to rise up, suspecting correctly that Y-Bham Enuol had not sent it—so nothing happened.[10]

Attacking forces outside Ban Me Thuot and Cheo Reo melted away.[11]

Cheo Reo was Kpa Doh's home and the source of many Jarai recruits to FULRO. I was certain he had been leading the attacking force, so went back to my notes from 1973.

The weather had been a disaster:

> Couldn't reach in time because of [the] roads ... [By then] the Vietnamese were alerted ... Had to cross a river to get [back] to Cambodia, but it was too high.[12]

In Vietnam's Central Highlands, dry season usually begins in December but, in 1965, December saw a deluge. (On the coast, rainfall was almost 8 times normal[13]), which turned roads to mud wallows and rivers to impassible barriers. This made the Americans' jamming of radio signals even more consequential.

FULRO knew that its neatly choreographed schedule was turning to soup, but it had just moved the rebellion's start date forward to December 17, having gotten wind of a visit on that date to Pleiku by South Vietnam's prime minister. Given the fragility of its communications, however, this was like moving a house of cards. Secrecy and deception were essential to the rebellion's success, yet, on December 14 or 15, FULRO held a meeting in a Montagnard schoolhouse on the Pleiku outskirts to hand out new orders face-to-face. It was too clamorous, and one participant believes all secrecy was lost at that time.[14]

If this rebellion was so important to FULRO, how could it have been allowed to fail?

Certainly, FULRO had its primitive aspects. One example—its invisible ink was lemon juice, developed with iodine. And some of its troops looked to have arrived from a different century, e.g., 90 barefoot Mnong in loincloths and Ike-jackets, some with white Prell bottlecaps in their earlobes, emerged to take one provincial capital. However, FULRO's leaders were intelligent and capable men, quick to master modern tools, and many of its NCOs and officers had had years of combat experience. (Perhaps not incidentally, the 90 barefoot Mnong scored the rebellion's only success, taking Gia Nghia without a shot and holding it for 30 hours.)[15]

Lack of sophistication may have been evident in that too-obvious schoolhouse meeting, but other factors combined to make the Second Rebellion fail—American betrayal, bad weather, and, most significantly, that last-minute decision to move the rebellion ahead.

The jammed radio broadcast would have been a serious blow no matter the date, but FULRO was on its toes, expecting some betrayals by Americans, thus might have compensated. Bad weather could have been finessed by delaying everything until late December or early January when the roads would dry out, but the decision to go early had the exact opposite effect.

The idea appears to have been Kosem's. Po Dharma credits him with ordering the rebellion to start on the 17th, hoping that a revolt in the prime minister's face could finally shock the government into granting limited sovereignty to Montagnards. (Po Dharma overstates Kosem's role. More likely Kosem simply suggested the change rather than "ordered" it.)[16]

The Montagnard militants shared Kosem's goal but, in late 1965, there was one significant difference between their approach and his: they could imagine an alliance with the Americans, but Kosem could not. (Sihanouk and France were behind him at this point.) It is unlikely Kosem intentionally sabotaged the rebellion, but its ultimate success would have been less important to him than to the Montagnard militants.[17]

***

Kpa Doh did mention the Second Rebellion to me in 1973, but I did not realize its—or his—importance, so my notes are sparse.

The plan in Cheo Reo appears to have been for a Jarai RF/PF company to attack a Vietnamese district post at Phu Thien, north of Cheo Reo, thus draw elements of the ARVN Division out from town;[18] the main FULRO force would then attack the relief column or occupy Cheo Reo in its absence. But the Ruff-Puffs jumped the gun and machine-gunned a Vietnamese platoon emerging from its barracks. They then sought refuge with FULRO Montagnards at a nearby Special Forces camp but were turned away.

Kpa Doh had personally recruited many of the Ruff-Puffs. He was disgusted with the Jarai CIDG captain who had turned away the fleeing rebels, describing him as a *poule mouillée* (wet hen). Clearly, Kpa Doh felt responsible for all of Cheo Reo.

Without more notes, I can only conjure images from my own memories—of white-capped rivers and soiled, sodden skies.

I can almost see Kpa Doh and his men waiting in the gray–green forest twilight before turning to vanish into the trees.

Choosing to run instead of fight may have been one of his defining virtues. The Jarai clan name, Kpa, is the name of a river fish known for being slippery and hard to catch.

***

The RF/PFs who had machine-gunned the Vietnamese had killed 32 and wounded 22—a massacre. With the Vietnamese Army hot on their heels, they showed up at the nearest Special Forces camp, though it is unclear why. Were they hoping for help and firepower to fight off the Vietnamese and make their escape, or were they hoping to make a glorious last stand? (During the 1964 rebellion, some of the Rhadé troops had fully expected to die for the cause.)[19] In any case, they were turned away and captured. Their leaders were subsequently tried and sentenced to death, two in Pleiku, two in Cheo Reo.

A strange, sad coda to all this was recorded by an American missionary, Bob Reed, of the Christian and Missionary Alliance, who was fluent in Jarai, already having worked in Cheo Reo for nine years:

> The Vietnamese Province Chief asked that I go … meet with the [condemned] men … I found them, still shackled, sitting at a table, their last meal before them, untouched. One of them turned and said,
>
> "O, *Ama* (father), we are going to die today. We have sinned, can *Oi Adai* (God) help us?"
>
> One man had been in our chapel, the other had heard us preach in his village.
>
> I told them that I could not save them from the Government's punishment, but that Jesus, *Oi Adai*'s son, had died to pay for their sin. I told them that Jesus had risen from the dead and would provide forgiveness and eternal life even for them, if they would believe in Him. Oh yes, they wanted forgiveness and this eternal life, whatever that meant. They wanted to believe in Jesus, *Oi Adai*'s son. They bowed their heads as I prayed, and they joined me in prayer.

> The Vietnamese soldiers came to take them to the place of execution. As they stood up, they asked me to go with them …
>
> Tied to two posts, the two men faced a large hostile crowd of Vietnamese and nine ready rifles. Their eyes searched the crowd for the face of a friend. They must have seen [a few Montagnards]. One of the men cried out,
>
> "O, Uncle, come and take my hand before I die!"
>
> Nobody moved.
>
> I asked the captain of the execution squad if he could wait, and he agreed. I walked to the two men and placed my hands on [each of] their shoulders. With their hands tied to these trees of death, they bowed their heads. I prayed again, committing their souls to God. As I finished, I bid each one goodbye, assuring them of God's faithfulness in granting them new life in His land.
>
> Hoods were pulled over their heads. The Captain raised his arm. Rifles were aimed. No one spoke, no one breathed. The arm came down, the rifles roared, and those two men died.[20]

A rumor subsequently spread throughout the Highlands that the spirits of the four executed men had flown to Cambodia to enter the body of Y-Bham Enuol, where "they made him invulnerable and endowed him with magic powers to wreak vengeance on the Vietnamese immigrants and expel them from Montagnard lands."[21]

***

Despite its failure, the Second Rebellion proved that "FULRO had greater political and military potential then either the Vietnamese or the Americans previously believed."[22]

FULRO had been growing within South Vietnam. A Cham trader who travelled frequently to Central Vietnam on business reported in 1966 to the French military attaché in Phnom Penh that "90 percent of the population [in the Highlands] call themselves FULRO." He estimated that only "2–3 percent of Montagnards [were still] in the Viet Cong," many having "begun to desert since 1965." This was in contrast to the period "prior to 1963 when the VC had succeeded in attracting many Rhadé and Jarai by promising autonomy and exploiting Saigon's faults."[23]

Two other sources, while no doubt exaggerations, give some idea of the extent of FULRO's membership within the CIDG:

In 1966, Y-Bham Enuol boasted to a French envoy that there were 20,000 FULRO partisans in the CIDG. (Intriguingly, he also claimed that, if necessary, he could count on the support of 10,000 ethnonationalists *within the Montagnard Viet Cong*.)[24]

In 1967, Cambodia's own military intelligence bureau estimated the CIDG number more soberly as 15,000 (though still probably inflated).[25]

At the same time, by 1966–67, it was fairly clear that FULRO had *not* cast its lot with the Vietnamese communists, which led to speculation as to whether FULRO might somehow help the Americans and South Vietnamese cut the Ho Chi Minh Trail.

To harass the Ho Chi Minh Trail was one thing, however: to actually cut it quite another. The CIA's secret army of Hmong in Laos had never gotten close. The best time to do it would have been much earlier, in 1964–65, but the tactics and technology—essentially helicopter-assisted guerilla warfare—did not yet exist. Large numbers of soldiers, not only Montagnards but American recon teams and helicopter crews, would have had to die on increasingly suicidal missions. Any sign they might actually succeed would have triggered vigorous opposition from the Russians and Chinese along with a worldwide clamor about Laotian and Cambodian sovereignty. Politically, to try to force Saigon to relinquish control of even a piece of the highlands risked destruction of South Vietnamese morale and a worldwide public-relations disaster—and was likely impossible anyway. Yet, fortune in war can turn on intangibles, and it is at least conceivable that territoriality and its effect on both Montagnard and North Vietnamese morale might have opened other paths.

But the problem was that, at the same time that FULRO was gathering strength within South Vietnam, it was weakening at its core in Cambodia.

In retrospect, FULRO's wave had come and gone.

***

In 2014, I found Kpa Doh mentioned in an online report of a battle only 11 months later, in November 1966 in the Plei Trap Valley between a company of Montagnards, with six Americans, and a North Vietnamese battalion.[26]

The Plei Trap lies along Vietnam's northernmost border with Cambodia, spearing into the high, dark Annamite Chain. Only a decade before, it had been wilderness so primeval that new species of large mammals were still being discovered, but now it concealed a skein of North Vietnamese infiltration routes because it was just across the border from their Base Area 702 in Cambodia. (Not much deeper into Cambodia was "Office 100," where Pol Pot was brewing a revolution that would take the lives of two million of his fellow Cambodians a decade later.)

The valley was an evil place. Over the next two years, it would become one of the most contested corners of South Vietnam, blistered with the pale pox of trees splayed outward like matchsticks from B-52 strikes. North Vietnamese soldiers would come to call it the "Jungle of the Screaming Souls."

I tracked down an American who had been in Kpa Doh's battle. From multiple phone interviews with him, plus a written exchange with the patrol leader, an American lieutenant, I obtained extraordinary detail.[27] In places I was able to fill in minor details because I had led patrols only 50 kilometers (30 miles) to the north, also near the border but without contact with the enemy. This book is plagued by a paucity of facts, but here was one place I could insert a few from my own memories.

The effort to summon those details pulled me back into the dark.

The details of the battle may also pull the reader into the dark. Both sides were fighting to the death to expel a hated invader. For the Vietnamese, the invader was the Americans. For the Montagnards, all of them FULRO, it was the Vietnamese. To this particular unit, which was made up entirely of Jarai—the invasion was literal: the Plei Trap was in Jarai country. By contrast, the North Vietnamese were largely from Hanoi; the highland forests must have felt as alien to them as to the Americans, perhaps even more so because all six Americans were professional soldiers and more prepared for the coming trial.

***

Nguyen Huu An, the North Vietnamese general at the battle of Ia Drang (see p. 138), had come to the conclusion there was a way to nullify the American advantage in air mobility.

By drawing the Americans into a forested area with only a few places for helicopters to land—unlike the Ia Drang valley, which had been savannah—he could construct traps at the most likely places. He envisaged attacking a Special Forces camp first, causing an American infantry division to respond, then leading the division down a daisy chain of small battles by seeming to retreat until, in a clearing he had prepared near the border, the Americans would leapfrog to block the North Vietnamese from reaching their sanctuary in Cambodia. At that point, hidden antiaircraft guns would blast the helicopters out of the sky, and his troops could annihilate any Americans left alive. ("Annihilate" (*tiêu diệt*) was the word used in North Vietnamese Army (NVA) mission orders. Hanoi saw early that US resolve would dwindle with every American killed. Hanoi's highest military award was the "Hero Killer of Americans Medal." Achillean rage, killing 20, garnered a First-Class ribbon. Though the word "annihilate" could also mean "wound, capture, cause to desert, or even send fleeing from battle,[28] in practice it meant kill, and that included executing the wounded.)[29]

Nguyen Huu An decided on the Plei Trap Valley.

He and his staff had spent months personally walking the terrain, identifying and numbering likely landing zones, deciding whether each would be a killing zone itself or a gateway to a fortified ambush some distance away. For killing zones, he ordered pits dug to hide antiaircraft machine guns on tall tripods, with bullets as thick and heavy as the butt of an Altamont pool cue. The largest clearing had 12 pits within it, beneath straw mats, placed downwind so as to target the choppers' underbellies when they lilted up to land.[30]

The general was acutely aware the Americans had 24-hour photographic surveillance from high altitude, not simply from the daily buzz of low-flying aircraft, so he insisted no leaves be allowed to wither above his hidden roads, no streams be muddied even briefly, and nothing edged or straight or pale leap from the dark holes below to strike American eyes. As the time for his trap approached, he ordered the laying of dummy telephone wire and the construction of a dummy footbridge to misdirect the Americans.

He was confident his men had a psychological edge over American soldiers, which he attributed to "superior morale and politics." He was probably right. Convinced their country's survival depended on expelling the Americans, they had an advantage in that most terrible of combat, hand-to-hand. In turn, hand-to-hand combat was crucial because the general had deduced one other thing from Ia Drang—that the only way to escape the ripping metal and roasting petrol dropped from airplanes was to "grip the Americans' belt," closing as rapidly as possible with the GIs, literally throwing themselves forward into one-on-one combat.

In the coming battle, he was sure that earth would defeat sky.

He probably did not give much thought to the Americans' Montagnard troops, whom he referred to as "puppet commandos."

***

On the morning of November 8, 1966, almost exactly one year after Ia Drang, 160 Jarai soldiers of the Mike Force were suited up and lounging back against their packs in loose formation on Pleiku's runway. Despite their relaxed pose, every man felt a tension inside that wound tighter with the up-whine of starting helicopters.

Moving among them in the billowing red dust was Kpa Doh, half-smiling but deadly serious, checking their equipment, himself bullous with grenades and pouches. As chief interpreter, he had no military rank, but his military experience was at least on a par with the Montagnard company officers, if not greater, having spent three years going out on patrols with Americans.

By virtue of his FULRO rank, he was the company's political officer, essentially its commissar because the Mike Force was almost 100-percent FULRO. Every pay day, he would circulate, collecting everyone's FULRO dues, one-tenth of their pay. All Montagnard CIDG camps had a significant proportion of FULRO members. However, the Mike Force units had the highest numbers because they contained no Vietnamese at all, whereas each CIDG camp had a team of Vietnamese Green Berets.[31]

The Vietnamese Security Police accepted this situation, because it made the troublemakers easier to watch, and sent them all more often into the jungle, where they were less likely to infect other Montagnards with their ideas and more likely to die. The police knew Kpa Doh had been instrumental in the Second Rebellion and would have liked to quietly kill him, but when he took refuge in the Mike Force, they sat back to let the enemy do it for them.

He had just informed the soldiers of their mission, going into the Plei Trap, which they all knew was occupied by North Vietnamese. Some even had relatives there who worked for the occupiers as bearers. But what Kpa Doh told them was even more ominous, that they would be screening the American 4th Infantry Division, moving along its flank, wedged between it and the border. They would be first to make contact with the enemy, at which point they needed to stay alive long enough to bring in the airplanes or American soldiers from the division. In other words, they were bait.

The six American Green Berets were their link to the sky, to its life-saving bombs or artillery shells directed onto the enemy, not onto them. However, they had heard this was sometimes an impossible distinction. (Indeed, four months later, Kpa Doh and the Pleiku Mike Force went out on an operation during which 14 Jarai and one American were killed by an errant US bomb.)

No doubt the excellent pay had drawn many to sign up, but so had social pressure, warrior tradition, hatred of Vietnamese, and, like my own wish at 18 to jump out of airplanes, a desire to test themselves. But to stay in, especially to go out repeatedly on dangerous operations, with no end in sight, required something more. For all soldiers, loyalty to comrades is usually part of that. But for most a higher motive is also needed, an idea or a cause. For this group of Jarai, it almost certainly was FULRO, for which they needed to hone themselves in battle against Vietnam's best soldiers, preparing for the day that the Americans left.

***

Passing over the massif below, the Jarai shuddered as cold, pure air whipped through helicopter doors, open for the machine guns. Raised in hamlets with no machines more complicated than manual water pumps, they had gotten used to this bounding, bird-like flight in no time, or casually pretended they had, but were happy to return to warm, moist air as the choppers dropped back down to skim the treetops. A brown, frothy river flashed by below, then strobing glimpses into the jungle's depths.

In the distance to the north, razor-crested mountains marked the border with Cambodia. In the flatlands to the west—where they were heading—the border was anyone's guess. As a dividing line, a figment of some Frenchman's imagination long ago, it had been irrelevant until war came along.

The choppers slowed to circle a clearing below. A forest-covered hill jutted up just to the north. It showed no reflections of sunlight through its leaves, but the landing zone itself certainly had a North Vietnamese watcher, who would have stayed long enough to see the first choppers disgorge six Montagnards and two Americans each, then hurry to report the arrival of "commandos." The sight of these small, dark men, with grins and gold teeth, and armed to within an ounce of staggering, cannot have been reassuring to him.

The whump-whump of choppers faded to blood's thudding in the ears. One of the Americans was exhibiting signs of excess adrenaline. Kpa Doh kept ostentatiously calm to protect his Jarais from contagion.

The morning was still cool. This was the beginning of tropical winter when dryness plays the same role as dying light at higher latitudes. As they set out, chinks of clear blue sky were visible through the canopy far above. There was little undergrowth. They moved quickly to get away from the landing zone. Behind them, they heard the clatter of another two units of CIDG arriving, who headed off in a different direction, then silence.

General Nguyen Huu An would have learned by radio within minutes of their landing. But the successive arrival of more units at the same landing zone was too many for watchers to track. The Mike Force left without being followed. A rear guard, put out by the Jarai, made sure.

Over the next half hour, the forest began to drowse. Nearing midday, bird calls ceased. The point man—the most experienced Montagnard, chosen by the Jarai themselves—needed no instructions to slow down. Move, stop, and listen. Move, then stop, then listen. The pauses grew longer as the heat suffocated sound.

The point man froze as he came round a large tree.

Those behind him knew instantly that he had enemy in front. For long seconds, no one breathed, then the point man ducked as he jerked his rifle up to begin firing. The first three Montagnards scrambled forward to join him. The roar went on and on, then diminished to scattered popping—shots being fired back by escaping enemy—then silence.

In a depression below was one dead soldier amid a large number of packs and helmets and parts of antiaircraft guns, and blood trails leading up the other side. Following the blood, they found more gun parts and eventually assembled three antiaircraft guns and their tripods.

The dead man had no rank or insignia but was much bigger than the average Vietnamese, thus likely a Chinese artillery advisor. The fact that he was killed outright, but none of the others were, was hard to explain unless he had tricked the point man into giving him time to get off a first shot himself—perhaps their eyes had met for an instant then, with superhuman self-control, he had kept his eyes sweeping the jungle foliage. This had bought him only a few more seconds of life but somehow saved the others.

First blood was a shock, as was the sudden din that had ripped the midday heat. Until now, they could hope the Plei Trap was empty, but the presence of an antiaircraft detachment meant a very large number of North Vietnamese was somewhere around, perhaps 2,000 men. Even the Montagnards guessed this and were unnerved.

Kpa Doh's remedy was to put on one of the NVA helmets and stroll about as though nothing had happened. As he came around a tree, the hyped-up American almost shot him.

Awareness of the beast jumped a notch two hours later when they found its lair, a wide area of bamboo huts with sleeping platforms and classrooms, even a small firing range—all ringed by foxholes. Despite the gloom of late afternoon, deepened by a forest canopy purposefully woven overhead, the bamboo had the gleam of recent construction. The lieutenant decided to spend the night, taking advantage of the defenses, setting out Claymores, explosives that spray shrapnel in one direction on detonation by signal down a wire.

Three of the Americans brought out a deck of cards and played Hearts until dark, a calming thing to do, at least for those calm enough already. Kpa Doh watched them intently, occasionally asking questions as to the rules. (On subsequent Mike Force operations, some Jarai played Hearts too.)

***

Night was the worst. The North Vietnamese preferred to attack at dawn. They would maneuver as close as possible to American lines after nightfall, during the forest's slow-building frenzy of creature calls. Scouts would crawl in first to cut the Claymore wires, then unspool telephone wire back out to guide them back with their comrades. Then they would wait in the hours of dead silence after midnight, to attack in a rush at daybreak.

Sometimes, but not tonight, the two sides could smell each other in the moist air. Americans thought the Vietnamese smelled like wet clothes. The Montagnards claimed they could tell North Vietnamese by their sickness smell, from malaria and/or months on the Ho Chi Minh Trail.

Bothersome to all were the mosquitoes wafting in the air around midnight. Unknown to any of them, *Anopheles* was making blood brothers of men about to kill each other.[32]

Close to the equator, the sun drops like a rock and daylight comes up with a rush. Americans were poor at gauging this, but the Montagnards knew exactly when to get ready. If any American still slept, they nudged him awake in the last black hour.

Along the backbone of Southeast Asia, it got cold overnight. Men shivered as they watched the blackness slip away between the trees. But no attack came.

***

The next morning, they set off west toward the Cambodia border, about 8 kilometers (5 miles) away. Undergrowth thickened, slowing progress. The point man would drop to the ground from time to time to peer beneath the brush ahead. More worrisome, the canopy overhead was thickening too. Their sky was disappearing, which meant that, if they met a large enemy force, they could not count on bombing because it required visual contact through the canopy.

By now, the general knew exactly where the Mike Force was, and sometime after noon, they started catching glimpses of small groups of North Vietnamese in the distance, eerily motionless, looking right at them. If anyone went in pursuit, the watchers would disappear.

They rested that night on a knoll, again setting out listeners who were instructed to pull back in if any strange noise occurred, a cluck or mournful cry, something that did not belong in the cacophony after dark. They again set out Claymores, like shotguns primed with lead nuggets, but they waited until it was too dark to be seen doing this. The Americans had been issued Dexedrine, to stay awake. No one needed it.

Unknown to them, the general had given orders to ignore them for the time being, to be ready instead for an American infantry battalion that would arrive any time now, about two miles away. At one prominent clearing, the crews of 12 camouflaged antiaircraft guns had been waiting *for a full month*, sitting at the bottom of earthen pits. Positioned just across the border to pounce on the arriving division were soldiers of the 88th Regiment.

However, word had failed to filter down to every North Vietnamese soldier that there was a company of "Saigon puppet-army commandos" out there in the forest, stealthier than the American infantry. The next day, two Vietnamese were captured. Grilled by a Vietnamese-speaking Jarai, one prisoner revealed he had been told Americans would cut his head off and eat his remains.

With no blood paid yet, Americans might have felt the bill mounting. But Kpa Doh and his Jarai could not have thought in those terms. Their war had no scales, no clocks, no substitutes running in from the sidelines. Their enemy would never cease taking over the highlands unless violently stopped. If they ever allowed themselves to imagine the day their war would be over, the span of time stretching out before them had only one metric—the number of enemy they could kill—just like the North Vietnamese.

***

General Nguyen Huu An had guessed right. A battalion of the American 4th Infantry Division did airlift the next day into one of the areas he had prepared.

However, by pure chance, the lead helicopter pilot chose to land in a clearing adjacent to the one with the antiaircraft guns, one that was brushy and uneven, letting his troops off at a 10-foot hover instead of settling down. No ground troops were killed during the landing, though three gunships were shot down. The Americans moved to a low hill 2.5 kilometers (1.5 miles) northeast of the Mike Force and started to dig in.

The next night, after an hour-long 120 mm mortar barrage, the 2nd Battalion of the 88th NVA Regiment breasted through head-high thorn bushes to attack the low hill, some reaching the Americans' foxholes to leap in with bayonets.

Surprisingly, the final count of US casualties in this battle was a low five killed, 41 wounded (not counting the helicopter crews).

***

The Plei Trap operation was Bob Ramsey's first combat experience, at age 26. Despite that, he found himself calm, which he attributes to extensive prior training. "Kpa Doh was the same way," he said, "Too busy thinking, taking everything in." (For both of them, however, it was more likely innate.)

The following is based on Bob's account, with contributions by Jake, the lieutenant.[33] It picks up the story on the fourth day:

They are still moving west toward the border. By midafternoon, they see light ahead through the trees—a large clearing. (General Nguyen Huu An had chosen not to include this clearing in his plan, possibly because it was so close to the border that the Americans would never use it as a major landing zone.)[34]

They hold back, sending out small patrols to reconnoiter around its edges. Bob takes one to the right, around the northern end,[35] keeping the white shimmer to his left. The forest is triple canopy, thus with little undergrowth, and visibility is good, as far as 50 yards. The sun is still high enough for sunlight to filter through. At one point, he sees two motionless North Vietnamese scouts' watching them. When the scouts finally move, seen through the trees, they flicker.

Coming around the northern tip, he finds a dirt road coming out of Cambodia, wide enough for vehicles. He then continues his recon down the western side of the lakebed, returning by the same route to report to Jake. The road looks certain to be used. Jake wants Bob to set up an ambush there, but not until after dark. In the waning light of afternoon, Bob retraces his steps to decide on a position, taking key Jarai with him (but not Kpa Doh, who is with Jake).

Because they are being watched, the only possibility for deception is to change location when it is pitch black. Sometime after 7:00 pm, with only a sliver of waning moon in the west and clouds blotting the stars, Bob takes 50 men straight across the bare hardpan of the lake to the location scouted earlier, where they put out Claymores facing the road. He tells the Montagnards that a red flare will be his signal to withdraw straight back across the lakebed. Otherwise, they need little instruction, certainly not in ambushes. Bob sits with his back against a tree, certain something is going to happen, and begins a very long night.

Meanwhile, Jake and the main body of the Mike Force, with Kpa Doh, move further away from Bob, down the eastern edge of the lakebed and set up their perimeter, a semicircle looking out into the forest. Tactically and psychologically, the open space and sky at their backs belong to them and the forest belongs to the North Vietnamese, especially when Jake learns, on a radio call to preregister artillery support, that the Mike Force is now out of range. So, no artillery, just air.

Sometime after midnight, the Montagnards break out shouting—a violent, startling cacophony—then stop, their bellows echoing into the forest. One of the men heard or smelled the enemy. They were sending a message: "We are Jarai. We dare you."

As daylight creeps through the trees, Jake feels, then hears, the distant drone of the forward air controller (FAC) and raises its pilot on the radio. (A small, vulnerable airplane that flits and swoops, the FAC is a crucial intercessor between earth and sky if troops get in trouble, by directing airstrikes.) The pilot asks for help determining their exact location, as there are one or two other clearings in the area. Jake begins directing him to the correct lakebed. It is about 6:00 am.

Bob had been watching the road appear out of the night, as if the remainder of his fated life—short or long—were in a film bath.

Suddenly, firing breaks out to his front. It is from the men furthest forward at his listening post, then from the rest of his troops. In the gray light, he can make out enemy in a column-of-three coming from Cambodia. They had begun scattering and dropping when he fired the Claymores, and, in his mind's eye forever, he sees more of them fall like bowling pins. They begin returning fire. Its volume grows, and he realizes there are more enemy than he thought (later he figures out this was a weapons platoon, with mortars, preparing to set up at the northern end of the lakebed). He fires the red flare, yelling for his men to withdraw. The North Vietnamese fire a red flare, too, which results in their ceasing fire, then pulling back. This makes no sense—unless two red flares meant "withdraw" to them. Their temporary mistake gives his group time to get across 200 yards of dangerously open ground. Last to cross, he helps one Jarai who has been hit. Bullets are kicking up dust around them as they reach the tree line.

Meanwhile, Jake is on the radio to the FAC when he hears Bob's explosions and the rattle of gunfire. Less than a minute later, his own perimeter is attacked. The North Vietnamese had been out there in the forest all night, waiting to attack, when Bob's encounter forced their hand. They are only coming from the south, suggesting they did not have time to encircle him. The first wave of attackers comes in a ragged rank toward the ring of Jarai, who are belly down on the ground in pairs, firing from behind small trees.

The Montagnards have been trained to fire one bullet at a time, but rapidly, aiming at the enemies' legs because their carbines kick upward. Some do just that, some fire wildly on automatic, and a few do not fire at all, paralyzed. Out of some perverse pride—mirroring the Americans, or perhaps it was the other way around—the Montagnards are not dug in and have no helmets, which costs some their lives, but the North Vietnamese tend to fire high which saves many others. With time, gaps appear in the defensive line as Montagnards are killed or wounded. In the din, they yell to each other. Even the simplest of men grasp quickly what it takes to survive and, from time to time, someone rises to a crouch and moves to fill in.

For their part, the North Vietnamese have been trained to throw themselves forward—to hug the Americans' belt—to avoid the napalm and bombs sure to come behind them. They have been told the Americans will cower like rabbits, but it is unlikely many believe that, plus they know they are also facing Jarai. They do know that the faster they attack and encircle their enemy, the better their chances of survival. Some are impelled as well by hatred of the invaders. But the rifle fire is more deadly than expected, and the Mike Force has two .30-caliber machine guns. One stops firing early, but the other puts up a murderous wall across the front of half the perimeter until it stops abruptly—there are shouts in Jarai and one brave soul stands up to change barrels (the other barrel having grown too hot)—then resumes fire.

The first attack seems confused and hesitant. Jake has the sense of enemy "just moving around" to his front. Eventually, the North Vietnamese withdraw. They have lost the advantage of surprise, and the minutes are ticking down until the American planes arrive. By attacking from a different direction, they might still derive some advantage, and this is probably what delays their second attack.

Meanwhile, Bob has been making his way south just inside the treeline toward the sounds of battle. His men having preceded him, he is alone, in brushy forest, and beginning to think that all enemy are further south when he comes across a dead Jarai in dark, black-striped fatigues, glistening with blood.

Suddenly two Vietnamese in khaki emerge in front of him. They are sideways to him, but one begins to turn. He shoots both dead with his carbine only half up from the hip. Shortly afterward, he comes across a Vietnamese crawling, with his pants down at his knees "as though gut-shot"—wounded in the abdomen. Their eyes meet. Bob lets him go and keeps moving south, joining the northeastern part of the Mike Force perimeter.

Around 7:30 am, the first airplanes arrive, propeller-driven Skyraiders, ground-attack aircraft from the Korean War that drop napalm and cluster bombs, the latter loosing a stream of bomblets that explode on large branches, showering shrapnel in a rolling wave. For now, it kills only North Vietnamese on the other side of the lakebed.

Mortar rounds start landing near the Mike Force position, the hollow sound of their tube-launches coming from the northern end of the lakebed. Jake and a Montagnard step out of the tree line to fire grenades toward the mortars, and the mortaring stops. Meanwhile, the Americans have guessed the size of the North Vietnamese force—almost four times their own number—and are beginning to worry about running out of ammunition.

A second attack begins, now from the east. Bob takes cover behind a large log, with a nearby eight-foot hedge. Down the line he can see the lone machine gun, already with a large number of enemy dead to its front, not quite a pile yet but two North Vietnamese are using the corpses as cover. One throws a Chinese potato-masher grenade that fails to explode. The attackers come crouching at a trot, screaming, an inhuman sound. Bullets crack in the branches. Trees splinter. Leaves rain. It feels to Bob like the roaring approach of a giant lawnmower. He sees a rocket-propelled grenade zipping toward him for a half-second before hitting a nearby tree with a deafening explosion that blows him several feet to the ground. Again, the enemy's attack slows, many now firing from behind nearby trees or on their bellies. He can hear their officers urging them onward in high-pitched voices. He begins lofting grenades over the top of the hedge at concentrations of them. This has the added advantage of killing without giving away his own position. He has eight grenades; when he runs out, he scuttles to collect more from dead Jarai.

On the radio with the FAC, Jake calls for an airstrike "danger close." When he gets it, some hot fragments strike within the Mike Force perimeter. The FAC needs to know better where they are. Jake steps out from the tree line to throw two colored smoke canisters onto the lakebed. Suddenly, he feels as though a baseball bat hits him full force in the abdomen, dropping him. He cannot move his legs. Under fire, Bob and another sergeant drag him to a safer location.

Around 8:00 am, jets arrive with 500-pound bombs that blast whole trees into the air a second after their screaming runs. This only makes the enemy's attempt to get close more insistent, with attacks coming from the east, then the north.

However, now the FAC knows exactly where the Mike Force is located. Skyraiders can strafe close to its perimeter with 20 mm cannon, shells that explode on impact and light fires, adding to the haze. The Mike Force reports 50 percent casualties over the radio and requests reinforcements and more ammunition.

In the distance, Bob sees Kpa Doh moving upright through the smoke, which looks first to Bob as if he has lost his mind. Then he realizes Kpa Doh is walking behind a line of his men, probably reminding them to aim low or to save ammunition, or maybe steadying them because they have become agitated by how close the bombing is getting. A couple of them already have minor wounds from hot fragments.

Suddenly, Kpa Doh shakes his head, as though stung by a wasp. Dropping his carbine, he tears off his web gear as if angry, throwing it to the ground. Then, after a pause, he picks up a big stick and resumes walking, tapping his men's boots as he passes. He has been struck in the neck by an AK-47 bullet. Barely able to speak, he is letting his men know he is still there.

Bob cannot pinpoint exactly when this happened, except that the feeling there were enemy soldiers everywhere was lessening.

"It didn't even knock him down," Bob says. "It just looked like it pissed him off."

Until I heard this, Kpa Doh had seemed inauthentic to me—a cultural hybrid out of place in a story about Montagnard agency. But this—this was 100 percent Jarai. News of it would have spread to Jarai and Rhadé everywhere, instantly raising his status within FULRO.

In the eroded words on a Cham stela, describing a forgotten king from a thousand years ago, "His only armor was his heroism."[36]

***

The battle was essentially over by midmorning. Fourteen Jarai were killed, 40 were wounded, some badly, and got medevac'd out around noon. Kpa Doh waited till last, then went out too.

Fifty-eight North Vietnamese were found dead, scattered about the battlefield. Some ten to twenty lay in front of the machine gun. Further out, some had been killed by airstrikes. Others—dead or dying—had been dragged away by their comrades.

Elements of the American division began to arrive around noon, airlifting in a small bulldozer to dig a burial pit on the dry lakebed. There were so many North Vietnamese dead that they also brought in a front-end loader to carry their bodies.

Bob watched from a distance as it tipped the lifeless bodies into the pit, heads lolling, still gangly youth.

***

All six American Green Berets survived despite being in the thick of battle while one-third of the Mike Force Jarai were killed or wounded.

This suggests that the Montagnards had served as a barrier. I wondered if it had been psychological as well as physical, whether the same territorial instinct that amplified hatred of American invaders had the opposite effect when the North Vietnamese from Hanoi found themselves confronted by Montagnards in the highlands.[37] This looked to be impossible to verify, but I went looking anyway.

I found nothing at first in Hanoi's publications about this small battle on November 11. Instead, Hanoi focused on the large battle the next day, November 12th, against American infantry near the clearing with the antiaircraft guns, in which the North Vietnamese unit was the 2nd Battalion (of the 88th Regiment).

Then I found one snippet that said, "On November 11th, when one enemy commando company arrived [at the dry lakebed], the *Third* Battalion ... blocked their way and attacked them, wiping out most of their company."[38]

I could raise no one from the 3rd Battalion, but I did make email contact with the English-speaking son of a veteran of the 2nd Battalion and the next day's battle.

Over the course of many back-and-forth exchanges, I learned that his father's sole interest in talking with me about the earlier battle was to learn the exact location of its burial pit (I sent him back a diagram marking Bob's best guess).[39] Somewhat later, I learned that he and his comrades were convinced the Americans had buried 21 wounded North Vietnamese soldiers alive in that pit, "standing in a deep bomb crater, arms bound behind their backs with Claymore wires" (Bob had watched the front-end loader dump the corpses. "No question," Bob said, "they were dead," adding, with irritation, "We don't do stuff like that.") The Vietnamese also believed that, two days before the battle, some outlying Jarai had captured four unarmed Vietnamese, slit their throats and stuffed their rations in their mouths. This at least seemed possible.[40] True or not, it reportedly inflamed the entire NVA.[41]

But their greatest anger—as veterans of the next day's battle—was reserved for what they believed to be falsely low American casualty figures of that battle. Realistically, the final number of American KIA likely did exceed five. I pointed out that the disproportionately high number of wounded probably included men who died later. That got no reply.

I pressed the son again to find a veteran of the 3rd Battalion, someone who had fought the Jarai. He hoped to encounter one at an upcoming reunion of the 88th Regiment, held annually on the date they had set off down the Ho Chi Minh Trail some 55 years before. After a long delay, he sent me color photos of two white-haired, uniformed men with beribboned chests, making me glad I could not differentiate the ribbon of a Hero Killer of Americans. Included was a written version of the November 11 battle against the Mike Force Jarai:

> On the night of 10 November, the Third Battalion hid its troops on the other side of a stream, directly across from the enemy commandos. In some places the two sides were separated by a distance of only about 15 meters. The next morning a cook went out to wash his pots to prepare to move out. He spotted the commandos. [*Sic? This makes more sense if the commandos' cook spots the North Vietnamese.*] The cook and the other soldiers

> opened fire and the engagement and pursuit lasted from early in the morning until the late afternoon. … Although it was only a small battle, it was a ferocious one.
>
> We are prepared to meet face-to-face to see what the Americans have to say. They were not political, not [conscientized]. They were just simple soldiers, and during the firefights they were unable to see the evil hearts of their leaders.

No response seemed adequate.

We both think the other was misled—brave but ultimately sad puppets of propaganda. The difference between their reality and Bob's and mine will accompany all of us to our graves.

It was no surprise, then, to read what the embarrassed son wrote next:

> Unfortunately, [they are] unhappy with the book you want to write because it will celebrate their enemy.

And, of course, they were right.

Notes

1 The other interpreter, Phillipe Drouin, aka "Cowboy," is described in an eponymous book by Daniel Ford (*Cowboy: The Interpreter Who Became a Soldier, a Warlord, and One More Casualty of Our War in Vietnam* (Durham, NH: Warbird Books, 2018)). Four years later, Drouin was assassinated/executed by FULRO for suspected corruption. Kpa Doh may have played a role.

2 Nay Luett (photos on pp. 46 and 143; note 12, p. 48) with whom he served in combat later and remained very close despite divergent political paths

3 Kpa Doh, interviews with author, April 1973; plus interview with his 90-year-old sister, H'mian (with author, July 2015).

4 At one point he, Paul, and Dhon were all singing together in the Dalat cathedral on Sunday mornings.

5 Crews McCulloch, A-Team commander at Buon Beng, interview with author, July 18, 2016; plus Jim Morris, A-Team executive officer, interviews with author over a span of 15 years, 2009–2024.

6 Crews McCulloch

7 CIA, *The Highlanders of South Vietnam: A Review of Political Developments and Forces*, CIA-RDP80T01719R000300010003-8 (Washington, D.C., 1966), 88.

8 Demeure says this was common knowledge in Ban Me Thuot in November–December 1965.

9 Captain Jackie Schmidt, Plei Djereng After-Action Report, accessed online 2015, no longer accessible.

10 Pierre K'Briuh, interviews with author over span of ten years, 2014–2024. The leader was Paul Nur.

11 CIA, *The Highlanders of South Vietnam*, 90.

12 Kpa Doh, interview with author, April 1973

13 At Cam Ranh Bay, rainfall was 23" as opposed to the usual 3".

14 Y-Tlur was present at the schoolhouse.

15 At 4:00 am on December 18, ninety Mnong emerged from the forest and passed through the town gate of Gia Nghia without opposition. Less than half had rifles, old French ones at that. Fortunately for everyone, Y-Thih Eban—a moderate Montagnard leader

(see p. 54)—was in town and had convinced the Montagnard gate guards to stand down. (This may not have been difficult because ARVN's troops in Gia Nghia appear to have been largely Montagnard. See note 19, p. 230 re Quang Duc.) His relations with the Vietnamese province chief were excellent, thus the chief let FULRO run up its flag, then the chief felt he had to "bracket" them with one artillery round and one mortar round (which set fire to a church), and then everybody was content except an American infantry advisor who had been made to look bad by the takeover and grumbled about "bombing the bastards". The next day, a Vietnamese airborne battalion flew in and accepted a FULRO "surrender." However, the "oh, what a lovely war" picture here is belied by a later CIA report saying that a deputy province chief had been killed. Y-Thih's account says only that the man had "hidden in the jungle." As often happened elsewhere in situations where FULRO's soldiers surrendered, their subsequent fate is unclear. Y-Thih himself ultimately spent 2½ years in prison for this. Y-Thih Eban and George "Speedy" Gaspard, interview with author, May 19, 2017, plus CIA, *The Highlanders of South Vietnam*, 91. Also, thanks to Jim Morris for the Prell bottlecaps.

16 Po Dharma and Mak Phoen, *Du FLM à FULRO: Une Lutte des Minorités du Sud Indochinois 1955–1975* (Paris: Les Indes Savantes, 2006). Po Dharma, being Cham and loyal to Kosem, credits Kosem with more control over FULRO and events in general than was probably the case. Here this results in an inaccuracy—he has Kosem commanding Dhon, Bhan, and Y-Nam to unleash the Second Rebellion, but Dhon was already in jail (see Ch. 13). I am aware that Po Dharma and Mak Phoen say a few things contrary to what I say, and several things in addition to what I say. I respect Po Dharma as a historian, particularly of Champa, but suspect that his version of FULRO's history is slanted by his pro-Cham, pro-Kosem bias and/or loyalty to the person who gave him access to the documents, Kosem's widow.

17 The CIA wondered from afar if the militants themselves were trying "to provoke an adverse government reaction and final break" (CIA-RDP79T00472A001800060004-3, -December 25, 1965).

18 Current-day Phu Thien has been moved some 22 kilometers west.

19 Y-Tlur Thomas Eban, interviews with author, November 8, 2009 onward.

20 Thanks to Juris Jurjevics, editor/publisher/novelist who died in 2018, for this typed manuscript given to him by Reverend Reed (1929–2010) whom Juris knew personally from his own time in the Army in Cheo Reo.

21 Dharma & Phoeum, *Du FLM au Fulro*, p. 95

22 CIA, *The Highlanders of South Vietnam*, 91.

23 *Monthly Report, French Embassy in Cambodia, November 5 1966*. Carton 14 S 367, Service Historique de L'Armée de la Terre, Vincennes, (author's translation, researched and provided to me by an individual who prefers anonymity).

24 He also said that he could count on 10,000 ethnonationalist Montagnards within the Montagnard Viet Cong if necessary (document dated September 7, 1966, entitled *Entretien Avec Son Excellence Etienne Manac'h* in Les Kosem trove).

25 Document dated May 1967, entitled *FICHE à l'attention de Monsieur.le Lieutenant Général* in Les Kosem trove). It too is boasting, in this case of what it saw as Kosem's achievement in convincing the Montagnards that they were Cham.

26 Clyde J. Sincere Jr., "II Corps Task Force Prong, 11/8/1966," MikeForceHistory.org, accessed 2013, at facebook.com/100064702057947/posts/160986460775705/. It was unusual to find individual Montagnards named in after-action reports, but this was a quasi-official account that mentioned Kpa Doh as having been heroic. The French Army's relationship with Montagnards was very similar to that of the US Army, but its behavior toward them was considerably more

recognizant. Not only did Montagnards get mention, but they received medals and, years later, pensions from the French.

27 Sergeant First Class Bob Ramsey, later sergeant major of the Special Forces Schools, and Lieutenant Robert "Jake" Jacobelli, later colonel in command of the 7th Special Forces Group.

28 Merle Pribbenow, interview with author, November 28, 2017.

29 As Merle Pribbenow pointed out to me, there is some irony in the fact that the North Vietnamese Army also had a body count.

30 Phil Courts, "Shootout on the Cambodian Border," Vietnam Helicopter Pilots' Association, at www.vhpa.org/stories/Shootout.pdf; and Phil Courts, interview with author, December 7, 2017.

31 A sympathetic US master sergeant (Frank Quinn) knew about the dues because he stored the piastres in the unit safe until Kpa Doh made his next trip to Mondulkiri. That virtually all the Montagnard CIDG were FULRO was common knowledge, supported by Jim Morris (*War Story* (Boulder: Paladin Press, 1979), p. 21) and Y-Tlur Eban (interviews with author, 2009 onward) who quotes one FULRO leader (Phillipe Drouin) as boasting, "Any camp where there are Montagnards, these are our troops." My own Project *Omega* Mike Force battalion was said to have been "rented" from FULRO. Regarding the Vietnamese Special Forces, these were the LLDB (Luc Luong Dac Biet), who were nominally in command of the Montagnard troops, with the American Special Forces team in an advisory role only. Apparently one of their functions was to keep an eye on the Americans, particularly in regard to possible encouragement of FULRO. They were in a difficult position, and many of them were good men. Later in the war, enough Montagnards had become officers that the LLDB team might have a Montagnard captain.

32 Some Jarai on this operation, with known (previously quantified) immunity to local *Falciparum* strains built up over a lifetime in the Central Highlands, nevertheless came down with acute malaria, either because the stress of combat temporarily weakened their immune system and thus allowed the malaria always lurking within them to escape immune control, or because they had been bitten by mosquitoes freshly laden with unfamiliar *Falciparum* strains from the Northern Highlands, i.e., picked up by the North Vietnamese on the Ho Chi Minh Trail and brought south. The timing of these cases' onset tends to suggest the latter. Note: though Kpa Doh's unit and its battle are not specifically named in the journal articles from which I extracted this information, it is clear they refer to the Pleiku Mike Force and its major operation in western II Corps in November 1966. Stephen C. Hembree, "Malaria Among the Civilian Irregular Defense Group During the Vietnam Conflict: An Account of a Major Outbreak," *Military Medicine* 145 (1980), 751–52.

33 The other three Americans were Frank Huff, Frank Quinn, and Danny Panfil. All three were equally important to the outcome of the battle, but I was unable to interview Frank Huff, killed in action five months later, or Frank Quinn, who was especially close to Kpa Doh and who died of natural causes in New York City only a few years ago. Danny Panfil preferred not to be interviewed. During the battle, Danny helped Bob drag the wounded Jake to safety under fire, and later, as a medic, worked to save Jake. Frank Huff was with Bob on the night ambush and then, during the battle, took over the radio, calling in airstrikes after Jake was wounded.

34 No one is exactly sure today which clearing it was. Some believe it was bisected by the border. For unclear reasons, it was named "Pali Wali" by the Americans.

35 The lakebed was roughly banana shaped and actually on a northeast–southwest slant, but I refer to "northern" end and "western" and "eastern" sides for clarity.

36 Georges Maspero, *The Champa Kingdom*, translated by Walter E. J. Tips (Bangkok: White Lotus Press, 2002), 168.

37 Another explanation may be that five of the six Americans had seen combat before while the soldiers of the 88th Regiment had seen little (or none?), having left Hanoi for the long march down the Ho Chi Minh Trail only 11 months before.

38 Merle Pribbenow translated these sources and brought them to my attention. He also gave me the contact that led to the son of the 2nd Battalion veteran.

39 Two years later the North Vietnamese MIA apparatus began serious attempts to locate the pit.

40 The Jarai were also said by the NVA to have burned their prisoners' canvas web gear, which makes no sense. Killing prisoners, on the other hand, might have made sense to them, being so deep in enemy territory.

41 "Political sessions were [then] conducted to incite hatred of the enemy, and the news spread quickly throughout virtually the entire [army in the] Central Highlands."

CHAPTER II

Outsiders

The Mysterious Les Kosem

Les Kosem is clearly central to the FULRO story, but little exists in writing about him. What there is derives from the controversial years of the Khmer Republic and usually describes him as "mysterious" or "enigmatic" or "*insaisissable* (elusive)," then hints at some nefarious core to his mystery.

What I sought was evidence of his character.

From a fellow parent at the lycée, I learned Kosem's widow was still alive and living in Phnom Penh. She was key, but I needed to know a great deal more about him before approaching her. Having met her for two minutes over four decades ago was not enough.

He had been the highest-ranking Cham in the army, thus the most prominent secular Cham in Cambodia. To have risen so high was extraordinary because Chams were an impoverished, undereducated ethnic minority, disdained and/or feared by most Cambodians, who saw them as sinister—a fisher people grouped with pirates, which had at least some historical basis, but also as having black-magic abilities (e.g., with a script more easily adapted to incantations in the air). Paradoxically, Chams were also mistrusted by Cambodians because their Islamic faith espoused austerity, very unlike Cambodian Buddhism. Finally, they were thought to have superior martial qualities, having been recruited as mercenaries for a millennium. The walls of Bayon temple show Chams, wearing strange flowery helmets, in war canoes bearing down on Angkor with fierce scowls.

Two Western authors had met Kosem. One—Gerald Hickey, the American anthropologist—found him pleasant from a brief meeting but concluded that he had "blunted" the Montagnard ethnonationalist movement by co-opting it.[1] The other—Charles Meyer, advisor to Sihanouk whom we have met before, referred to Kosem as "Lon Nol's assistant in mysterious affairs" and claimed FULRO was under CIA control. The former was certainly true but there are reasons to discount the latter as either misinformed paranoia or deliberate disinformation.[2]

The remaining reports about Kosem were second or thirdhand, most faintly echoing the Cambodians' sinister view of Chams. Yet, even with that factored out, the reports were disturbing, linking him to atrocities said to have been committed by troops under his command in the Republican years from 1970 onward (though one purported episode had occurred under Sihanouk in 1967 during an uprising in Samlaut subdistrict).

The most widely repeated accusation was that the so-called Cham Battalion had indiscriminately killed civilians in "Khmer Rouge" villages. Almost without exception, "Khmer Rouge" had quotes around it, conveying disbelief the dead truly had been Khmer Rouge combatants, but instead had been innocent civilians.

Through Bhan, I had met a Cham my age who had been in the battalion. I invited him to join me on a trip up-country in search of a Cham temple (see p. 21). En route, I danced around the atrocity question. I did ask what Kosem was like as a commander and got an unexpected answer: "He was too high up" to command a battalion.

On the way back, the Cham suddenly had me turn off the highway and head up a long straight road to a Buddhist temple on a low hill. This was the first time he had seen this place in 40 years. It had been the bivouac site for his unit the night before his own first combat. From the temple, he led me downhill on foot, following his memories.

There was haze that morning, smoke and fog. They received fire in this place here, from behind that stone wall over there. They had almost reached this schoolyard here, when firing broke out all over—an ambush by the North Vietnamese.

Turning to me, he said, "They shot at us. We shot at them."

This proved nothing, though it did suggest the difficulty in fighting an enemy who habitually bivouacked within villages. I needed more. The near ubiquity of quotation marks around "Khmer Rouge" suggested a single source. I tracked this down to an author whose few paragraphs had been repeated without attribution by others, an author who made no secret of his far-left sympathies.[3] When I queried him initially by email about his source, he replied it had been "conversations in Phnom Penh in 1970–72." Eventually, I met him in person, over coffee at a Mekong riverfront brasserie, and found him pleasant and accessible. Rakish in a beret at age 84, he flirted with the waitress. Asked about those conversations in 1970–72, he replied, "Much of the negative information about Les Kosem was secondhand." The way he put this, with a smile, followed by an admonition not to put too much faith in the writings of another well-known leftist writer—"She had a Cambodian boyfriend, a leftist intellectual later killed by the Khmer Rouge, and much of her information was hearsay from such people"—left me with no doubt he was discounting his own sources.[4]

The next most common accusation was that Kosem had massacred demonstrators protesting the ouster of Sihanouk.[5] The coup on March 18, 1970, had angered many peasants, traditionally the group most loyal to the monarchy, and large numbers had started marching toward the capital. On March 27, they seized and killed two hapless government officials, eating their livers. The next day, they reached the other end of the main bridge into the city. Kosem had been given command of the Phnom Penh Military Region by Lon Nol in the wake of the coup, thus was assumed to have been in charge of the troops defending the bridge—but in fact he was not: another officer was in charge.[6] Moreover, when I tracked down the figures of this "massacre," I discovered only one demonstrator was killed, suggesting orders had been given to fire over their heads. Meanwhile, on the same day, a real massacre had taken place, in Snoul, with 40–60 dead.[7]

It looked as if history had only bad to say about Kosem—but I had just discovered soft ground beneath not one but two of its pillars. In one case, the record was based on an assumption. In the other, secondary sources had accepted hearsay evidence from someone openly in favor of the Khmer Rouge, which had the effect now of vouching to the ages that his information was unbiased. More than forty years later, this has become history, with nothing to suggest questionable provenance.

Next, I stumbled onto two reports about Kosem on an entirely different plane.

***

The first was a scurrilous book published by Hanoi's security-police press in 1983—*FULRO #1 (A Criminal Organization)*—apparently based on interrogations of ex-FULRO members in Vietnam after 1975 and then wildly embellished to make FULRO's leaders look venal, and/or stooges of the US or France, and/or, in the case of several young Cham leaders, salaciously oversexed. Despite the obvious slander, one item in the book rings partially true—that Kosem was a spymaster whose use of fellow Chams as agents did bring Khmer Rouge wrath upon Chams.[8] However, the main reason was not Kosem's effectiveness as a spymaster but the fact that their Muslim faith was both a competing ideology and a particularly overt one, in ritual, dress, and diet.

That said, we can imagine that Kosem did infuriate the Khmer Rouge. Enormously popular among Chams, he must have found it easier and easier to recruit agents as the Khmer Rouge began suppressing Muslim practices in areas under their control, possibly even recruiting those Chams who originally had been enthusiastic partisans of the Khmer Rouge.[9]

***

The second was more stunning, however, and entirely true.

I found it online, a declassified analysis by the CIA of its four-year failure (1966–70) to detect a seaborne route by which arms reached communist forces in Vietnam, called the Sihanoukville Trail. From late 1966 onward, every two months, a Chinese freighter docked at the western Cambodian port of Sihanoukville to unload arms and ammunition onto trucks at night. These then trundled northeast along Friendship Highway, ironically recently built by the Americans, to a transfer depot near Phnom Penh, where Cambodian soldiers skimmed a portion for Sihanouk's army, then trucked the rest eastward to waiting North Vietnamese or Viet Cong forces at points along the Cambodia–Vietnam border. The trail's inception had been in November 1965 when Sihanouk met in Beijing with Zhou Enlai and the North Vietnamese, presumably agreeing to this in return for North Vietnamese promises not to support Cambodian communists. Despite mounting evidence of Cambodian complicity, CIA analysts, blinded by long-time obsession with the Ho Chi Minh Trail, continued to believe the main supply route was from the north through Laos.

The online document opens with:

> The neutralist government of Prince Norodom Sihanouk fell to a cabal of Cambodian army officers on 18 March 1970. Driven by a combination of anticommunism and traditional Cambodian antipathy for the Vietnamese, the new junta acted at once to cut the flow of Chinese munitions that, since late 1966, had flowed through the port of Sihanoukville to communist forces in South Vietnam. One of the group [Lt. Col. Les Kosem] … detailed the Sihanoukville deliveries and onward shipment of war materiel by road into the southern provinces.

It goes on to describe how there had been numerous indications over the previous four years of such traffic, notably in June 1968 when:

> A new source in Les Kosem's tribal entourage came online with a detailed description of [a] transfer depot … and of the mechanics of both the arms traffic and the rice shipments into South Vietnam.

Though the new source might have been Kosem's wife's brother,[10] I believe that Kpa Doh was more likely, fitting better into the category of "tribal entourage."

From 1966–70, this route was practically the sole source of enemy firepower in the lower part of South Vietnam, delivering some 20,000–30,000 tons of weapons and ammunition. The Cambodian Army skimmed from one-tenth to one-third of that, and the North Vietnamese paid some 36–50 million dollars to Cambodia for its services. (Sources disagree, and Hanoi's official histories are not totally reliable.)[11]

Kosem was a professional soldier and member of Sihanouk's outer circle, as well as his own people's most successful representative and source of pride. Later, in 1967 or 1968, he would risk death by joining a small group of plotters dedicated to overthrowing Sihanouk, but in 1966 when his sovereign asked him to run the Sihanoukville Trail, to decline would not have crossed his mind.

A very large amount of cash must have crossed his palms, however.

***

After about 1971, Kosem had one last pivotal role to play in the fate of his country. Ironically, it was thanks to his marginality, his Muslim faith. Sihanouk, living in exile in Beijing and deeply in the pocket of the Khmer Rouge, was agitating on the world stage to replace the Khmer Republic at the United Nations (UN), claiming he and his government-in-exile represented the true Cambodia. Kosem was tapped by Lon Nol to try to sway the votes of Islamic countries by pointing out how the Khmer Rouge were oppressing Islam in "liberated" areas of Cambodia. Most of these countries were proudly non-aligned and anti-American, so it is testament in part to Kosem's skill that the UN voted in 1974 to keep the American-backed government of Lon Nol.[12]

All this was in Wikileaks' trove of diplomatic cables to and from Henry Kissinger, 1970–75. A final cable mentioning Kosem was sent on April 3, 1975, two weeks before the fall of Phnom Penh, in which Cambodia's foreign minister instructed Kosem to "[fly to Bali to see Lon Nol ... before leaving on [your] Middle East Trip." (Lon Nol was in Bali en route to exile in the US.)[13]

Kosem left Cambodia six days later, six days before the fall of Phnom Penh. His family had gotten out much earlier.

***

Thus, the atrocity rumors were wrong, if only because he had been elsewhere or too high up, and Hanoi's accusation about bringing retribution on the Cham people was too obvious an attempt to shift blame. His single overt role—representing the Republic at the United Nations—was beyond reproach. Three others—shepherding FULRO, running intelligence nets, and helping to overthrow Sihanouk—had an unsavory aura due to their secrecy, but in each case, Kosem was acting as a servant of a legitimate state with a right to defend itself, including against its own monarch. His fourth covert role—running the Sihanoukville arms traffic—indirectly caused the death of tens of thousands but was in support of a war effort considered moral by half the people on this planet.

Which left the swag problem to ponder, and the fact that he got his family out of Cambodia alive when hundreds of thousands could not.

Then my wife and I rented a house in Phnom Penh because the neighborhood looked like something out of *Travel & Leisure*, with high, white walls and bougainvillea and two Buddhist temples. We failed to notice the razor wire on every wall or the swarm of cats in one temple, a sign not of Buddhist compassion but of rats and garbage nearby. With time we learned that the other temple was a squatters' warren, seized during Cambodia's overtly lawless time and still a dangerous place. Down one alley from us was a building sunk in its own jungle, antennae still visible on its roof—the US Ambassador's residence, empty since April 12, 1975. Down another was a house with sightless windows behind which lay dying the "First Lady" of the Khmer Rouge, Ieng Thirith.[14] And beyond her was an alley-level apartment where—no less a vestige of the past than the razor wire or squatters or Ieng Thirith—a murder took place shortly after we arrived: an expat woman *and* her baby were slain by an aimless thief-intruder, with a screwdriver. Without explaining why to our children, we began to sleep the four of us in the only room in our house with bars on the windows and a heavy, lockable door. The atmosphere of menace was only a whisper compared to what it had been as Cambodian society was crumbling, but this was the first time that, as a father, I had felt anything like it.

From that I realized that, to Kosem, holding on to as much money as possible and keeping his wife and ten children alive were the same thing. Nothing suggests he had been corrupt before the communists started handing him cash. Nothing about his character suggests greed. And as an intelligence officer, he knew better than almost anyone else what the Khmer Rouge were doing in areas they controlled, thus what lay ahead for Cambodia and for Chams.

The money was a windfall from Hanoi. Unable to guess how much money his family might need in extremis, Kosem must have felt obligated to keep it all. His family today lives on three continents, but to my knowledge only his widow has any trappings of wealth, and these are subdued. It is hard to see how anyone else was hurt by this.

That said, it was good to learn that Kosem continued to bankroll FULRO in South Vietnam after 1970 with some of this money (see p. 182).

But what about getting his family out? I imagined their taking airplane seats from others until I learned that his six oldest children were already at school outside the country and that he had rented a private plane from Thailand to come in for his wife and four little children. In other words, he got them out—when hundreds of thousands of others could not get out—because he *could.* Because for years he had been gaining power and friends and money by being who he was—sober, honest, discreet, and effective.

Near the end, he was among the 10 most powerful men in the Republic, attending a meeting in the house of the Foreign Minister five weeks before the fall of Phnom Penh, where evacuation was discussed. The minutes, in Kosem's hand, list refugees first, then the elderly, women, and children, then the general population. At the bottom, he has written "P.S. Chams and Montagnards toward Koh Kong [Island], 1st stage."[15]

The fact that Kosem's family of eleven is alive and comfortable despite his having died at age 49 strikes me, as an 80-year-old, as a slam-dunk success. I cannot guess whether that "P.S." down at the bottom represents failure or just reality, because I do not know how possible it would have been at that point to save any Chams and Montagnards. I am glad, and a touch surprised, at this evidence that he saw them as equally deserving.

***

His widow had a home less than 200 meters from us, but in a better neighborhood. She was away a lot—at homes in France or Australia or a slightly rundown resort she owned on the sea-coast—but eventually we met.

We would talk in her living room, seated at a glass coffee table with orchids, the room dim and cool with dark wood ceiling and light slanting in through closed white curtains. Among framed photos near the entrance was one of Kosem seated in uniform, she lovely and youthful next to him, and 10 children around them of almost perfectly graduated sizes.

She had become the doyenne of the worldwide Cham diaspora, having made it her mission to "complete what he started," which meant picking up the postwar pieces and trying to hold them together until it became apparent in the 1990s that the Cham irredentist dream was dead.

She was of course sensitive to the litany of slander against his reputation. The relative importance of each item in her mind showed in how often she returned to each over the course of many interviews, most frequent being the swag problem and its corollary, the Sihanoukville Trail. (She insisted she was responsible for the family's current wealth, earned with her own business acumen; though no doubt partially true, a number of people report having seen suitcases of $100 bills in Kosem's possession.) Next was her husband's role in getting rid of Sihanouk (possibly of some importance to contemporary peers in a Cambodia where Sihanouk in essence had been restored as king), and last was his role in bringing the FULRO Montagnards to Phnom Penh. She seemed genuinely fond of Bhan. Her continued support for him over the decades suggested she rued his fate, if not exactly her husband's role in it. Never once did she mention any of the atrocity rumors.

There are obvious problems in accepting the testimony of a man's widow. However, nothing I learned from her got contradicted by others who had known him. Over time, the single most impressive thing to me was the consistency of peoples' impressions. The adjectives were always the same: upright, dignified, calm, soft-spoken, abstemious, courteous. The question was whether these were only a façade.

The following is what she told me of his life, fleshed out with pieces of information from elsewhere.

In the 1880s, the French, already in colonial possession of Vietnam's southern Delta, maneuvered to take control of the middle part of the country. The Vietnamese resisted with a movement called "Save the Emperor," their first in a series of anticolonial movements that culminated with Ho Chi Minh's.

However, one ethnic minority, the Chams, sided with the French for reasons similar to the Montagnards' 70 years later: they were losing their ancestral lands to the Vietnamese. (Only 50 years before, the Chams had lost their last kingdom, Panduranga.) In later decolonization wars worldwide, this was common—minorities' siding with foreigners against an anti-colonialist majority—and a source of enduring bitterness.

Kosem was born in 1927 in a small village on the Mekong. His great-grandparents had escaped from Vietnam for political reasons, chased by Vietnamese. He knew little about them other than they had fled overland, stopping only long enough in a field of tall elephant grass to give birth to his grandmother.

Their flight was probably related to the 1886–87 troubles between French and anticolonialist Vietnamese. Kosem inherited his great-grandfather's sword, with its suggestions of aristocracy and command. As a teenager, Kosem would figuratively don that sword for life.

His grandmother, the one born in the grass, had married a Frenchman, a coffee planter, though this only seemed important genetically, source of

Kosem's unusual 6'1" (185 cm) height, broad shoulders, gangling liquid gait, and large eyes that gave his long face a mournful look.

It appears he started secular school at age 12, not counting a presumed village madrassah earlier. The Chams of Cambodia, unlike their forbears in Vietnam, are strict Muslims, but Kosem's other grandfather, village *hakem*, was an unusually enlightened man who insisted his grandson attend the secular French primary school downriver in Kompong Cham. The villagers grumbled, especially about his school uniform's shorts, but, as *hakem,* his grandfather could weather it. Kosem's name shows up in administrative rolls of his last year there, 5th grade in 1944–45 when he was 17–18.[16]

The French governor of Kompong Cham may also have played a role in this. Why the governor had always been solicitous of him and his family, visiting them often, was never explained. Kosem referred to it as "the family mystery."

He stood out at school, initially for awkward reasons, being older and much taller than his classmates. What he remembered, however, was the Cambodian boys' singing in derision "The Cambodian flag marches row on row toward Angor Wat / While little Cham pennants flutter in the prows of boats," and he dated his dream of reviving and reclaiming Champa to that first year, at age 13.

No doubt he stood out academically, too, because family lore has it that he was 16 when the governor asked him to work as his interpreter with the Chams.[17] He became an intermediary between the governor and communities along the river, accruing more and more reflected power. Performing services for his people, he began to build up patronage networks, the sinews of Cambodian society. Precocious experience of power and leadership, at an age when delusions are still normal, may partly explain the quixotic core of his later politics.

He then did two more years at an unknown school in Phnom Penh, meaning he only had seven years total of secular schooling. His later intellectual confidence suggests he made the most of these two years, plus continued lifelong self-study. It is also testament to an extraordinary will.[18]

There is a suggestion of a first marriage, perhaps two. One wife, betrothed too young, turned out to be unsuited to the life of a future Cham statesman. Another (or perhaps the same) died in childbirth, though the baby survived.[19] Grief was connected with his decision to become a soldier.

An Army career promised better—perhaps the only—advancement for a minority. Among Cambodians the popular view of Chams was sinister. He joined the military as a cadet at age 22 (in 1949). Two years later, he started reserve officers' training. In late 1952, due to a sudden expansion of the Army, he was assigned to a newly formed battalion[20] as a second lieutenant even though he had not finished training. The reason: America, increasingly worried the French might lose Indochina to the Viet Minh, had just given Cambodia its first infusion of military aid.

At least one Army unit saw combat against the Viet Minh in 1953; it is not clear if Kosem's unit did, though he was given a significant decoration in August 1953 and immediately after that was selected for training in France, undoubtably a plum posting.

In France, from 1953–55, he toured the country when off duty with another young Cambodian officer, taking photos of each other in ill-fitting suits, but he likely went alone, as to church, to the *Musée Guimet* of Asian Art in Paris and the nearby *Ecole Français d'Extreme Orient.* Among Cham sculpture of unique sophistication and tomes detailing Cham kings going back 1,700 years, he confirmed his belief in Champa's greatness.

He came back from France a fully qualified paratrooper/instructor/rigger, subsequently setting a Cambodian national free-fall parachuting record.[21] (This was more dangerous at the time than today's sport of skydiving, requiring that he carefully clean, fold, and pack his own parachute, else one wrong pleat send him streaming to earth.)

His country became independent while he was gone, and the Royal Army—no longer officered by the French—clashed hard with the Viet Minh in April 1954, a battle in which a young fellow officer, Um Savuth, was wounded. Savuth would be paired with Kosem throughout their careers and become his great friend, despite being physically and temperamentally his opposite (see photo, next page).[22] The pairing was because Kosem was an ethnic minority, kept one rank and one post behind the Cambodian Savuth. However, in matters that were secret—like FULRO and the Sihanoukville Trail—Kosem appears to have been given the lead.[23]

After two years as a paratroop captain, he began to look for a wife. She had to be Muslim but not a village girl, which narrowed things severely. She also had to be tall, educated, pretty, and smart—practically asymptotic. A number of people told him about the daughter of an Indian from Pondicherry and his Cambodian wife, who sold fabrics from the premium shops around the new art-deco Central Market.

He stopped by discreetly but left disappointed. Only later, by life-altering chance, did he learn he had gone to the wrong shop and spied the wrong girl. He returned, found the right girl, haggling hard to see if she got flustered. Coolly, she told him to get lost. Definitely the right girl.

He married Meidine Natchear in April 1958. He was 31, she 18. From her father, she had inherited dark good looks and a mind for business. During childhood, she lived briefly in Saigon where her father had dealings, thus

Les Kosem (standing, second from left), Um Savuth (standing, center). (Photo courtesy of Meidine Natchear)

learned to speak Vietnamese. She would always seem a bit too exotic for Cambodia, which, along with her husband's secretive ways and projects, gave the Les Kosems an air of mystery.

To Sihanouk, she was a potential conquest. Once, at a sporting event, word arrived from the royal box requesting her presence. Kosem knew exactly what was happening, silently took her by the hand, and exited the arena.

Meidine and Kosem. (Photo courtesy of Meidine Natchear)

***

As noted before, in the late 1950s, a clandestine duel between President Diem of South Vietnam and Prince Sihanouk of Cambodia began, with the CIA and French Intelligence as seconds. Diem, galled by Sihanouk providing sanctuary to the Viet Cong, gave sanctuary to an antimonarchist guerilla movement to gall Sihanouk in return.[24]

In 1958, the South Vietnamese Army pushed into Ratanakiri Province, in Cambodia's far northeast, uprooting border markers and replanting them eight miles further in.[25] Sihanouk's response was to send lowland Cambodians to colonize Ratanakiri, exactly as Diem had done in the Vietnam highlands. This caused friction with Cambodia's highlanders, and, in 1959, some attacked police with crossbows, killing several.[26] Kosem, still a captain and in command of a company, parachuted in to surround a Jarai village suspected of being about to rebel. To his surprise, he understood the Jarai tongue because so many Jarai words are also Cham. Smoothing everything over without bloodshed, he invited one of the Jarai leaders to Phnom Penh where his wife and brother-in-law escorted the man about the city, attracting a crowd at the Central Market because of his exotic attire.[27] This is exactly the kind of exploit—a combat jump with diplomatic success—that delights military superiors and may have broken the ethnic glass ceiling above Kosem.

In 1959, as Diem instigated one attempt on Sihanouk's life and one coup attempt. As mentioned earlier (p. 129), Sihanouk tasked his defense minister, Lon Nol, with stirring up trouble among Vietnam's ethnic minorities.

Um Savuth was the obvious choice to inflame secessionism among the ethnic Cambodians living in Vietnam's Mekong Delta, as he was from a neighboring Cambodian province and was close to Lon Nol (who was also from the region).[28] Savuth was reliable because, unlike some of his contemporaries, he was a soldier first and last, uninterested in money.

Kosem was the obvious choice to inflame ethnonationalism among Vietnam's Chams and to keep it growing among Montagnards. By character and outsider status, he was likely to be discreet, and Lon Nol must have felt he knew exactly what made Kosem tick. The younger man's singular devotion to the Champa cause, plus his Muslim faith, which his abstemiousness showed he took seriously, made him predictable. Lon Nol would have understood this better than most, being monomaniacal himself about the origin and destiny of the Cambodians.

Whether or not Kosem actually saw the Jarai and Rhadé as "highland Cham," he was a true believer in the irredentist cause, no matter how fantastical. If getting back territory from the Vietnamese were ever possible, it was now, in the hothouse of the 1960s, with war looming. To him, the five adjacent provinces of Vietnam's Central Highlands had been conjured out of no man's land by French explorers and administrators and only recently had been under Vietnamese control.[29] The Vietnamese grasp might still be weak. That the UN and/or world opinion might somehow create a more just world for ethnic minorities was still a tantalizing hope in 1960.[30] If so, autonomy or even independence might be wrested away or mandated by a supranational referee. Sihanouk and Lon Nol, for their part, could hope that, with the highlands as a wedge, the Mekong Delta provinces would follow. In any case, the coming war might Balkanize southern Vietnam. They needed to be ready to snatch up the pieces.

While Um Savuth created a front to liberate *Kampuchea Krom* (southern Cambodia, meaning the Mekong Delta), Kosem created a front to liberate Champa, meaning more-or-less the middle third of both coastal and highland Vietnam, inhabited by Chams or Chamic-speaking Montagnards. From the beginning, a third front was imagined in order to represent all the *non*-Chamic speaking Montagnards, i.e., those above and below the swath claimed for Champa (see map on p. 13). This was the inaccurately-named Front to Liberate Northern Cambodia. To Lon Nol, these Mon-Khmer-speaking Montagnards were highland Cambodians,[31] a belief exactly analogous to Kosem's belief that Chamic-speaking Montagnards were highland Cham. The two ideas were so similar, and grandiose, as to have a flavor of schoolyard boasts, with a similar potential for conflict.[32] Lon Nol was, if anything, more mystical than Kosem, with bizarre takes on the past greatness of Indochina's brown-skinned peoples stretching from Burma to Vietnam's highlands. (A recent author with some perspective points out that Elizabeth Becker was one of the few members of the international press who took Lon Nol's ideas seriously, noting "how these fantasies had long haunted Cambodia's vision of national identity and could appeal to common people.")[33]

In May 1960, Zhou Enlai came to Phnom Penh, cementing a personal, almost avuncular, relationship with Sihanouk. Kosem was in charge of Zhou's security and took the opportunity to remind him of Champa's history. All those hours in the Paris library must have paid off with references to Chinese court records dating back to AD 192.

This was a pivotal time in Indochina. Diem's harsh reactions to the communist threat had brought little security but lots of enemies. Many of those enemies united in December 1960 to form the National Liberation Front—the Viet Cong (VC)—but they had trouble gaining traction in the highlands, which they themselves attributed to failing to do enough political work before showing up in the Montagnards' midst carrying guns.[34] However, it may be that their biggest problem was simply being Vietnamese. Accordingly, the VC sprouted a Montagnard branch, led by Y-Bih Aleo (whom we last saw in 1958 mounting a Bajaraka demonstration with Dhon, then being interrogated with Bhan). Y-Bih's movement explicitly promised autonomy to South Vietnam's Montagnards, pointing to the existence of two autonomous

Zhou Enlai (second from left), Kosem (middle, looking to his right), and Sihanouk (looking to his left). Zhou looks jarringly colonialist in a white linen suit but is actually showing sympathy for the recent death of Sihanouk's father (white being Asia's color of mourning). (Photo courtesy of Meidine Natchear)

zones already created in North Vietnam (though these turned out at the end of the war to have been for show).[35]

Cambodian Chams were largely apolitical, but Kosem single-handedly tried to change that, speaking in mosques up and down the Mekong about the dream of reviving Champa. One listener remembered Kosem saying Chams might need to ally with the VC if that resulted in the Chams getting what they wanted (but to the listener's knowledge, it never happened).[36] Kosem had been a disciple of Tuan Sales, a renowned Muslim teacher from his village who, attracted by the arguments of the Viet Minh, had studied in Hanoi, then created a Cham "struggle-movement for the oppressed races in collaboration with the Viet Minh in 1948."[37] Tuan Sales had fired Kosem to the irredentist cause and passed the mantle to him, telling him, "Only you can do it." However, in 1954, the victorious Viet Minh—being Vietnamese first—had rejected Sales's requests for help getting back Cham territory from Vietnam, and Sales had supposedly died in Saudi Arabia, from sorrow.[38]

Around this time, too, his wife remembered stapling shut one of his notebooks because she was not supposed to see its contents. Kosem had begun making regular trips to the Vietnam border, 160 kilometers (100 miles) southeast of Phnom Penh, where he was running agent nets into Vietnam.[39] (Kosem had to be worth more to Lon Nol and Sihanouk as an intelligence officer than as an infantry officer. This, plus his added responsibility by 1967 for the Sihanoukville Trail, is strong circumstantial evidence he had nothing to do with suppressing the Samlaut Rebellion—another vague accusation against him because of his association with paratroops.)

For Kosem the spymaster, Vietnamese Chams were ideal agents. Some were traditional traders plying waterways throughout southern Vietnam; one family even peddled magic herbs all over Indochina. But it was the younger, better-educated ones who became important to FULRO. Unlike Cambodia's Chams, those of Vietnam's central coast were partway politicized already, conscious of the rebellions of the 1880s and the Chams' still-extant royal line, plus more aware of the outside world, having been educated in secular schools.[40] A number of young Chams joined FULRO, either as soldiers in the forests of Mondulkiri, such as Po Dharma,[41] or as cross-border agents. Because Chams look Vietnamese, and the young ones could speak Vietnamese perfectly, they could cross back and forth across the Mekong Delta border between Cambodia and Vietnam, using flashlight and baguette codes, then successfully pass multiple checkpoints on the 250-mile stretch between the Delta and the Cham coast, where they recruited fellow youths to come to Mondulkiri and/or delivered support payments to the families of those who had already gone.

An important agent was Wa Hap, the mysterious Cham in *National Geographic*'s article on the September 1964 rebellion (see pp. 4–5).[42] The article's author sensed Wa Hap's intensity and assumed he was communist (the American colonel who inserted himself at one of the camps reported being "heckled" by him).[43] In fact, he was a radical ethnonationalist and Kosem's chosen representative.

Another was Nara Vija,[44] educated at the Lycée Yersin and University of Dalat, who had served as a combat interpreter with the US 101st Airborne Division before joining Kosem in Phnom Penh in 1969. Po Dharma and Nara Vija went onward to France in 1972 to get a doctorate and masters, respectively. The former became a renowned Cham scholar and leader of the Cham diaspora, as well as co-author of the only inside book about FULRO, *Du FLM à FULRO*.[45] Nara Vija translated a major classical Cham work before moving onward to the US. Until late 1974, Kosem must have paid all their travel and living expenses in France out of his own pocket. (Two more in France included a woman, about whom we will hear later, and her husband.)

In 1971, before leaving for France, Nara Vija found himself carrying a suitcase with "half a million dollars in piastres"[46] to a rendezvous in a Saigon bar with another agent, the money to support FULRO activities in South Vietnam. The year is significant because Cambodia was now an ally of South Vietnam and the US. No more money was coming from Phnom Penh. The French would have tried to keep their hand in, but with dwindling funds. Thus the money for this had to be coming from Kosem himself. Bankrolling FULRO and supporting the young Chams in France cannot have been cheap.

***

As we have seen (p. 57), Americans arrived in the highlands in late 1961, and the Rhadé responded enthusiastically to a chance to regain agency. As the number of enrolled villages jumped from 40 to 200 between April and August 1962, the South Vietnamese Government started getting nervous about the army at its back.

Sihanouk had similar concerns about this irregular army at his doorstep.[47] Sometime in the first half of 1962, he and Kosem must have come to the same conclusion: that Kosem's Champa Front should start co-opting the growing Montagnard force.

Perhaps establishing his bona fides, Kosem sent a letter to the UN protesting Diem's colonization of the highlands. He also set in motion a plan to break Y-Bham Enuol out of prison, using Cham soldiers, though nothing came of it.[48] And he sought out Y-Bih Aleo at a VC conference in Phnom Penh in February 1962, probably to verify what he had heard—that the leader of the Montagnard VC had an equal or higher loyalty to the Montagnard cause than to Communism. He may also have been coordinating possible joint actions in the future.

***

Then Kosem disappeared from the scene. Just as events in Indochina were gathering speed, he left for eight months in Paris at the French Army's War College for Staff Officers (*l'Ecole Superieure de Guerre et Ecole d'Etat-Major*), accompanied by his pregnant wife. Dropping out at this crucial time makes no sense unless Lon Nol and Sihanouk expected the training to make him a more effective thorn in Saigon's side. For France, he would have been a potential asset, especially useful as a source of information. For Kosem, using the French in return must have made sense, and there is evidence he continued to receive advice and funds for FULRO from the French military attaché in Phnom Penh into the 1970s.

By 1963, Cambodia had become France's last bastion of significant influence in Indochina and its only lever on the new war in Vietnam. De Gaulle's government was calling for the "neutralization" of Indochina, a prescient idea but a proposal America would never accept, largely because it so clearly meant handing all of Vietnam over to Ho Chi Minh, but also, at least in part, because it seemed so blatantly/irritatingly in the self-interest of France, which was hoping to retain commercial relations with a communist Vietnam. While de Gaulle's attitude toward America's military involvement in Vietnam may not have hardened yet into outright enmity, anything that impeded the US at this point, causing trouble for the Americans, was probably welcome. As mentioned earlier (p. 51, and note 6, p. 59), this would have been especially true at the level of secret services.

The Kosems' time in France, from September 1962 to sometime after May 1963, is the one period in which Kosem's life comes into sharper focus because his wife knew where he was. They lived in the 17th Arrondissement in a one-room government hostel near Saint-Lazare. This was her first trip away from Indochina. While he was at school, she took French lessons at the *Alliance Francaise* and studied to be a beautician. He would cook if he got home before her. On weekends, they would go to the Guimet Museum of Asian Art to see the Cham sculptures.

As her due date approached, they discussed names for the baby. She knew what was coming because this was their fifth child; he was going to tire her out with lists of names until she said, irritatedly, "You choose." It was a boy, born May 10. Kosem named him "Mohammed Gandhi," an interesting choice.

In February 1963, the CIA got word that Montagnard firebrands were about to ally themselves with the Montagnard Viet Cong (MVC). However, Y-Bih Aleo, leader of the MVC, then sent contrary word that he might rally to Saigon, but only if his old friend, Y-Bham Enuol, convinced him to do so. The CIA pulled Y-Bham Enuol out of jail and was heading to the remote meeting site when it was bombed by a South Vietnamese plane.[49] That the site was the Cham tower of Yang Prong suggests Kosem was pulling strings from afar. The best explanation of this puzzling episode is that Kosem was trying to increase cohesion between rebellious Montagnards—FULRO and the MVC—and that Saigon caught wind of this.

Kosem impressed his instructors at *l'Ecole d'Etat-Major*. His final evaluation lauded him as "an officer of quality, with exemplary bearing and sociability who demonstrates a moral force and faultless dignity. Extremely conscientious and serious, he did considerable, careful work with very satisfactory results (including a remarkable report on Cambodia)." His highest grades are in "Bearing," "Discipline," and "Moral standing."[50] In retrospect, Kosem had one advantage over most of his classmates. For him, there was nothing theoretical about this schooling. He was going to use it soon.

We have to assume that 1964's First Rebellion—unlike the second one in 1965—was planned largely by Kosem. An interesting question is whether he should have foreseen its failing because of Montagnard deference to Americans.

Kosem's focus shifted to the Sihanoukville Trail in 1966. Hs wife believes Sihanouk took Kosem away from FULRO on purpose, because the prince's worries about FULRO's participation in a coup against him had only grown.

From our point of view, reliable information about FULRO's history from 1966 onward was harder to come by because Kosem's wife and brother-in-law were now out of the loop.

She only had vignettes as to his Sihanoukville role.

On the occasions when he accompanied a shipment, he took it right to the border, instead of leaving it at depots inside Cambodia safe from American capture, because he detested the idea of Vietnamese setting foot on Cambodian soil. From the beginning, he documented everything about the arms traffic, sending the papers onward to Malaysia for safekeeping in case Sihanouk someday disavowed the trail and blamed his subordinates for it. By the end, Kosem's mistrust exploded in anger, throwing a framed photo of Sihanouk to the floor at home and stamping on it, exclaiming, "*Roi fou!*" ("Crazy King!").

If her picture of him as unhappy with his role and angry at Sihanouk seems defensive, it is supported by the fact he was a founding member, in 1967 or 1968, of a small, ultra-secret group of anti-Sihanouk officials and high-ranking military officers who initially tried to rein in Sihanouk by building up parliamentary opposition to his policies, but finally engineered his removal by parliamentary vote in March 1970.[51] This was deadly serious. If caught, he and the others likely would have been executed.

***

I met Kosem in 1973 and liked him. When I started serious research in 2008, I was predisposed to look for the good in him. Repeated meetings over the years with his family predisposed me further, and I have gradually become his apologist. That said, his reputation was dark enough that I never stopped expecting to turn over one more rock and find something incontrovertibly ugly. But I never did. The closest it got was his sometime association with one nefarious individual,[52] but this had many explanations. Nothing I found proved he was other than what he seemed—an extraordinary, decent, and flawed man.

He stood out—by appearance, ethnicity, and religion—yet his secretive occupation made him a blank slate on which almost anything could be written. These made him a target for lazy calumny. Moreover, from the point of view of the Khmer Rouge, he was a dangerous opponent—their single-most important adversary in winning and keeping the allegiance of the Cham people from May 1970 when they took over his home district of Krautchmar, where he was idolized, until and beyond his death in Malaysia in 1976.[53] We can imagine that at least some of his negative reputation was from conscious efforts by the Khmer Rouge to malign him.

A question important to this book is whether Kosem manipulated FULRO's leaders. Being a decent man does not preclude that, and my central thesis is that the leaders, while influenced by outsiders and sometimes flimflammed, were no one's puppets, not even Kosem's.

Hanoi's thesis was/is the exact opposite, that Kosem was an agent of France and/or the US and that he duped FULRO's leaders. Hanoi clearly had a political agenda—to discredit a potentially dangerous foe.

I do, too—though it feels to me like a position toward which I have been led by the facts—which is that Montagnard ethnonationalism was spontaneous and more authentically Montagnard than any competing ideology, thus more consequential than either Saigon or Hanoi admitted.

Neither thesis can be proven or disproven, but, on this issue at least, it seems to me the single-issue fanaticism of both Kosem and the younger FULRO leaders makes them easy to read. Monomania opts for the pragmatic—even Y-Bham Enuol, in his early radical phase, was open to joining forces with communist Montagnards—thus is transparent. Kosem probably did serve as a French asset, but only because, and only for as long as, France contributed to his irredentist dream. Likewise, it is reasonable to assume the FULRO leaders' relationship with Kosem was also transactional, so long as his single-issue goal overlapped with theirs. They were using each other and aware of it.

True tragedy in the classical sense is seldom found in real life. Its criteria are too sublime: a high-born protagonist, or one risen high, with overweening pride as a tragic flaw and a moment of awful "What have I done?" recognition at the end. Usually, the protagonist, like King Lear or Captain Ahab, is so blinded by his flaws that such a moment almost fails to come. Rare figures like this exist in real life but without the painful epiphany. We like to think they have one but, in fact, given the psychology necessary to rise to dizzying heights, most of them probably do not.

Remarkably, FULRO's story contains two such figures—Sihanouk and Kosem.

Prince Sihanouk, the last absolute monarch on the planet, succumbed like Lear to petulant anger that destroyed what he loved, only it was some 1–2 million times worse than Lear—instead of one daughter, it was his country and many of his subjects—all because he sought revenge on those who deposed him by allying himself with the Khmer Rouge. We cannot know if he ever admitted error to himself, much less had a flash of awareness of the human condition, but it seems extremely doubtful.

Kosem, who rose to become the highest secular Cham in Cambodia, brought at least 80 FULRO Montagnards to Phnom Penh, in pursuit of a goal only slightly less mad than Ahab's white whale, and all, except Bhan, went down with the ship (the French Embassy). Without Kosem, their peril would not have existed. (By contrast, FULRO itself probably would have.) His hubris was in his belief he could almost single-handedly reverse history and bring a kingdom back to life. There is reason to believe he felt regret for bringing the FULRO Montagnards to Phnom Penh, but it seems unlikely he ever questioned the cause that made him do it.

The French

The French had the most to gain by supporting Montagnard ethnonationalism.

Before 1955, they did so to divide in order to rule (*diviser pour regner*, the classic colonialist tactic). Initially, the CIA saw the value of this, too, and started monitoring if not encouraging Montagnard ethnonationalism as early as 1956–57[54], but the fact that this went against America's larger objective—supporting Saigon—became increasingly apparent, whereas for the French it was the opposite, i.e., after 1955, it was a way for the French to keep their hand in the politics of their ex-colony. As America became more and more involved in Vietnam, de Gaulle and Sihanouk saw their hopes for "neutralization" of Indochina dwindle. Somehow, they had to get the Americans to pack up and leave, which meant causing problems for the Saigon–Washington alliance. The September 1964 FULRO rebellion fit that bill perfectly, at least initially. Murdering 73 Vietnamese in cold blood was an extraordinary act of wartime sedition that, in the eyes of the Vietnamese, would demand harsh and immediate punishment, while the Americans—given their investment in the Civilian Irregular Defense Group program—would certainly counsel restraint, at least until FULRO's potential became clearer.

This is exactly what happened, though Saigon damped the rebellion's effects on the alliance by swallowing its anger.

The French had close relationships with Kosem and Dhon, both key figures in the 1964 rebellion. One authoritative French source refers almost crowingly to Kosem as a French agent. At least one American source makes the same claim.[55]

We know that the three bearded Caucasians at the church were French. One must have been Roger Bianchetti. He was closest to Dhon and had been a military chaplain, the latter making him the most likely of the priests to be close to the SDECE (*Service de documentation extérieure et de contre-espionnage*). The other two must have been French planters known to be agents of the SDECE.[56] It was common knowledge the planters supplied the rebels with food during the rebellion.[57]

Jacques Dournes—the priest to the Jarai who converted none—claimed FULRO was a creation of the French in the 1950s.[58]

In the years 1964–68, Phnom Penh was known to be the center of French intelligence operations.[59]

Multiple sources report the French gave money to FULRO, along with sending communiques on its behalf to the outside world, via the Phnom Penh military attaché. This may have extended into the 1970s.[60]

Even deeper into a hall of mirrors, Barry Peterson, the Australian captain who worked closely with Rhadé soldiers in 1964, saw sinister French fingerprints everywhere. He even made a case for the French having murdered an American intelligence agent.[61]

In some contradiction to all the above, the VC and North Vietnamese—who had the greatest stake in knowing—believed that both France and America were behind it, but that America's role was greater. (Some South Vietnamese believed this, too). But their reasoning feels forced, and a touch paranoid. One captured document said FULRO was "a tool of US imperialism, with some French involvement" because FULRO's "anti-people's policy"—which can only mean its anti-ethnic-Vietnamese policy—showed it was under "external control."[62] Another said an eventual communist victory over the Americans was so certain—thus no doubt obvious to the Americans—that FULRO must have been created to serve as the nucleus of an eventual stay-behind resistance.[63]

Two things are clear, however, from documents to be discussed further on: 1) the CIA did not have a good handle on what was going on at the heart of FULRO; and 2) whether or not the French actually did, they were confident that FULRO was *not* in the Americans' pocket. In September 1966, de Gaulle's righthand man in dealing with all of Asia, Etienne Manac'h, had a private meeting with Y-Bham Enuol, which suggests an avuncular, if not paternal, relationship from the point of view of both parties. Again, this never would have taken place if the French were not confident of being number one.

France was supposed to open its secret service files to researchers in 2023, after a legally mandated wait of 60 years. However, in 2023, President Macron amended that policy to 70 years, essentially blacking out France's covert actions during the entire period of the Vietnam War.

All the above suggests France played an important role in the FULRO phenomenon, particularly in stimulating and supporting the First Rebellion.

But we are still left with the question: to what degree did they actually control FULRO, as opposed to believing they did?

Notes

1 Gerald Hickey, interview with author, April 1973. I later found a corroborating quote with the word "blunted" but can no longer locate it.

2 Meyer's exact words are, "[FULRO in Cambodia] … always remained under American command, ordered to stay on Cambodian soil and to gather as much intelligence as possible … We can be sure that the CIA took advantage of [this] to engage in subversion of the Cambodian general staff." In the next paragraph, he maintains that FULRO's delegations to the Indochina Peoples' Conference consisted of "poor buggers appointed by Lon Nol and his assistant in mysterious affairs, the Cham colonel, Les Kosem" (Charles Meyer, *Derrière Le Sourire Khmer* (Paris: Plon, 1971), 269). Meyer was writing after the ouster of Sihanouk, his patron. Surprisingly, Stéphanie Benzaquen-Gautier ("The Relational Archive of the Khmer Republic (1970–1975): Re-visiting the 'Coup' and the 'Civil War' in Cambodia Through Written Sources," *South East Asia Research* 29, no. 4 (2021): 456) said Meyer was one of the few who thought the "coup" was mostly an internal, Cambodian affair. He no doubt suspected, correctly, that Kosem was involved. This is likely what he had in mind with "subversion of the … general staff", i.e., supposedly convincing higher-ranking officers to participate in Sihanouk's overthrow, which in any case must have been a bitter pill for Meyer. If we assume France's relations with FULRO were closer than America's, then this statement by Meyer is deliberate disinformation.

3 This was Michael Vickery, who wrote a defense of the Khmer Rouge in 1984.

4 Michael Vickery, email correspondence with author, January 15, 2014; Michael Vickery, conversation with author, June 16, 2015.

5 "All the peasants I interviewed … were very angry. The massacre of the peasants who went in protest to Phnom Penh instigated by Colonel Les Kacem, roused great indignation among them." Serge Thion, *Watching Cambodia* (Bangkok: White Lotus, 1993), 16.

6 CIA cable TDCS-314/05323-70 from May 12 mentions that "even when LK was nominally in charge of Secy for the Phnom Penh Region," in fact it was Major Thach Chan who was really in charge. It goes on to say that "Les Kossem has been fully occupied in attempting to obtain arms and other aid from Indonesia and in the recruiting of ethnic Cham forces for the expanding Cambodian army." In other words, again, he was too high up.

7 Ben Kiernan and Chan Boua, *Peasants and Politics in Kampuchea 1942–1981* (London: Zed Press, 1982), 208.

8 Ironically, Chams were among the earliest supporters of the Khmer Rouge because of their allegiance to Sihanouk, which in turn was due to their ancestors having been welcomed to Cambodia by the Cambodian monarchy in the 19th century. Many joined the Khmer Rouge after Sihanouk's deposition in 1970. Farina So, interview with author, June 17, 2015.

9 Chek Brahim, *Confession*, Catalogue #D02687 (1975–76), S-21 (Khmer Rouge torture center), Phnom Penh: Documentation Center of Cambodia (translated to English by Chenda Seang); Nasir, interview with author, December 13, 2013; and Raymond Scupin, "Historical, Ethnographic, and Contemporary Political Analyses of the Muslims of Kampuchea and Vietnam," *Sojourn* 10, no. 2 (1995): 321.

10 Ken Conboy, *The Cambodia Wars: Clashing Armies and CIA Covert Operations* (Lawrence: University Press of Kansas, 2013), 32.

11 Regarding sources: the CIA estimated "26,000 tons of supplies, just over 21,000 tons of it ordnance [but] … even more might have slipped through." Dang Phong (*Five Ho Chi Minh Trails* (Hanoi: The Gioi Publishers, 2012), 314) said "Cambodian authorities [were paid] … $36,642,653 and 52 cents, [which bought] 20,478 tons of weapons, 2,015 tons of military equipment and uniforms, and 70,810 tons of food (rice and some salt)." Doan Khuc (*Review of the Resistance War Against the Americans to Save the Nation: Victories and Lessons* (Hanoi: National Political Publishing House, 1995), 221), quoted by the CIA, said "we shipped 21,400 tons of supplies through the port of Sihanoukville and paid the government more than 50 million USD in port fees and transportation charges." The CIA document said 10 percent was set aside for Cambodia's Army. However, Um Savuth, in another CIA debriefing, claimed to have taken off one third for Cambodia, then cached one-third of that for FULRO—though Bhan said FULRO only received some uniforms and Chinese grenades. (CIA document dated 20 July 1970, TDCS-DB-315/08715-70. Regarding the millions: Sihanouk and the royal family likely took the lion's share. Regarding unreliability: For apparent reason of current politics, Hanoi claims the arms and ammunition came from Russia, not China. Multiple Cambodian sources from the time disagree.

12 Kissinger's cables for the Khmer Republic years (1970–75) in Wikileaks online (https://search.wikileaks.org/?query=kosem). Kosem (or Kossem or Kassem) is frequently mentioned in these as Cambodia's point man with Islamic countries.

13 The exact words of the cable are, "PRIERE EN VOYAGE GEN LES KOSSEM VOIR NOTRE PRESIDENT A BALI AVANT SON DEPART TOUR MOYEN ORIENT" (Long Boret, Public Library of US Diplomacy, 1975 wikileaks.org/plusd/cables/1975JAKART03915_b.html). The "*priere en voyage*" is not completely clear but, since Kosem himself was in Phnom Penh at the time, it appears to mean "please, while [Lon Nol is] travelling." The foreign minister himself, Long Boret, was in Bali with Lon Nol and had two weeks to live, returning to Cambodia and being among those immediately executed by the Khmer Rouge, most likely on the 17th.

14 Wife of Ieng Sary and Minister Social Affairs under the Khmer Rouge

15 Document in long-hand entitled "CHEZ LONG BORET le 9/3/75 de 24H à 02H00" in Les Kosem trove. See also note 10, p. 203. Here, though, it is clear that Koh Kong was for Montagnards too.

16 *Bulletin Administratif du Cambodge 7 October 1943*, thanks to Jean-Pierre Chazal.

17 The governor was probably a different appointee in 1946 than the one in 1944.

18 This was not the French school for the Cambodian élite, the Lycée Sisowath, though he allowed the author, Gerald Hickey, to believe this, probably more a matter of habitual misdirection than ego. I find it interesting that his actual education level, not counting self-study, was

similar or less than that of the Montagnard leaders. This, plus his having risen from the very lowest social rung, as they had done, may explain a lot.

19 An army document from September 1956 (*Feuille de Notes pour 1er Semestre,* in Les Kosem trove) lists him as a "widower with one child."

20 The 2nd Batallion of Cambodian *Chasseurs (Raiders)*, or the 2 BCC. His typed service record (author's collection) actually says "4 BCC", a battalion that saw significant combat in April 1953, but it appears that Kosem himself corrected the "4" to read "2." I could not learn whether the 2nd Battalion saw combat.

21 His service record says he was assigned first to the infantry school at Saint-Maixent, then to an administration school at Coëtquidan. There is no mention of jump school at Pau. However, my notes from another source (since lost) state clearly that he was at Pau from Feb–May 1955, part of that for training as a jump-master. Ken Conboy (*FANK: A History of the Cambodian Armed Forces, 1970–75* (Jakarta: Equinox Publishing, 2011) mentions the free-fall record, in August 1957.

22 Savuth and Kosem seem to have functioned as alter egos in supervising both the Sihanoukville Trail and FULRO. (Though himself closer to the Khmer Krom, Savuth shared Kosem's dream and named his daughter Champa.) His reputation colors his life story. As a dashing young paratroop officer, he married a beautiful Eurasian. Given to drink, one evening he challenged a comrade to shoot a can off his head; the comrade missed, leaving Savuth with a bad limp and speech impediment. No longer dashing, he turned more to drink, losing his wife. Despite this, he continued to rise in rank, always in tandem with Kosem who, despite his own abstemiousness, would accompany his friend to bars where Savuth would loudly order drinks, ending with the affectionate flourish, "And milk for the baby!" After war broke out against the North Vietnamese, word soon spread among the international press that "Savuth was a better general drunk than the others sober," though Americans who fought beside him for weeks never saw him intoxicated; rather, they remember him best for, one night during a mortar attack, sitting in a lawn chair on top of a bunker and giving orders calmly to his troops through a megaphone. (Rocky Farr, interview with author, September 25, 2014, and Steve Spoerry, interview with author, January 27, 2014). Uninterested in money, he was known for his incorruptibility and largesse. At his funeral in November 1972 after a jeep accident, *cyclo-pousse* drivers from all over the city showed up out of gratitude and respect.

23 The CIA thought Savuth was his assistant in running the arms traffic.

24 Called the Khmer Serei, they were particularly maddening to Sihanouk. In 1963, he ordered that the execution by firing squad of a captured guerilla be filmed and shown for a month in the nation's movie theaters. This was a glimpse into the furnace that, from 1970 onward, would consume his entire people. To Sihanouk, *lese majeste,* causing injury to the monarchy, was the ultimate crime, sparking his bad judgment. We can only speculate where this came from. Perhaps from his grandfather, Norodom, who put girls from his harem to death for infidelity. Or perhaps more banally, from an upbringing in which he never dressed himself and in which courtiers in his presence referred to themselves as "his Majesty's footstool" or "lower than the dust beneath his Majesty's feet."

25 International Control Commission in Cambodia, 7th report (HMSO, Cmd 887), 27–8, via Christine Nabias, "Neutralism in Indochina: A Comparative Study of Neutralism in Cambodia, Laos, and Vietnam, 1954–65" (Master's thesis, Ithaca, NY: Cornell University, 1971).

26 Sara Colm and Sorya Sim, *Khmer Rouge Purges in the Mondul Kiri Highlands*, Documentation Series no. 14 (Phnom Penh: Documentation Center of Cambodia, 2009), 20.

27 Ibrahim Mohmmed Keo, interview with author, January 26, 2015. I watched and heard this 84-year-old tell this story and am certain that he believed it.

28 This cause—clawing back part of the Delta from Vietnam—was probably the one closest to Sihanouk's heart. It was certainly the one that fired a disproportionate number of Cambodia's leaders (including Lon Nol) who had been born in the region. (The fact that "Southern Cambodians" figured prominently in Cambodia's leadership is thought to have come from their better education, because the region's schools in the 1920s–30s were secular and French, as opposed to the Buddhist academies in Cambodia).

29 Though debatable, many Montagnards believe this today. The question is whether the lowland Vietnamese had political claim to the highlands before or during the time of the French. The five provinces were Darlac, Quang Duc, Pleiku, Kontum, and Haut Donnai.

30 My guess is that this hopeful ethos—now quaint—is what motivated Dhon as well.

31 Scholar George Coedes had roughly the same idea: "[Cambodians] are Hinduized Montagnards" (Meyer, *Derrière Le Sourire Khmer*, 47). Whether this is true or not has yet been studied genetically.

32 At one point, it sounds to have gotten close to ugly, with Lon Nol—standing over a map—threatening to replace Kosem. The problem was that Kosem's claim, for Champa, looked to include part of Cambodia itself. The eventual solution was apparently to de-emphasize "Northern Cambodia" and to make it very clear that "Champa" included nothing west of the Vietnam–Cambodia border except a chunk of southern Laos, called Champassak. The latter, at least, was entirely true: Wat Phou, a marvelously evocative ruined temple there, high on one bank of the Mekong, recalls the reach of ancient Champa.

33 Benzaquen-Gautier, "The Relational Archive of the Khmer Republic (1970–1975)": 450–68. Benzaquen-Gautier provides needed perspective on the Khmer Republic, among other things pointing out the "tendency among international correspondents to paint the Republic in a farcical light. The patronizing, even condescending tone of American governmental records and, to some extent, of the media is striking … [This] is nowhere more evident than in the treatment of the Republic's leader, … Lon Nol, often depicted as a mystical loon." This made me correct my own use of that phrase: he was definitely mystical, but he was no loon.

34 Giap, quoted by David Marr. See note 20, p. 38.

35 Actually there had been three, but one disappeared without notice in 1959. The other two lasted until December 1975, when, with the war won, Hanoi no longer needed them to attract southern Montagnards to the revolutionary/unification cause. Walker Connor, *The National Question in Marxist-Leninist Theory and Strategy* (Princeton: Princeton University Press, 1984), 119.

36 Sen Tith, interview with author, December 13, 2013.

37 Page 14 of a document entitled PREFACE in Kosem's papers, written by him and listing every event in the history of Champa from BC to a month or two before the Indochina Peoples' Conference. ("*Des le début de 1948 sous la direction de [Son Excellence] Haji Sales … les Chams avaient créé, en collaboration avec les Viet-Minh, un mouvement de lutte pour les races opprimées.*") The document dispels any suspicion that Kosem's irredentism could have been a pose, or cover, for Sihanouk's anti-Vietnam policies, because it is so clearly the loving creation of Kosem himself, a bookish fanatic.

38 "Tuan" is honorific (as in Joseph Conrad's "Tuan Jim"). Sales learned Arabic in Malaysia and opened a school to teach it in Cambodia in the 1940s, then saw alliance with the Viet Minh as the best hope for Chams. A popular version of what happened in 1954 is that, when he asked for Viet Minh help in reclaiming Champa from Vietnam, the Viet Minh declined but

with an uncharacteristic lack of diplomacy. Over time and repeated tellings, this became derision ("Laughing, they pointed toward Angkor Wat, saying 'You can go squat with your people there'"). This is considered the ultimate cause of his death. Deeply disappointed, he went off to Mecca, praying "Please let me die in the Holy Land," which he did, possibly by his own hand. (From a combination of interviews with Sen Tith and Ibrahim Keo, plus S-21 confession of Chek Brahim, plus the document mentioned in note 37 above.

39 Les Kosem told Jim Morris that FULRO "grew out of an intelligence operation." Jim Morris, interview with author, August 16, 2019.

40 Their elders practiced either a nearly unrecognizable brand of Islam, called Bani, or a nearly unrecognizable form of Brahmanism, called Balomon. Exactly how the younger ones caught the irredentist contagion is unknown—perhaps Vietnamese Chams passing through Phnom Penh to Mecca in the 1950s brought Kosem's message home, or perhaps it was part of the fifties' general awakening of consciousness, usually revolutionary, in the Global South. In the Malay world, this was driven by Indonesia's Sukarno, one of the giant figures of the 20th century, who defeated Dutch colonialism after World War II, sponsored the Non-Aligned Movement (hosting the Bandung Conference in 1955), and put down a CIA-aided rebellion against him in early 1958. According to a CIA-officer I met in 1973, who had served in Indonesia, Sukarno's agents fanned out through Southeast Asia in the early 1950s to keep tabs on overseas Chinese and the rice market (Bob Pierson, interview with author, March 1973). We can imagine they sought out Kosem who, even as a young man was among the most prominent secular Chams in Cambodia, and that these early contacts were at the root of his closeness with Indonesia in later years.

41 Po Dharma, *nom de guerre* of Quang van Du, became an officer in the Cham unit and, much later, when the unit became the Cham Battalion, was badly wounded fighting against the Khmer Rouge.

42 Wa Hap (or Wa Hab, or Eli) were Muslim *noms de guerre* of Hoang Minh Mo.

43 Peter Grose, "US Saigon Aides Split on the Revolt," *The New York Times*, September 30, 1964. The colonel reported being "heckled by a stranger in the camp, a member of another tribe, who was later identified as one of the persons who brought in the pro-Communist leaflets." This can only be Wa Hap, not Dhon. Allowing for some self-dramatization by the colonel, Wa Hap sounds to have been the colonel's primary antagonist: "I offered to let him be the one to shoot me if he wanted to … I handed him my weapon in front of everyone, but he ran away without taking it." This is interesting because it sounds like a deliberate attempt to anger the American military brass, as opposed to simply making their alliance difficult with the South Vietnamese.

44 Nara Vija (*nom de guerre* of Nhuan Nguy) became a computer programmer for Unisys in the United States, then returned to Phan Rang, Vietnam, in his old age, dying there in 2024.

45 Po Dharma and Mak Phoen, *Du FLM à FULRO: Une Lutte des Minorités du Sud Indochinois 1955–1975* (Paris: Les Indes Savantes, 2006).

46 Nara Vija, interview with author, July 7, 2015. I am sure this is what he said, but it seems impossibly high. If true, it would have required many, many suitcases, even in large denomination bills. On the other hand, if he really meant "a half-million piastres," that would have been too small for one suitcase unless in small denomination bills amounting to as little as ~$5,000. We have to assume from Nara Vija's whole attitude that it was worth considerably more.

47 Meidine Natchear, interviews with author, February 4, 2011 onward to 2018. Later, Sihanouk began to actively worry about a coup against him.

48 It was either a contingency plan or entirely for show. Sen Tith heard it was attempted, but this seems unlikely because during this period Sihanouk still hoped to get international recognition

of his borders and was unlikely to have risked injuring his carefully constructed image as the aggrieved party in cross-border incidents.

49 Po Dharma and Mak Phoen, *Du FLM à* FULRO, 42.

50 His evaluator was one Colonel Offel de Villaucourt (author's collection).

51 Central Intelligence Agency, "Background leading up to the 18 March change of government in Cambodia," TDCS-DB-315/04151-70, August 14, 1970, 1–12.

52 Lon Non, younger brother of Lon Nol. The usual take on Lon Non was that he was a corrupt, hyperactive schemer, with a finger in every pie and wild ideas, the last of which was a colossally failed attempt to preempt the Khmer Rouge capture of Phnom Penh through fakery ("googleable" under Hem Keth Dara). Yet, after the press had looked away, he faced his end with dignity.

53 People lined the roads when he came home. His wife found it difficult to take showers because of ever-present crowds around the house when he was in residence.

54 Francis S. Sherry III, known CIA agent, Harvard graduate, born to a French mother and American father, began visiting Ban Me Thuot in 1957 under cover as a big-game hunter and is believably reported to have contacted Y-Bham Enuol and others, presumably encouraging their ethnonationalism. (*Du FLM* as well as the writings of General Vinh Loc).

55 Roger Faligot, Jean Guisnel, and Rémi Kauffer refer to him as "a choice recruit by the SDECE in the 1960s" (*Histoire Politique des Services Secrets Français* (Paris: Editions La Découverte, 2012), 326). My guess is he was contacted while at the Staff College in Paris in 1963. Terry White says that Kosem [and Um Savuth] were "double-agents, working for both the Cambodian secret service and the French SDECE" (*Swords of Lightning: Special Forces and the Changing Face of Warfare* (London: Brassey's, 1992), 143). I do not doubt these are true statements. However, my guess is "transactional, temporary source" would have been more accurate than "agent."

56 Both Barry Peterson (*Tiger Men: A Young Australian Soldier Among the Rhade Montagnards of Vietnam* (Bangkok: Orchid Press Publishing Ltd, 1994)) and François Demeure (*Memoires d'Avenir: La Fondation à Ban Me Thuot, Vietnam 1954–1975* (Paris: Bénédictines Missionaires de Vanves)) assume that the main French planters—actually Corsicans—were SDECE agents.

57 Article by Thanh-Thuong-Hoang in the Saigon daily *Tiếng Vang (Echo)* #224, September 30, 1964, quoted in FULRO's own handout, *HISTORIQUE,* distributed at the Indochina Peoples' Conference.

58 Jacques Dournes, *Minorities of Central Vietnam: Autochthonous Indochinese Peoples*, Report no. 18 (London: New Edition, Minority Rights Group, 1980). Dournes's primary purpose in writing this article four years *after* the communists' victory was—without any doubt—to take some of Hanoi's vengeful heat off the Montagnards, particularly his beloved Jarai. To that end, he blames FULRO's creation wholly on the French and its continuation on the Rhadé and Bahnar. To try to erase the idea that anti-Vietnamese ethnonationalism was a spontaneous Montagnard phenomenon, he disdains Dhon and other ethnonationalists as "gallicized [Natives]." Yet we know that at one time Dournes had supported FULRO. (Nay Rong, interview with author, August 15, 2013.)

59 Arthur J. Dommen, *The Indochinese Experience of the French and the Americans* (Bloomington: Indiana University Press, 2001), 580.

60 Chek Brahim, *Confession*, 4, 18; among others.

61 Frank Walker, *Tiger Man of Vietnam* (Sydney, Australia: Hachette, 2009), 113; and Peterson, *Tiger Men*, 92.

62 CIA Memorandum, *The Situation in Vietnam, 22 May*, Directorate of Intelligence, 1967. Describes a captured Viet Cong document, probably from 1965/early 1966, [that] states

FULRO is "a tool of US imperialism, with some French involvement," that its "external control is manifest in [its] anti-people's policy" [which can only mean anti-ethnic-Vietnamese policy], and thus that the [VC and NVA's] objective should be "the destruction of FULRO so that it can not be used to US advantage." Appended to this is a comment by the CIA itself that this analysis appears to be "the *least* accurate" of several other analyses made in the document, but does not elaborate. As late as February 1969, a captured document states the North Vietnamese Army's belief that "whether in Cambodia or back in Vietnam, FULROs are merely the faithful servants of the French and American imperialists who act against the revolutionary forces" (DOD Intell Info Rpt #6028268769, 11 May 69). The Khmer Rouge appear to have inherited this belief, with sometimes fatal results for FULRO partisans who took refuge in Cambodia before 1979. Colm and Sim, *Khmer Rouge Purges in the Mondul Kiri Highlands*, 112; and Henri Locard, "Jungle Heart of the Khmer Rouge," NIAS Monographs no. 157 (Copenhagen: University of Copenhagen, 2023), 273.

63 The two underlying beliefs here—that Montagnard enmity toward Vietnamese was created by colonialists and that it was obvious even in 1964 that the communists would win—were shared by many who were sympathetic to Hanoi. Most notable of these was the distinguished anthropologist, Oscar Salemink (*The Ethnography of Vietnam's Central Highlanders* (Honolulu: University of Hawai'i Press, 2003), 255. That said, thoughts about future resistance of course must have crossed some minds.

CHAPTER 12

Leaving Asia

By 2015, it was time for us to move on from Cambodia. Among other things, my children needed American schooling. I found a job in Brooklyn, and my family packed out.

I had two stops to make first, in Saigon and Cheo Reo.

Last Stand

Bhan had told me once about being attacked by "the VC" and sent running, but he was vague on context, and we never did pin it down. (From him, "VC" could mean either Khmer Rouge, Viet Cong, or North Vietnamese.) I assumed it was a skirmish in Mondulkiri, either with the Viet Cong or with the North Vietnamese Army (NVA). Sihanouk had made it clear to the Vietnamese communists that they were his guests and should give FULRO a wide berth, but firefights occurred when FULRO troops crossed NVA Base Area 740 to get to Vietnam.[1] The North Vietnamese then had no qualms about shooting at the people they referred to as "armed bandits."

With time, however, I met three other people who had been in the same encounter as Bhan and got an entirely different picture.

It happened over two nights, May 6–7, 1970.

Seven weeks previously, on March 18, Prince Sihanouk had been deposed by a group of Army officers and civilian leaders fed up with his allowing the Vietnamese to occupy eastern Cambodia. This was immediately labelled a right-wing coup, and it was assumed, incorrectly, to be the work of the CIA. Cambodia—now called the Khmer Republic—was suddenly in America's camp and an ally of South Vietnam. This neutered FULRO and made Cambodia less safe as a sanctuary for the VC and NVA. It also shut off the communists' access to arms and supplies via Sihanoukville.

The NVA immediately started moving west, deeper into Cambodia, to position itself to take Phnom Penh. It also began rolling up small Cambodian outposts in the border provinces of Rattanakiri and Mondulkiri. Among the latter was Sem Monorom, guarded by a platoon of Cambodians, but it was also FULRO headquarters, and the area had become literal home for about 250 FULRO troops, 200 Montagnards and 50 Cham, including wives and some children. Anticipating difficulty taking it, the NVA began digging zig-zag trenches in early April to approach it.[2] (Sem Monorom was relatively bare; perhaps the numerically superior NVA could not mass for fear of American bombing.)[3]

In response to NVA movements, Vietnamese and American units crossed into Cambodia on April 29 and May 1 in what came to be called the "Cambodian Incursion" (more accurate than "Invasion," at least literally, because penetration was limited to 30 kilometers/19 miles). Neither crossing was close enough to Sem Monorom to be of help. FULRO was on its own.

Kosem sent a C-46 to evacuate wives and children. Another was due the next day, but the NVA took the airfield.

FULRO withdrew to a low double-humped mountain just north of town,[4] where they set up at the top of a gradual slope with their backs to a cliff, FULRO in front because they had Claymores and good weapons, Cambodians in the rear as reserve. On the first night, they fought the North Vietnamese off. On the second night, the enemy somehow came from behind, the Cambodian platoon disappeared, and FULRO only barely beat the NVA back. They decided to evade at first light, breaking into small groups, with a designated rendezvous point short of the Mekong, some 85 miles away. They keyed on a big trail heading northwest, hoping the enemy would assume they had gone southwest toward Phnom Penh.[5]

Traveling overland at night on trails, they had to dodge North Vietnamese who themselves were on the move away from the Americans. But their more pressing problem soon became hunger. Because the NVA made a habit of sleeping in the homes of peasants, the sparse settlements they encountered represented danger; they could not ask locals for food. They began to starve, and their memories today focus on food. This was the stretch labelled "SOLITUDE and DESERT, without water, without anything of life" on 19th-century maps.

After several days, they all met up again at the rendezvous point, then turned south, moving in one larger group of both Montagnards and Chams.

One night, someone shot a wild buffalo, but then they saw the lights of approaching trucks and had to scatter. The next morning, some Cham inadvisedly went back for the meat and were next seen, hands bound, standing in a truck being driven away. At another point they were tempted to rob a peasant's food cart, but, after disagreement, desisted. Last, they encountered a Cambodian who offered to take them to food. It turned out to be a trap, and several more men, all Cham, were killed before everyone could plunge back into the forest.

After 14 days, they heard the sound of American .50-caliber machine guns on personnel carriers. To get the Americans' attention, they had to go up to one and pound on its side.

Hearing this, my impression was that this was one more sad case of Montagnards being overmatched, crushed in the gleaming coils of history. In my mind, I saw it as the The Rout.

However, there was one more person to interview who had participated. Intriguingly, it was a woman. Evidently someone who elicited strong emotions, she had once been an object of romantic desire but was now the target of political anger.

Hannafiah

She had been the only female Cham with FULRO in the Cambodian forest, drawn from coastal Vietnam to Mondulkiri like the young men politicized in high school in the mid-1960s. At FULRO headquarters in Sem Monorom, two young leaders fell in love with her and had to be prevented from killing each other by Kosem. She eventually married the intellectual instead of the man of action,[6] had two children with him and moved to France with him—where he committed suicide, depressed by FULRO's fading fortunes after 1970.

She had returned from France with her toddlers to Saigon before the communist victory in 1975. Word among the Cham diaspora—and its preeminent figure, Po Dharma[7]—was that, after the communist victory, she at best made accommodations with the victors, at worst embraced them, based on her clearly having been the source of details in the scurrilous book mentioned previously (note 17, p. 39), published in Hanoi after the war to discredit FULRO.[8]

She eventually married again, to a Cham poet of some renown. When I visited their one-room apartment, he retreated behind a curtain where he occasionally shouted translations of a Vietnamese word to English. I knew from old photographs that she had been pretty but not drop-dead beautiful, thus expected some other kind of fire. At first, she banked it. However, over the next six hours, with her 40-year-old son translating, she revealed a sharp intelligence, and I realized how extraordinary it had been for a Cham woman of her time to be passionately political.

She considered Kosem "a wonderful man" (though I never met a Cham who did not).

From a unique perspective, she remembered Y-Bham Enuol as a "gentleman"—from dancing with him on homespun musical evenings at Sem Monorom headquarters.

On May 5, 1970, she had refused evacuation by C-46 airplane with the other women.

On the 6th, the first night, she endured an eternity of explosions and bullets fizzing overhead as she crouched in a waist-high foxhole. The next day, she went out to get water and saw "a lot" of North Vietnamese dead. With horror, she spied one body being eviscerated. Later, one of the young Cham men thrust a piece of liver in her face. When she recoiled, he taunted, "So, you like the Vietnamese?"

The next night, the attack was even stronger, barely repulsed by 3:00 am. The leaders decided they could not withstand a third assault, so everyone escaped, initially in two groups, Cham in one, Montagnards in the other, until rejoining several days later. They had little to eat but did get some food by fishing, and at one point she was able to get rice and chicken by bartering her jewelry.

During the second part, while heading south where they hoped to meet the invading Americans, food became an increasingly desperate matter, which led to a series of incidents. First was the wild buffalo. She claimed Po Dharma ordered it shot, but I had heard other versions and doubted this. In any case, 12 Cham were taken away as a result and never seen again.

Next, there was the incident involving a cart with food belonging to local farmers, which Po Dharma advocated taking at gunpoint, but a Montagnard said no because doing so would alienate the local people.

Finally, they encountered a peasant who promised to take them to food. Both Chams and Montagnards were following him when, at the last moment, the same Montagnard leader spotted the trap in time for everyone to scatter. They ran a long way through the forest. When they regrouped, her feet were bloody. Nine Cham soldiers were captured. Three of them escaped two days later, but the others were executed.

There was an obvious drumbeat to her *ad hominem* accusations against Po Dharma. She was open about hating him (presumably he had been chief judge and accuser against her in the Cham diaspora). On the other hand, 18 Cham died, while no Montagnards did (corroborated by other versions).

I asked who the Montagnard leader was. She could only recall that he was "someone who knew the forest well," because she had not been very conscious of the Montagnards as a group.

However, a little later she came up with it: 'His name was Pa-Tuh. We were all lucky he was there."

This was Kpa Doh. She cannot have guessed that I was interested in him.

***

I took two things away from all this.

First, that it was a lot more than a rout, a lot more than simply one more example of the Montagnards' and Chams' relative weakness as history left them behind.

It was FULRO's Last Stand and the last stand of an alliance between Montagnards and Chams against the Vietnamese that had lasted, off and on, for 800 years, since the 12th century.[9]

(Though its participants would fight again later against the NVA as members of the Khmer Republican Army, the Chams and Montagnards would do so in separate units, in different areas—no longer side by side.)

They were literally fighting a final battle against the *Nam tiến* (southward expansion by the Vietnamese out of the Red River Delta) that began in the 11th century. It is usually dated as ending in 1834 when the last Cham polity, Panduranga (Phan Rang), fell to Vietnamese rule; however, in 1886, there was a significant Cham uprising against the Vietnamese, and now, 84 years later, FULRO had risen up one last time against Hanoi's final erasure of Champa.

It also confirmed Kpa Doh's skills as a survivor, raising the question again as to whether he might have survived the Khmer Rouge. Given his Ulyssean wiles and luck, he and/or his family seemed the most likely of all the FULRO Montagnards at the embassy to have done so. The Cham connection, particularly, might have been a way out.[10] He was the sole FULRO leader whom I could see as white-haired president of a small, land-locked Asian nation, not because of any preternatural brilliance, but because he seemed more capable of growth than the others, more curious, more independent. In the early Republic years, he had become factotum to Um Savuth, the Republic's best general, a step up that suggested he was growing beyond and outside of FULRO. (This was cut short, however, when Savuth died in a jeep accident in 1972.)

***

Sometime in the latter 1980s, a Rhadé nurse, working for Doctors Without Borders at a refugee camp just inside the Thai border, was making idle conversation with a wounded combatant/refugee from one of the five armies fighting for control of Cambodia at that time, when the wounded man mentioned a Jarai battalion commander killed sometime before who was not in the Khmer Rouge faction. (This made it more likely the commander was a Jarai from Vietnam, not Cambodia.)

The nurse, who had been with FULRO, believed he was hearing about Kpa Doh.[11]

If it was Kpa Doh, he was on Hanoi's wanted list, thus could not have returned to Vietnam. He could not have entered Thailand either, because the Thais forced refugees like him to stay in Cambodia and fight on behalf of one of the factions that Thailand favored. The Thais did exactly that to other Montagnards escaping across Cambodia.[12]

I could not imagine his agreeing to fight for anyone until I realized that maybe he had lost his wife and children.

The possibility of his surviving was practically nonexistent. However, there was a way to be sure. His relatives would have heard by now—somehow—if he had done so.

I needed to stop by Cheo Reo anyway on my way home, driving from Pleiku to the coast in order to view the actual terrain, as opposed to topographical maps. Was the Cheo Reo Valley truly different ecologically from the plateau, and was the Song Ba Valley truly the best route to the highlands? I was particularly interested to see how hard it was to climb up the escarpment onto the plateau.

I had seen the escarpment once before, but only in a flash passing over it by helicopter. It was 1973 and I had just come from Phnom Penh, where Kpa Doh had told me he was born beneath a volcano. Suddenly, there the volcano was, ahead, an unmistakable cinder cone in the distance, the single-most striking feature in a broad, flat valley, across the river from Cheo Reo town. That night I waded the river, longhouses looming ahead like barns under the stars, and awoke the next morning to the astonishing sight of a hamlet with no sandbags or foxholes, and longhouses with thick, gray-thatch roofs decades old, meaning that no VC had ever fortified the hamlet, no GIs like me had ever come with cigarette lighters.

Cheo Reo had been cradle to a number of high-ranking communist Montagnards, which suggests there had been at least a unilateral effort to protect it on the communists' part.

***

The cone is known as Chu Mo, meaning "wife mountain" in Jarai.[13] "Husband mountain" is said to be about halfway down the Song Ba Valley to the coast (Song Ba is the Vietnamese name now for the river the Jarai called A/Pa).

The names are all we know now of a long-ago battle by Chams against the Vietnamese, in which the Chams were retreating up the valley and the Cham king sent his wife on ahead to safety in Cheo Reo.

Today, the valley is largely populated by the Jarai Hroi, whose dialect is even closer to Cham than that of the Cheo Reo Jarai. That their stilt houses continue all the way down to about 40 kilometers (25 miles) of the coast validates the idea this was a major route for the Cham to and from the highlands.

The Cheo Reo Jarai, unlike their brethren on the plateau, must have been quite aware of their Cham heritage.

Kpa Doh was known to say he was Cham.[14] Some of that may have been political smoke (the person who told me this was Cham), but I suspect he meant it.

The strength of his cultural identity—plus chance, plus personality—may explain why he did not choose Communism like some of his contemporaries, even though he had the right background. ("Very poor—and despised by other Montagnards" were his exact words.) He was the classic talent-ed-but-very-marginal individual who could have gone either way at a time when traditional culture was crumbling. If he had not won a scholarship to the Lycée Yersin, he probably would have chosen Communism.[15] Instead, he met Dhon and felt the sting of racist epithets, thus chose militant ethnonationalism.

In either case, militancy would have been part of the appeal.

***

As expected, the Cheo Reo Valley was mostly scrub vegetation and the climb out manageable (40-stories up but not so steep). But the plateau above was unexpectedly bare, meaning my argument about colonization might need tweaking. Then I realized that the Chams—to guard against the attack from the west, from above—*had to have a military outpost on the plateau.* That Pleiku's "prairie" extended to the valley's rim made it that much more possible to maintain one, and that a tendril of the Ayun snakes within three kilometers of the temple probably clinched it for them. While a permanent outpost-plus-temple might meet some definitions of "colonization," it is hard to imagine the Jarai—a people who hunted over this territory on horseback by moonlight with crossbows—feeling dominated.

***

I found Kpa Doh's 90-year-old older sister, H'niam,[16] living in a stilt house, though one closer to the ground than the custom long ago. Its walls were of gray boards, its roof tin (not thatch), and it was too close to others like it—as though a capitalist developer had maximized his profit—but I knew that some of these changes had once functioned, on purpose, to lessen obvious disparity in wealth and to weaken the Jarai matriarchy. However, some were simply modern reality, as in nobody had an elephant anymore to lug in big logs for pilings. On balance, the changes must have benefitted poor families like Kpa Doh's.

She was a big woman in a long skirt and shawl, who received me sitting on her dusty floor. She never smiled. There was no warmth in her memories of him, but she had been 13 years older.

He was *mất tích* (lost, missing). Never heard from.

She knew his end had come in Cambodia. At first, I took hope from that, then realized he must have come back to Cheo Reo in the early 1970s and told people where he was.

Did she have any personal memories of him?

Not really, because he had left home at age 10. On his own, he had decided.

He had walked 100 kilometers (60 miles) to Pleiku. He wanted to become a teacher.

I asked again to make sure I had heard right—yes, age 10.

And that was it.

To say goodbye, she refused help getting up, crawled away to hide her struggle for a foothold, scrabbled again and again, lurched, then finally rose.

A small crowd was waiting outside. Knowing more questions would occur to me later, I pulled out my pen and notebook, asking if anyone would give me their mailing address. A young woman pulled out her smartphone and asked my email. Hers was Gmail, mine was still AOL.

A final surprise was learning Kpa Doh had had another child with another woman, a son who was still alive in one of the highland cities, but no one knew his name. The main surprise, though, was that he was a veterinarian.

Getting a professional degree had been highly unusual before, for a Montagnard, especially one who was poor.

Notes

1 Kok Ksor, interviews with author over the span of 16 years, from 2002–2018 (Kok died in 2019), and Sen Tith, interview with author, February 3, 2014.

2 The main camp, PC2, had been near Buon Bu Dreng, about an hour's walk. Everyone must have withdrawn from there to the town. There had also been a camp at Bu Sra (PC3), much closer to Vietnam, largely so that wives could cross back and forth. This no doubt had shut down even earlier.

3 Po Dharma, interview with author, July 1, 2014.

4 Photographs of this low mountain can be googled, under "Sen Monorom," then find "Hilltop View" north of the town.

5 This is a composite tale from four sources: Puih H'loanh, interview with author, December 29, 2015; Po Dharma, July 1, 2014; Kok Ksor, from 2002–2022. Also, Bhan (interviews with author), who was at Sem Monorom, too, but at a different location, stuck in the town itself. When it was surrounded, he and some others escaped out a ravine at daybreak. They headed west, too, but, being slower than the main group, were blocked by rising rivers. Starving, he and his companions eventually turned around and went all the way back through a now-deserted Sem Monorom to a border camp in Vietnam, where he was recognized and arrested. The South Vietnamese helicoptered him to Ban Me Thuot and kept him blindfolded in a Conex container for eight days. His mother came to see him but was sent away. The CIA came to ask him questions about FULRO in Phnom Penh. When released after 1–2 months, he needed money to make it back to Cambodia and thought he might get it from his wife's family because he still owned 25 cows in their keep. He asked them to sell one but—now understandably disenchanted with their son-in-law—they refused, "If she comes here, we'll do it." So, he spent the next two weeks catching fish by leaving many rods overnight at the river's edge. He then bought a plane ticket to Saigon and, with the help of Chams, crossed the border the way you do it today, by bus to Phnom Penh.

6 The intellectual was Yang Neh. The man of action was Jaya Marang, who joined the resistance after 1975 against the new government, was eventually caught and died in prison.

7 Po Dharma went on to fight against the North Vietnamese as an officer in the Cham Battalion (5th BIS) in 1970–71, was badly wounded, and was eventually sent to France by Kosem to get a PhD.

8 *FULRO: A Criminal Organization* (Ngon Vinh, 1983, HCM City). One neutral observer says Hanafiah earned the enmity in which she was held; among other things she bad-mouthed a longtime friend of the Chams, French priest Father Moussay, who had given her considerable help.

9 Po Dharma, "Le FULRO: Moment de l'Histoire" (1993), p 273

10 Kosem had investigated Koh Kong Island, off the coast on the Thai border, as a possible site for resettling Chams, apparently on the model of Taiwan as a refuge for Chinese Nationalists in 1949. Pailin, on the Thai border, was also discussed, though it was probably unreachable by 1975. Steve Heder, interview with author, September 22, 2013.

11 Y-Tlur Eban got this from the Rhadé nurse, Y-Yok Ayun. Y-Tlur and one other also heard about this Jarai from a Cambodian officer high up in Son Sann's faction (the FNLPK), presumably the faction for which Kpa Doh fought.

12 The story of FULRO after 1975 is literally a whole, other story. In 1992, a group of Montagnards who had escaped Vietnam emerged from the forests of Cambodia. Announcing they were FULRO, they asked if Y-Bham Enuol were still alive, unaware that he had been executed 17 years before by the Khmer Rouge (Nate Thayer, "Montagnard Army Seeks U.N. Help," *Phnom Penh Post*, September 12, 1992). They had gone into the jungle after Hanoi's victory in 1975 to continue their fight. Instead, they found themselves mostly on the run. Their enemies knew the terrain from 30 years as guerillas themselves, plus the Montagnards lacked what the North Vietnamese had enjoyed—sanctuary in Cambodia and support from outside powers. Prior to the fall of the Khmer Rouge in 1979, it was usually fatal for FULRO to seek sanctuary there. After 1979 they could cross the border, but then Hanoi's troops could, also; gradually the Montagnards ran out of ammunition. At one particularly bitter moment following a Vietnamese sweep, survivors could not spare bullets to drive off tigers feasting on

their dead. (Y-Hin Nie, interview with author, July 4, 2020). A small number escaped across Cambodia to the Thai border where they were held up for *six years* by "Great Power" politics, reaching the United States only in 1986 (Y-Tlur Thomas Eban, interviews with author, 2009 onward). The rest remained behind in the highlands, where Hanoi's grip tightened to the point the only resistance available to them was increasingly fervent Christianity. In 1992, despite their travails—which could largely be laid at America's doorstep—the American Embassy balked at accepting them as refugees. Angry ex-Green Berets flew to Cambodia to intercede, brandishing a copy of the minutes of a 1975 meeting at the US Embassy in Saigon in which Montagnard leaders had asked what to tell their million-plus people to do when the government fell and specifically what to say to individuals who might be marked for elimination by the communists (one questioner's father had already been executed). The embassy official stalled, saying he needed time to carefully consider their questions, then never gave them an answer. In part due to this document, they were finally admitted to the US in 1993. The document was "Memorandum of Conversation April 4, 1975." Pierre K'Briuh, (interviews with author) participated in 1992 in convincing the State Department to do the right thing.

13 It has always been considered sacred. Children are told to protect themselves, if they get close, by stooping to get a finger of dirt and writing their name on a knee (Hip Ksor, interview with author, August 15, 2013). In the 1930s, when the Cham temple near Cheo Ro was being dismantled by the French to build a guardhouse, the Jarai salvaged the statue of an elephant, the size of a dog, and buried it on the slopes of Chu Mo, thereafter holding secret ceremonies at the site.

14 Nara Vija, interview with author, April 15, 2015.

15 In Guatemala, where I worked in the 1990s, the same kind of marginal but mentally lively individual would have been torn between Communism and evangelical Protestantism, but the latter was late in reaching Montagnards compared to the Maya, plus Kpa Doh's personality was decidedly secular. (See Sheldon Annis's great book, *God and Production in a Guatemalan Town*.)

16 Kpa H'mian, interview with author, July 6, 2015.

CHAPTER 13

The Trove

In 2017, I published an op-ed in *The New York Times* about FULRO as part of the newspaper's Vietnam War 50th Anniversary series.[1] The next year, I sent it on to Madame Kosem via one of her daughters, one of the little girls I had seen playing in the dirt in 1973, now a statuesque woman of the world with dry humor, a British accent, and American ways from four years at Cornell. Months later, she reported back that her mother was about to donate a long-rumored trove of Kosem's papers to the Documentation Center of Cambodia but that I was invited to come have a look first. I jumped at the chance and, anticipating frantic photocopying, took along my now-teenage children.

Documents and photographs were bundled into two, dusty extra-large suitcases,[2] the kind people use when they emigrate. Only one out of many folders was labeled "FULRO," and it was missing a good number of sequential documents.[3] Two folders were labeled "VC/NVA/PRG"[4] but contained nothing—unclear if meaningful because Kosem was in the habit of re-using folders. The suitcases had been in Australia, which echoed another of Kosem's habits, storing documents outside Cambodia. By their dates, the papers had left Cambodia sometime in 1974 but, according to Kosem's wife, this habit began during the 1966–70 period of running arms when he suspected Sihanouk might one day disclaim knowledge of the traffic, leaving him holding the bag—so he documented everything, then periodically sent the records to Malaysia.

Most of the papers in the suitcases were in French, the official language of both FULRO and the Cambodian Government/military. They are all now in the Documentation Center of Cambodia Library, most likely catalogued. However, because I saw them before that, I refer to them here by their titles or headings.

They range from Kosem's 1950s service records through to some personal correspondence in 1976 before his death. The ones that concern us here are mostly from late 1964, all of 1965, and early 1966.

Here I should mention one written at the very end, by Y-Bham Enuol to Kosem on March 20, 1975, less than a month before the fall of Phnom Penh and his own death. He is asking Kosem to tell Kpa Doh not to put him and his family on the list of families hoping to leave the country because he had decided "to stay in Phnom Penh whatever happens."

May–September 1964

A small number of notebook pages, stapled together, are in Kosem's handwriting, difficult to read. One page is dated May 1964—four months *before* the First Rebellion, thus of considerable interest. Initially, only fragments of ideas are legible, like rocks jutting up from surf. After decoding some of his stenographic symbols, I could make out mentions of minorities undergoing racial awakening, gaining autonomy, then gathering into confederations—which sounds like the result of research into which political structure would be best for an alliance between minority groups (ancient Champa was itself a confederation). There are mentions of creating a political front of Cham in Thailand, Laos, and Vietnam (the extent of ancient Champa), then getting recognition from the embassies of the USSR and China, which could then be used as propaganda. "Material aid might follow." Excluding the US appears meaningful but probably was not; at the time, there was no longer an American Embassy in Phnom Penh.[5]

More intriguingly, there are mentions of the Americans' training and recruiting ethnic minorities as soldiers in South Vietnam [a reference to the CIDG program], with the comment, "The situation is evolving favorably. The future is ours. The recruitment … is *valable* [valid, significant, meaningful]." Another quote seems to say that FULRO Montagnards were being inserted as interpreters into the CIDG (*nous les nommons interprets en quoi [que] c'est possible*), which corresponds with the fact that all five of Bajaraka's leaders released from jail in August 1962 had become interpreters at Special Forces camps.

Kosem's own name pops up twice along with 2–3 others, which was puzzling until I realized these were the minutes of meeting(s). He is noting his own comments, as well as others.' Someone else besides him was commenting on American recruitment of Montagnards, thus this particular batch of papers might be Kosem's memento of what he was being told to do, possibly by Lon Nol or his brother, Lon Non. If so, this implies that the papers in the two suitcases may have been selected by Kosem with an eye to history.

***

There are several versions of FULRO's September manifesto, the one read by Dhon to the Green Berets by lamplight.

Their principal author is clearly Dhon.

Only a Montagnard would express horror at assimilation, repeatedly insisting on never turning into Vietnamese. Only a Montagnard would feel compelled to protest that Montagnards are NOT savages—if they are backward, it is because of racial discrimination by the Vietnamese.

Dhon. (Photo courtesy of Meidine Natchear)

Its writing is good but not perfect. Kosem could not have written it because, in a second version, he corrects the French of the first.

No other Montagnard could have been the author.[6] It fits Dhon's character and background—the smartest boy in school, the most political, the one with the most social consciousness, the one who stood up arrogantly to the French governor at age 17. An angry document, its tone and worldview fit best with Dhon and what he wrote later. More than most of his peers, anger and idealism were fused in him, probably from the example of his father. His own progression had been from gentle reformer in the Legion of Marie, to earnest, would-be med student, to warrior. (Françoise the nun's last image of him—before the cage—was standing in a jeep with bandoliers of bullets over his shoulders.)

He was the most likely of his peers to have heard the growing worldwide call for liberation of minority peoples. Echoes of the 1948 Universal Declaration of Human Rights reverberate in the manifesto, with mentions of rights to peaceful assembly, to use native languages, and to social progress, plus freedom from arbitrary arrest. There are other echoes—the Vietnamese's "barbarous acts," rebellion as "a last resort," and FULRO's legitimacy deriving from "the will of the people." One can imagine Dhon reading the United Nations Charter over and over, especially its "principle of equal rights and self-determination of peoples," scribbling furiously in libraries at the lycée or the French Cultural Center in Dalat, inflamed by this revolutionary idea.

Like many ethnic minorities before and since, he interpreted "peoples" to mean "nations within nation states," and he saw the occupation of Montagnard lands by lowland Vietnamese as colonialism. He would not live long enough to learn that the international community, including Vietnam before and after 1975, defined "peoples" as nation states and "colonialism" as something imposed by white people from overseas.

He was the most likely to be aware of anticolonial successes after the French loss of Indochina, from the Bandung conference in 1955 that gathered Asian and African countries to support "unfinished struggles for liberation,"[7] to the Algerian rebels' brilliant declaration of independence in 1958,[8] to Castro's takeover of Cuba in 1959 under the very nose of the United States, especially exciting to those who favored armed struggle, which without question included Dhon. (Could he have read Frantz Fanon, published three years before, in 1961? One of the reasons he gives for FULRO's taking up arms is so that Montagnards become "aware that [they] are not an inferior race"—a possible echo of Fanon's prescription of violence as "a cleansing force … [that] rids the colonized of their inferiority complex, of their passive and despairing attitude."[9] To a certain kind of individual, of course, the idea is instinctively obvious: Kpa Doh described his near-constant brawls with his Vietnamese classmates as "*pour la dignité* (for dignity)." Even if Dhon did not read Fanon, the rebellion itself—FULRO's intentionally/excessively murderous opening act—was very much in Fanon's spirit.)

Exasperated by aged leaders unaware of the outside world, he assured his audience FULRO was in the hands of Montagnard youth, not elders—an emphasis peculiar to him and Paul.

The manifesto mocks American attempts to enlist FULRO in the anti-communist cause, saying Montagnards had no stake in that fight. This is a clear echo of the French view.

Yet his larger allegiance is clear: he talks of both camps of Vietnamese being the enemy. All evidence points to enmity toward the Vietnamese being his driving emotion, trumping any leftist sympathies or French influence. It is likely he and his friend and ex-teammate, Kpa Doh—his American-influenced stereoisomer—shared the same expectation and fear, that the North Vietnamese, if victorious, would be "even more Vietnamese"[10] than the South Vietnamese, harsher and more thorough in reaching the Marxist–Leninist goal of creating a single national identity, i.e., turning Montagnards into brown-skinned Vietnamese.

February–July 1965

In an information packet called "HISTORIQUE" that FULRO handed out at the Indochina Peoples' Conference in late February/early March 1965, there is a third version of the manifesto, which is angrily anti-American.[11] More clear, rhetorically more powerful, and further to the left than the first two manifestos, it cannot have been written by the same author as those. Though it is dated September 20, 1964, it was probably written after the first American bombing of North Vietnam in February 1965, then backdated.

Sometime during the conference, Y-Bham Enuol met with his old friend, Y-Bih Aleo, head of the Montagnard Viet Cong (MVC). It is said the two agreed they were Montagnards first, ideologues second. Y-Bham Enuol is quoted as saying, "Anyone who helps my people is my friend."[12] Both men had been politicized in the 1930s–1940s, much earlier than most Montagnards. In the small community at that time of Rhadé with some schooling, this must have been an extraordinary bond between them. Thus, when Y-Bham Enuol claimed in 1966 to de Gaulle's emissary that, if push came to shove, he could call on the aid of 10,000 Montagnard communists,[13] he was probably referring to his friendship with Y-Bih Aleo if not an explicit agreement.

***

Right after the First Rebellion, FULRO partisans in Mondulkiri consisted of only about 200–300 soldiers—largely Mnong, the rest Rhadé—who had crossed the border for refuge, plus a few wives who had preceded them. Over succeeding months, however, that number swelled into the thousands, including wives and even children, many drawn by Y-Bham Enuol's mystique.

Initially, Y-Bham Enuol was Kosem's guest but, with the growing numbers, his power grew and the balance shifted. By the end of the Indochina Peoples' Conference, he had reason to believe his name had appeared in newspapers all over the world. Kosem's ability to influence him through reason alone was gone, leaving Kosem few levers—the quality and amount of rations delivered to FULRO, plus personal perks like transportation (aircraft vs. truck).

It was one thing for Y-Bham Enuol to accept that Montagnards were "highland Cham," quite another to believe FULRO's goal should be to resurrect a long-dead kingdom of absurd extent (three-quarters of modern Vietnam). He was not a pie-in-the-sky dreamer. Instead, he thought in terms of what he could do to improve the lot of his people in Vietnam now, not in some distant future. Though this did not exclude aiming for autonomy or independence, Y-Bham Enuol was never as fiery about it as Dhon or Kosem.

The earliest FULRO documents are stamped "Liberation Front of Champa" but, in early 1965, this changes to "The Liberation Front of the High Plateaus and Plains of Champa" because the Montagnards had begun to grumble about the Chams ("Where's *their* territory?").[14] The addition of "High Plateaus" was to mollify them.

Kosem's quite reasonable argument to Y-Bham Enuol and other Montagnards was that they were ethnically related to Chams, and together they constituted an ethnic "nation," which gave legal justification to FULRO's irredentist aims and could garner international support. In addition, this "nation" had once been part of a nation-state—Champa, far older than the Vietnamese state—which would make FULRO's irredentist claims even more solid in the eyes of the world, better than trying to create a state *de novo*. Dhon seems to have been an early convert to this logic.

In March 1965, American Marines landed in Da Nang. The FULRO documents do not mention it, but the FULRO leaders must have begun to recalibrate their strategy.

Hoping for US support, Y-Bham Enuol wrote to the American ambassador, promising:

> … to chase the Vietnamese invaders (wherever they come from) out of [FULRO's] country … [Our] hope is for independence but, if not, some sort of arrangement under tutelage of the US and France because our people are not ready for self-governance, also not strong enough to fight off aggressive communist Vietnamese and Viet Cong.[15]

Overtly, the Americans discouraged this thinking, conscious of their alliance with Saigon, but, covertly, they certainly did not oppose it.[16] No one at this time, except the communist Vietnamese, could imagine the possibility of American defeat and eventual collapse of support for the Montagnards.

As noted earlier, Dhon and Y-Bham Enuol clashed personally in mid-March about their dress code while touring Cambodia. In April, Dhon sent an ominous and enigmatic letter to his old mentor, Father Roger Bianchetti, saying "I have a clear view now but am under surveillance."[17]

Meanwhile, Kosem and Dhon—the radicals, along with Paul—would have seen the Americans' arrival and Y-Bham Enuol's drift towards reformism as threatening their revolutionary goals. In May, they convened an extraordinary session of the High Committee of FULRO—on which sat both Dhon and Paul Y-Bun Sur—to pull him back into line. (On paper, the committee had authority over him.) They threw figurative ropes over him by getting him to agree to and sign a statement that:

> FULRO's purpose is the liberation of Champa. The citizens of our country are called *Champois*. FULRO has only one goal, independence.[18]

But the ropes proved Lilliputian.

***

The documents in Kosem's trove say little about FULRO's military actions.

There is no mention at all of actions during the first six months of 1965, perhaps because these were frank terrorism, hauling Vietnamese civilians down off of buses and trucks to murder them.

At the end of June, a document called "Preparations" appears, an operations-order for ten-day armed propaganda missions into areas of Darlac and Quang Duc Provinces that Saigon—under American pressure—was expected to turn over to FULRO in return for FULRO's keeping them clear of Viet Cong. These would be FULRO's "tactical zones" (TAORs in American military parlance, Tactical Areas of Operational Responsibility). It lists necessary supplies, training, etc., then enumerates enemy forces (ARVN units plus settlements of ex-soldiers). An undated document in Kosem's handwriting seems to compliment this by enumerating friendly forces in those provinces.[19] In Darlac alone there were 2,150 partisans by apparent careful count, *not* counting CIDG.

The armed-propaganda missions, sounding like a page torn from the Viet Cong playbook, were to leave photos of Y-Bham Enuol behind. This seems rather benign, but a CIA document from September suggests that these missions also kidnapped Vietnamese, with no mention of their fate.[20]

Though Saigon had not yet agreed to the "tactical zones," in July FULRO moved a small Mnong battalion into Quang Duc and two large Rhadé battalions into Darlac, one into the wedge between the Sre Pok River and the border, the other into an area up by Buon Brieng camp (see maps on pp. 4 and 16). The latter caused growing tension with the Vietnamese that ended abruptly in September with the sudden encirclement and capture of the battalion by Vietnamese Marines. Details on this episode are conflicting, perhaps because it was embarrassing to FULRO. Its import here is that Dhon attributed it indirectly to poor leadership by Y-Bham Enuol and that Montagnards in general came to believe that the captured soldiers had been "disappeared."[21]

August–October 1965

A document from early August makes clear how deep the political and personal rift has become. Addressed to Y-Bham Enuol from his would-be superiors, the High Committee, it indignantly announces having just learned that three FULRO companies—which should have dispersed into tactical zones —instead went to Ban Me Thuot in late July to meet with Vietnamese and American negotiators. Its tone is scolding:

> The High Committee wants to know if *Monsieur le Président* [meaning Y-Bham Enuol] gave these missions to our envoys.[22]

Of course, the High Committee knew full well that he had. Its schoolmasterly tone and sarcasm mark it as Dhon's. This incident was more significant than Dhon realized, and ominously so. It showed that several hundred FULRO soldiers were already so loyal to Y-Bham Enuol that they would/could completely disguise their intent from their immediate superiors, the respected colonels, Bhan and Y-Nam. This did not bode well for those two officers, and it boded far worse for Dhon.

In mid-September, in another attempt to reign in Y-Bham Enuol, Kosem invited him to a meeting in Phnom Penh of a group intended to be a sort of board of directors for FULRO, consisting of influential Chams and Cambodians, the latter mostly southerners from the Mekong Delta and notably including Lon Nol himself, Cambodia's Defenser Minister at the time. The group's name, the Association of Austrien Peoples, reflected Lon Nol's half-baked theory that Indochina's peoples—excluding the Thais and Vietnamese—were all related.[23] The meeting appears to have been aimed at impressing on Y-Bham Enuol the need for solidarity between Chams and Montagnards. After listening quietly, he gave a short, flowery speech thanking Lon Nol and the others for "reviving the great Austrien race."[24] (Y-Bham Enuol was not the kind of man one imagines as capable of sarcasm, but if he was, this was it.)

However, at that very moment, Y-Bham's representatives were *again* negotiating unilaterally with Saigon. The minutes of these meetings show the chief Montagnard negotiator to have been hat-in-hand while the two Vietnamese lieutenant colonels—insultingly low in rank—had been patronizing and officious.[25]

Someone—unnamed but had to be Dhon—could not contain himself about this. A scathing "Analysis" of those minutes soon appears, bursting with sarcastic disdain, with the following a sampling:

> Either [the main negotiator] had an inferiority complex or he truly intended to ask for LITTLE THINGS … [never demanding] THE SLIGHTEST PIECE OF ANCESTRAL LAND TO BE UNDER THE ABSOLUTE SOVEREIGNTY OF MONTAGNARDS THEMSELVES … Now, as Montagnards and Revolutionaries, would you accept these minor requests … these Trifles? If we accept them, the popular Montagnard masses will surely accuse us of Cowardice … [because their] True Desires are:

> Our Country,
> our Lands,
> our Government,
> our Flag,
> our Language—and
> Out with [our Vietnamese] PAINS IN THE ASS!
> If one is not a strong debater, it would be … better [for one] to simply shut up … When all the points are made, we should wait for our adversary's response, and if he asks us again, we should keep repeating … and not babble on about subjects that were not recommended by the High Committee …

Dhon's youthful eye for absurdity makes him mockingly imagine the Vietnamese responses to each of FULRO's five insignificant demands:

> Sure thing!
> It's done!
> We'll look into it.
> Yes, it's very likely we'll do that!
> Good idea—let's unite!

The last leads him to an exasperated:

> Why are we always talking about [uniting] with the South Vietnamese to fight against The Communists? [Does this mean] only the VIETCONG, or all the Communists of the Socialist Camp, making up the population of half the globe …

He is almost gleeful in his shredding of Y-Bham Enuol's representative. He seems modern, though adolescent. He is funny. He is likeable. And yet one cringes for him, picturing him as a little too enamored of his own cleverness, not conscious enough of the danger around him, a bit too disdainful of less-educated older men and the enemies he is making.

Sure enough, the next document in Kosem's trove is Dhon's resignation from the vice-presidency on October 9. At first, it looks like a "you-can't-fire-me-because-I-quit" statement, then he mentions his arrest. He is writing from a FULRO jail, typing it himself, in a state of high emotion.[26] One's picture of him shifts. He must have had some idea of the danger ahead. To assume otherwise robs him of credit for courage.

The document's first section is Dhon's account of squabbling with Y-Bham Enuol over prerogatives, which they followed with angry public insults. It seems embarrassingly petty except that it was deadly serious to Montagnards. Versions of this incident are what those in North Carolina remember today, as though the two had shed blood.[27] Dhon then moves into substantive criticism of Y-Bhan Enuol's leadership, ending with some ad hominem slashes.

Dhon makes no effort to deny the charge against him, whatever that is. Instead, he makes a case to FULRO's leadership that Y-Bham Enuol is an unfit leader, hoping it will result in the older man's removal.

In essence, he is doubling down, trying to overthrow Y-Bham Enuol by convincing a small number of fellow leaders of the older man's unfitness.

The following version is shortened by removal of some of its more awkward outbursts, as well as slightly rearranged and reworded for comprehensibility:

> Of my free will, I have the honor to present my resignation to the HIGH COMMITTEE of the Champa Liberation Front. Without doubt, this decision, after much thought, causes my heart great regret because I love my country; but the following reasons force me to this decision … which I am revealing only to the HIGH COMMITTEE.
>
> I was the Vice-President, certified and known throughout the world because of the Indochina People's Conference, but I have just been stripped of my function by an arrest …
>
> I am treated badly … I AM INSULTED … first by Y-Bham Enuol's wife [who accused] me of plotting against her husband two months ago, then just now by Y-Bham Enuol himself … in front of the soldiers, then forbidden to talk back to him. HE INSULTED MY PARENTS AND WHOLE FAMILY. Try to imagine who is most dishonored, he who does the insulting or he who is insulted.
>
> Y-Bham Enuol [and his right-hand-man] … are raising themselves personally to the heights of power … They are beginning to eliminate Brothers-in-arms and put friends in their place.
>
> They propose changing the Front's by-laws, [to shrink] the Directorate … to three people.
>
> Allow me to analyze this: One Brother, Kosem is considered nul because, ***according to [Y-Bham Enuol], "No foreigner can have any power"*** [author's emphasis]. Another Brother, Bhan, is a soldier who, without discussion, carries out orders. Thus, there remains only one person, Y-Bham Enuol. So, why not say that the Directorate consists of only one person? …
>
> [Y-Bham Enuol's right-hand-man][28] … guides Y-Bham Enuol more and more toward the abyss, and the latter will throw the people into the chasm without their even guessing it.
>
> I can no longer conform to the President's desires because he constantly changes his mind, and now he is changing his mind again [about FULRO's goal being the liberation of Champa, agreed to on May 13th] … I think that he did not give the matter enough thought before adopting it, or maybe he is still in a hallucinatory state … He does not realize that to ask for negotiations without [being] in a POSITION OF STRENGTH is to submit to the enemy. He does not call on the High Committee [to make important] decisions jointly … Decisions whether to send men to the front are decided [without deliberation].

Finally, unforgivably, Dhon blurts out his long-festering grudges:

> [In] meetings … one person talks endlessly/absurdly for hour after hour while the others are obliged to remain mute like poor listeners.

> [Remembering] the press conference after Indochina Peoples' Conference ... all the FULRO delegations were ridiculed because of the maladroit speech of Y-Bham Enuol ... He makes excuses here and makes excuses there but finally admits that he does not know how to express himself correctly in French.

These were Dhon's last recorded words. Kosem appended a short, handwritten note at the bottom:

> I noticed that even before the IPC [Indochina Peoples' Conference] there existed signs of division. The sense of division was clearly revealed after the IPC.
>
> I do not know how the Brothers see this.

The last sentence in the present tense was presumably written shortly after Dhon's resignation. It is surprising because it suggests that Kosem was much further from the inner workings of FULRO than one might think (though this fits with "No foreigner can have any power").

November 1965–February 1966

This was in early October. The heat turns up in early November. With Dhon in jail, Y-Bham Enuol appears increasingly confident in his power and in the rightness of his moderate stance. He begins signing letters to the outside world with "Front for the Liberation of the Dega-Cham," with "Dega" a Rhadé word for Montagnards. From Phnom Penh, Kosem confronts him, attacking him for reformism, i.e., trying only to improve the economic and political lot of Montagnards and Chams within South Vietnam, not confronting Saigon.

The documents in Kosem's trove are like one side in divorce proceedings. Y-Bham Enuol is not represented. One begins to think of him as obstinate and power hungry, forgetting that neutral observers saw him as a good man in an impossible position. (The only negative I ever heard was that he had "a terrible temper," illustrated by his raging at a private secretary for typing errors).[29] His moderate stance began looking much stronger by mid-November with the Battle of Ia Drang; the Americans were now clearly here to stay; if FULRO continued to espouse violence against Saigon, Americans would side with Saigon. As a pragmatist, Y-Bham Enuol had good reason for his moderation.[30]

Thus, the next document, from November 30, comes as an even bigger shock: Dhon has been condemned to death.[31]

The judgment lists a drum roll of decisions against him. First, the officers of the garrison met and condemned him to death, then the headquarters officers and officers of Battalion 64 did likewise, then the secretary of state. Next was Y-Nam (Bhan's great friend, fellow militant, and ally of Dhon's), weighing in as head of national security, with a slightly more clement recommendation than the others—that Dhon be held in prison until after National Liberation, lest he intrigue with "the Foreigners" (*de peur qu'il s'arrange, s'unisse avec les Etrangers*),[32] then "condemned according to the oath he took before the Revolutionary Flag."

However, the consensus judgment was death, "because [Dhon] committed grave errors."

Exactly what these errors were is murky. Mentions of "[violating] his Revolutionary Oath" and "abandoning the Revolution" could mean anything. The document's exact words are: "According to his letters, [Dhon] sought so many things, slandered in order to be able to overthrow the President." Because the phrase "sought so many things" is slangy in French and can be translated as "looked for (into?) so much stuff," his main "error" appears to have been conspiring against Y-Bham Enuol, evidence for which had been found in letters. In turn, this fits with a story that a letter from Paul in France to Dhon had been mis-delivered to a man named Dhun, who happened to be Y-Bham Enuol's loyal private secretary.[33] Despite sounding like *The Princess of Cleves*, this has the ring of truth.

And what about Bhan? What judgment did he deliver, as chief of staff, against Dhon, his old friend and fellow militant?

> [Prison] in perpetuity because [he is a] <u>criminal</u>.

At best, one can imagine that both he and Y-Nam were hoping/expecting that passions would cool with time.

It is possible, of course, that all the legalistic arguments were window-dressing, that Y-Bham Enuol ordered Dhon's execution because it looked truly necessary to him, either for reasons of discipline in an army constantly threatened by anarchy, or because he truly believed that Dhon's way would lead to destruction of the Montagnard people. (It has been argued FULRO's militancy did just that.)[34]

I learned more about Dhon's death from Montagnards in North Carolina, triangulating among their hearsay accounts. It probably happened in early February 1966. Dhon was kept for days, even weeks, in a pit dug in the forest floor (a common form of temporary "jail"), possibly buried to his chest for an unknown period, then taken in his weakened state toward Vietnam, which would conform with "moving him elsewhere, to the Front." This meant crossing the turbulent Dak Dam River where, in his weakened state, he drowned.

Bhan's hearsay account of what happened used the phrase "stepped on," clearly suggesting Dhon was helped to drown. This strange delicacy/formality in choice of words may simply be Bhan's limited vocabulary in English, except that the entire November 30 document has a similar feel.

One can wonder if there were a parallel formality – almost ritualistic – in how Dhon finally died, maybe some connection with trials by water, to avoid committing outright murder.

***

The next official FULRO document in the trove feels like someone shaking off a confidence-draining nightmare. Probably written after Dhon's death, it is looking back at the recent Second Rebellion in December.[35]

The FULRO leadership is now split into two factions, a small group of militants and a much larger group of Y-Bham Enuol's followers, reflected spatially when Bhan and Y-Nam moved into their own small base camp in February.[36]

The document has been produced by the militant faction and is copied to "Patriot Paul Y-Bun Sur," who is in France. (If the moderate faction ever produced any documents, they are not in the Les Kosem trove.)

Its first shock is a claim that Y-Bham Enuol betrayed the Second Rebellion. Allegedly, FULRO forces never attacked Ban Me Thuot because Y-Bham Enuol's representative there, on receiving "a counter order from [Y-Bham Enuol]," tipped off the Vietnamese. Likewise, the Vietnamese in Pleiku were tipped off by the same man "five minutes before [the Prime Minister's plane landed]." (In reality, the Vietnamese in Pleiku had known about the rebellion for at least 24 hours.) Thus

> the patriotic group … Colonels [Bhan] and Y-Nam, plus top civilians [and] political commissars—noting that the President (Y-Bham Enuol] has no respect for the principles of Revolutionary Law, has decided to create a separate military force in order to continue the struggle, [given] the political and military failure of the faction led by the President.

This all-new version of FULRO is declaring itself to be a provisional government (echoes of the Viet Cong and Algeria's FLN) and thus will be establishing a shadow government down to commune level.

Then it lists FULRO's military forces, most of them supposedly stationed within Vietnam. Ten "battalions" of regulars from FULRO's army are identified by location, presumably in so-called tactical zones. As to the CIDG, the document says, simply: "*à nous*," meaning "ours," which echoes one leader's boast, "Any camp where there are Montagnards, these are our troops."[37] (Of course they are exaggerating, but even if their numbers were half what they claimed, the overall picture—including Kosem's count of irregular forces (see note 19, p. 230) is astonishing. FULRO's numbers were much greater than outsiders knew.)

Finally, it says that "liaison [between headquarters, probably a reference to Cambodia, and the tactical zones] will be supported by the Americans ... with transport by helicopter or vehicle." At first surprising, this actually makes sense. The Americans are hoping that FULRO, now occupying its tactical zones, will keep them clear of Viet Cong.[38]

What does *not* make sense, after this optimistic and chest-thumping document, is that FULRO's army apparently never mounted another significant military operation again, at least not on its own behalf. (Indirectly, its partisans continued to see a great deal of combat against VC and NVA as CIDG).

What happened to the idea of clearing the tactical zones of Viet Cong? Starting in early 1966, both Kosem's trove and *Du FLM au FULRO* (based on documents from Kosem) make no mention of any military action. Instead, they talk only of politics—antagonisms and negotiations, either between Kosem and Y-Bham Enuol, or between FULRO and Saigon. Likewise, the three men I interviewed in depth[39] who would have done the fighting against the VC or NVA never mentioned doing so except as accidental skirmishes within Cambodia. Their only actions within Vietnam itself had been a few raiding parties against South Vietnamese military. In other words, FULRO's own army—as opposed to its troops within the CIDG—appears never to have intentionally engaged in battle against the communists.

One possible explanation is that Saigon never accepted the American idea of tactical zones for FULRO.

Another possibility is that the French, pulling strings through Kosem, sabotaged the idea.

A third explanation is that FULRO never rediscovered its fighting spirit, sapped by the clash between militants and moderates, with fault lines that could only grow in a hothouse atmosphere of living cheek-to-jowl with thousands of strangers—men, women, and children—in the forest for prolonged periods, without custom to regulate behavior, often with nothing to do, That many of them were armed did not help. Marital infidelity could be fatal.

On one side of a psychological divide were the younger, more educated, more modern Montagnards, sometimes Christian, on the other side those who were older, less educated, more traditional, and usually animist. By the end of the Second Rebellion, another fault line had appeared—the most insidious—between the Jarai (allied with the Cham) and the Rhadé.

Ironically, in April of 1966, some three thousand *more* Montagnards, men and women, crossed the border to join FULRO in Cambodia, motivated by Saigon's harsh measures in response to the Second Rebellion.

Bhan and his step-granddaughter with the author. (Photo by Alma Chickering)

It begins to come together

I finally understood why Bhan's accounts skipped the forest period: he had voted to condemn Dhon.

In 2018, after considerable gnashing of teeth, I carried the document "Condemnation and Judgments Against Dhon" with me on a visit to see Bhan. By now, he was an old friend, not a source I could ambush, so I left it with him, asking him to read it overnight.

The next morning, he handed me his reply, a written version of his usual, "O-o-o-o, I don't know about that"—"About condemn [Dhon] …, I do not see and hear anything," with an added comment, "All in this paper I do not know nothing. Maybe from Les Kosem."

He was 85 years old; it had been half a century. His putting it all off on Kosem was a false note but, by now, he may have believed it. If I wanted to know how such a strong individual as Bhan could turn against his old friend and comrade, Dhon, I would have to figure it out myself.

It was comforting that, of all the condemnations of Dhon, Bhan's was the least harsh—almost clement.

***

The papers in Kosem's trove say nothing about Dhon's execution, much less its ugly details.

Even the old men in North Carolina—those who were there, in the forest—are silent on this subject. FULRO was as rigidly hierarchical as any 19th-century army, so they may have been too young and low-ranking to know what was going on higher up, or they simply do not wish to exhume passions long dead. They are all supporters of Y-Bham Enuol, selected by Fate to survive because they trekked back to Vietnam after he was deposed in 1968 (by contrast, Dhon's supporters stayed behind in Cambodia, thus died at the hands of the Khmer Rouge).

As to the details, Bhan and Paul had both mentioned burial to the chest. I was wondering if this were something fabricated for some obscure purpose, until I spoke with Françoise, the nun. Though she had known Dhon well, she had less to tell me about him than Paul. I sensed she was holding something back, so I probed.

"I saw a photo," she said.

"I had to look hard to see what it was … It was Dhon, *accroupi* (squatting) or very hunched. He was under a cage, in a forest. They told me he had been left like that for a long time before being *achevé* (finished off) by pistol."

Squatting, or buried? She had looked away so fast she could not tell.

The mind scurries to escape but keeps coming back to the question why they killed him that way, first burying him to his chest, then "stamping" him down in a river. Burial to the neck is a leitmotif in Southeast Asian legends,[40] a particularly terrible form of execution. But this was drawn out on purpose (depending on who you believe, "days" to "weeks").

So, the first puzzle is—why did they use such horrid methods to execute him?

One Montagnard in North Carolina ascribes this simply to his people's inherent cruelty, pointing out that the Cham language has a single word for "dying slowly at someone's hand." But he is a strong Catholic and the light of his faith may be casting too dark a shadow here.

According to what Paul told me, the generally accepted view among Montagnards was that rage was responsible. A similar idea is that pure, personal hatred explains it. No question, Dhon could be haughty. His scathing criticism and ridicule must have made bitter enemies among men in Y-Bham Enuol's entourage, to say nothing of Y-Bham himself. But hatred or rage would seem to burn too hot for slow murder by posse. (From the accumulated answers I heard over the years, I got the impression that a group of men was involved, a detachment of some sort.)

It looks more as if they thought he was hiding something.

In that case, the likeliest explanation of his slow death is that it was torture. "Intriguing with foreigners" would have been high on his torturers' list, but which ones? Not the Montagnard VC because Y-Bham Enuol was in contact with them himself. Not the Americans, because Y-Bham Enuol's thinking was increasingly aligned with theirs. Not the Vietnamese because no one who knew Dhon well could even imagine it. But Y-Bham Enuol was likely very worried about the French. From the moment that he began shifting away from revolutionary goals, he had reason to be. Dhon was as close to the French as anyone (except Kosem). Perhaps Dhon *had* been under surveillance since April.

Dhon's torturers would have tried to find out what plots were afoot, and who might be his hidden accomplices *within* FULRO. (Maybe Y-Nam was one and mentioned "foreigners" to deflect attention from himself.)

Anything that reduced the influence of the French on FULRO, especially something that permanently removed Dhon, would have been in the interest of the United States. It is easy to imagine that the CIA did its best to stir up paranoia and rage. From that, it is no stretch to wonder if they wanted him killed.

***

The November 30 document condemning Dhon has a Jacobin feel to it. When read closely, it provides two more shocks. The first lies coiled amid the list of judgments against Dhon: "Y-Bun Sur, according to the revolutionary citizens, should come work at Headquarters … to meet with Brother citizens and work with them," with a sudden strike at the end, "Y-Bun Sur is a true traitor, should meet with the citizens." This is paired with "Death to [Dhon]."

By Western standards, Paul Y-Bun Sur had risen highest of all FULRO Montagnards and was en route to become the only Montagnard with a university degree from France. If he had a moral lightness to him, it was the flipside of a flexibility that enabled him to venture far and high into alien worlds.[41] In this regard, it is notable that he got on well with Vietnamese (see p. 120).

Paul Y-Bun Sur. (Photo courtesy of Meidine Natchear)

Looking back now at his brief 36 years, one can see he lost the necessary bedrock of self, his character eroded by too much too soon, too easily gained. The images that exist of him, as the cloudiness and cold close over his memory, are stained by his behavior toward women and neglect of his children.

But he deserves a better epitaph than "playboy, handsomely paid by the Americans" (penned by the French author of *The Gate*). For one, he had little or nothing to do with Americans. The money for his lifestyle in Paris—student housing/carousing, but not the Ritz—came from Lon Nol, Sihanouk's defense minister, during a period when Cambodia's policies closely tracked with those of France. Paul was being groomed to run a Montagnard country someday, and the French must have been sponsoring it financially, if indirectly. (Only 11 months later, de Gaulle made his famous trip to Phnom Penh, and his foreign minister met with Y-Bham Enuol.)

Later, during the five-year civil war funded entirely by America, when Lon Nol was president of the Republic, Paul no doubt got spillovers from the common trough, but—from my memory of the man and his bungalow—his sins seem to have been carnal, not pecuniary.

Before Paris, there were signs of substance to Paul—courage, seriousness of purpose, and concern for social justice.

We know he wrote speeches in Phnom Penh for the Indochina Peoples' Conference in late 1964. In early 1965, he wrote out his specific ideas for the government of the Montagnard country-to-be. These can be fairly abridged to:

> In case the Vietnamese government [can be] forced to give Sovereignty to the Montagnards, [our] first item of business will be the expulsion of all Vietnamese arrived in the Highlands since 1949–50 … but without brutality, with justice and humanism. Because all races [meaning Montagnard ethnic groups] will keep their own languages, laws, and customs, the official language will be French, with school taught half in French for the first five years, wholly thereafter. After an artisanal stage, the economy will be agricultural but will need foreign aid, to be sought (*in order*) from France, Cambodia, Japan, and America. Profiteers, thieves, and political subversives will be cast out without pity … within 24 hours. A secret ombudsman will roam the country ferreting out corruption. The army will consist of elite soldiers (*arguably the only asset that Montagnards had in abundance*), but the citizenry will be able to take up arms. Past quarrels will be of no matter, likewise the ideology of neighboring states. Relations will be close with any country that respects our Integrity and National Sovereignty, even China and the USSR. In case of aggression, the United Nations will guarantee [our country's] survival, intervening militarily if necessary.

At the end—like Dhon's FULRO manifesto but clearly in a different voice—Paul emphasized the importance of youth in this new country and the removal of "incompetents," inserting a paragraph partly in Montagnard dialect about windbags in meetings, a probable swipe against Y-Bham Enuol.

The overall impression is of earnestness with flashes of originality, even brilliance, though with the occasional clunkiness of an undergraduate.[42]

Written in Kosem's hand at the top is *Par Paul dit Y-Bun (Saigon) le 7/2/65* (By Paul aka Y-Bun (Saigon) February 7, 1965), which suggests that Paul went back and forth at least once to Vietnam after having joined FULRO's top leadership in Mondulkiri, no small risk for someone so recognizable (capture by South Vietnam's Security Police was almost as feared as assassination).

It is unclear exactly when Paul left for Paris. In September 1965, he participated in the Phnom Penh meeting where Y-Bham Enuol acted compliant despite having begun unilateral negotiations with South Vietnam (see p. 212). On November 17, Paul's signature appeared on an angry document addressed to Y-Bham Enuol by the same Phnom Penh group, severely criticizing use of the phrase, "Dega-Cham," because it might give the outside world "the idea of division between the [Montagnards] and Cham."[43]

According to the story about the intercepted letter to Dhon—with a fatal mix-up of names, plotting a coup against Y-Bham Enuol—it was Paul who sent it. If true, it is likely this was the tip of the iceberg, and that Paul and Dhon—friends, ex-schoolmates, intellectual equals, and certain they were smarter than Y-Bham Enuol—had long seen eye to eye.

Whatever the exact date that he left for Cambodia, if it had been any later, he would have ended up in the jungle floor with Dhon.

***

The last shock provided by the November 30 document is a whiplash reversal in its final paragraph, proclaiming that:

> [Y-Bham Enuol] did not allow [Dhon's death sentence] to proceed; [instead, he] let it be known [through Y-Nam] … that the criminal should be moved elsewhere (to the Front) … to be judged in front of the People, after the liberation of the Country [*Selon le jugement precite, le Président n'a pas permis de le realiser; le Président a fait connaître aux Freres par intermediaire du Secretaire d'Etat au Departement de la Justice, que [le criminel sera deplacé] ailleurs (au Front) un jour près d'ici afin [qu'il soit jugé] devant le Peuple, apres la Liberation du Pays* …]

This is followed by a peculiar benediction above Y-Bham Enuol's signature:

> I allow myself to salute all the Brothers and ask them to avoid misunderstandings.
> [*Je me permets de saluer tous les Freres et leur demander d'éviter les malendus* [*sic*].]

Is this false magnanimity? The reference to misunderstandings may be paving the way for what has become the consensus explanation, blaming Dhon's death on overzealous followers of Y-Bham Enuol, call it the "Shakespearean version," ("Will no one rid me of this turbulent priest?")[44] This is the version Paul told me in 1973.[45]

On the other hand, maybe his commutation of Dhon's sentence was sincere. He was known for his decency and, except for one hint of bad temper, moderation. Even a close relative of Dhon's calls him "a nice man."[46] Maybe his stipulating "after Liberation" and his plea "to avoid misunderstandings" were signs that he sensed a growing lynch-mob mentality among his followers and hoped to let passions cool. Putting everything off until after an exceedingly distant liberation makes little sense otherwise.

***

A second puzzle, seemingly separate, is how both Bhan and Y-Nam could have turned against their old friend and ally, Dhon.

Bhan's confidences to me over the years were selective, evidently to protect and sculpt both his and FULRO's history. His principal motive seemed to be loyalty to, and/or concern for the opinion of, his remaining comrades, which fits with his stated reason for crossing the border into Cambodia so many years ago. His basic story never wavered, even when challenged at the end.[47] However, he did reveal a few things over the years that fit as pieces of the puzzle.

As commanders, both he and Y-Nam were especially hard and demanding. Father Bianchetti characterized Y-Nam as a martinet,[48] and Y-Nam himself adjudged Bhan to be even more of a disciplinarian than he was.

During the First Rebellion, the FULRO unit at Bu Prang had gone off and slaughtered Vietnamese civilians at a district post, clearly not part of their orders. Y-Nam had been in command there until shortly beforehand, when he moved onward to Ban Me Thuot, presumably to assume a more important role.[49] When Bhan arrived four months after the rebellion and asked him how the Bu Prong troops could have been such a loose cannon, Y-Nam replied they had been "too angry," essentially out of control.

To Bhan and Y-Nam—soldiers through and through—such behavior might have looked like a snake to be immediately crushed. Knowing better than civilians how hard it would be to someday face the Vietnamese Army without allies, they may have come to see Dhon as a loose cannon and his public insubordination toward Y-Bham Enuol—now General of FULRO's army—as dangerous, demanding at least a show of punishment.

In the tendrils of a dream

But there was something else going on here.

The trove contained a 15-page stapled booklet (overleaf), likely issued by the Association of Austrien Peoples and meant to be carried by Cham soldiers, which begins with rational (if incorrect) arguments as to why all the people of Southeast Asia are brothers except the three bullies (Vietnam, Thailand, and Laos), then talks of defending the United Nations' Declaration of Human Rights. But the last five pages veer into an entirely different dimension, listing four forms of *chaya* (literally "shadow," or protective magic) available to the soldiers that would make them invulnerable or invisible.

Page 14 of the document (translated, overleaf) is an explanation of what three of the *chaya*—"magic eyes/mouths/ears"—can do for "AGAS," i.e., soldiers of the vanguard:

> [the [magic] "eyes" watch and record
> the [magic] "mouths" communicate
> the [magic] ears listen and so you are informed and warned ...
>
> Invulnerability is thus obtained as is effectiveness because you can be invisible wherever you want to be yet you remain in contact with your companions

When I first saw this, I recognized the mysticism of Lon Nol, chairman of the association, but gave it no more thought. Then I remembered being told that, the day before the September 1964 rebellion, all the FULRO soldiers had been issued magic undershirts, with writing in Cham script to protect them from bullets.[50]

And, in front of me all along were FULRO's documents, which had disturbed me, but I could not put my finger on why. Despite the jungle heat and sweat-splotched vellum, a Montagnard scribe had typed them all in French, his second or third language, the language of modernity, making many mistakes but then painstakingly correcting every error with an X.

The Xs were like a barrier of thorns, as though something were prowling in the trees out beyond the light.

To some of Y-Bham Enuol's followers, there was one crime greater than betraying FULRO—that was to act against their leader. It was the worst crime because he was far more important to them than a military or secular leader would have been.

He was successor to 1937's Sambram. He was their next messiah.

To Y-Bham Enuol's most fervent and most primitive followers, questioning his authority—his identity as the once and future king—was worse than insubordination, worse even than *lese majesté*—it was heresy. Such heresy had to be dealt with harshly because it cast doubt on their own faith, darkening their hopes. Dhon's savage end, caged on the forest floor, was a purification—as

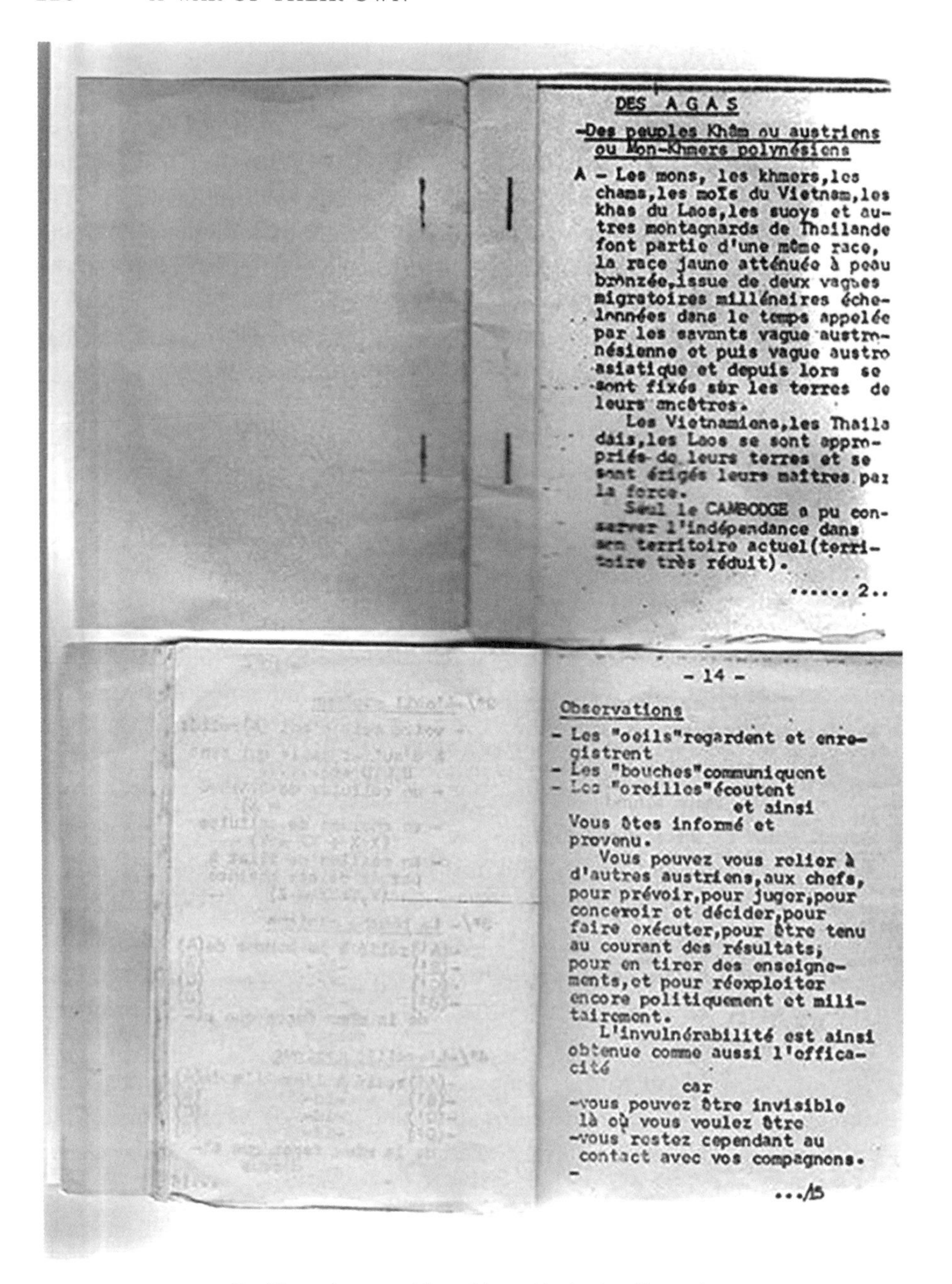

DES AGAS

-Des peuples Khâm ou austriens
ou Mon-Khmers polynésiens

A – Les mons, les khmers, les
chams, les moïs du Vietnam, les
khas du Laos, les suoys et autres montagnards de Thailande
font partie d'une même race,
la race jaune atténuée à peau
bronzée, issue de deux vagues
migratoires millénaires éche-
lonnées dans le temps appelée
par les savants vague austro-
nésienne et puis vague austro
asiatique et depuis lors se
sont fixés sur les terres de
leurs ancêtres.
Les Vietnamiens, les Thaila
dais, les Laos se sont appro-
priés de leurs terres et se
sont érigés leurs maîtres par
la force.
Seul le CAMBODGE a pu con-
server l'indépendance dans
son territoire actuel (territoire très réduit).

...... 2..

- 14 -

Observations

- Les "oeils" regardent et enre-
gistrent
- Les "bouches" communiquent
- Les "oreilles" écoutent
et ainsi
Vous êtes informé et
provenu.
Vous pouvez vous relier à
d'autres austriens, aux chefs,
pour prévoir, pour juger, pour
concevoir et décider, pour
faire exécuter, pour être tenu
au courant des résultats,
pour en tirer des enseigne-
ments, et pour réexploiter
encore politiquement et mili-
tairement.
L'invulnérabilité est ainsi
obtenue comme aussi l'effica-
cité
car
-vous pouvez être invisible
là où vous voulez être
-vous restez cependant au
contact avec vos compagnons.
-

...15

Booklet to be carried by soldiers. (Author's collection)

necessary as burning a witch at the stake. Though likely small in numbers, their fierce belief drew others into the abyss.

From this comes a cascade of realizations.

FULRO was a doubly millenarian movement. Though sparked by a mid-20th-century radicalism, it grew with almost fantastic rapidity—to thousands of Montagnards, including families, camped in the forest—then burned out of control on an ancient messianism. Rational nativism was swallowed whole by magical nativism. The Python God had returned.

There is irony in the fact that Dhon, Paul, and Kpa Doh were millenarians too, but of the modern, secular kind who saw revolution as the cataclysm to usher in a golden age. In the 1950s, this was still relatively hopeful and innocent, blind to how bitter and bloody the cataclysm would become.

Unfortunately for them, theirs was a small war within a global one, a Manichean struggle between true believers in Freedom and true believers in Social Justice, neither willing or able to imagine a blend of both.[51]

In a sense, then, FULRO's leaders were all burned at the stake, by those with fever dreams far greater than their own.

***

Bhan died the week I was rewriting these final paragraphs in December 2024. He was 91 years old. His Cambodian stepchildren had him cremated according to Buddhist custom. In April 2025, fifty years from when he lost his own family, I will travel with my family to pick up his ashes in Ban Lung and take them back to the hamlet where he was born. For political reasons—the main one a legacy of FULRO—it is a two-day trip by car and airplane, but it is only 200 kilometers (120 miles) away as the crow flies.

Despite his having travelled twice around the globe, Bhan once described an episode to me of when he had foolishly challenged himself at age 19 to swim the Sre Pok River at flood. He made it across but only barely because of something tugging at his ankle. Dragging himself up onto the other bank, gulping at the sky for a long time, he remembered the pull on his ankle and looked back, where he saw a horseman midriver, breasting up against the surge until both man and horse sank away, followed by water buffaloes dragged into the water from the other bank, then longhouses sliding into the water too, all attached to the horseman by an invisible fiber.

Having shared this with me, he added that one of the bonuses of having once been a Christian is the ability to banish such thoughts from his mind. It took me a while to realize that he was telling a rare joke, making fun of himself.

I have already mentioned my guess that he had been the ideal company or battalion commander and how, for a tiny subset of people, that is as high a compliment as there is. As his Vietnamese troops suspected, he was good at war. During his very first experience of combat, he had been able to call in airstrikes in good French because he carefully mastered every weapon available to him before he needed it. The more I heard him talk of his later experiences, the more I realized he could have led American soldiers too, not because he was modern but because part of him was ancient.

But this was a handicap for a people trying to cast off the yoke of colonialism, making them a tempting target for manipulation.

Even Kpa Doh, who had spent a half-year in the US, and Paul, who spent almost five years in Paris—penetrating further and higher than any other Montagnards into the modern world—even they must have had moments in which they could not be completely sure which side of reality's membrane they were on, still feeling that tug, still in the tendrils of a dream.

If they succeeded in avoiding manipulation—which I believe that all five Montagnard leaders of FULRO largely did—it makes their individual accomplishment that much more extraordinary, having done so without mentors, or, harder, with mentors who had ulterior motives.

Our situation is not that different. Yes, as individuals, we are far more informed than they were. But as social animals, we are still tribal, still easily manipulated—in fact, more so because social media amplifies our tribalism. One of these days, though, we will begin to feel and see our *own* yoke—not colonialism by force but domination by lies—and, on that day, may we find within ourselves what they found—courage despite awareness of their fallibility—to tear off that yoke and hurl it to the ground. We may not get another chance.

Denouement

In June 2023, a group of Rhadé and Jarai Montagnards attacked a police station "near Ban Me Thuot" and randomly killed nine Vietnamese, intending to sow terror.

No government news release mentioned it at the time, but, without one iota of doubt, the attackers identified themselves as FULRO.

It turns out that, of all the small-town police stations in the Central Highlands, this one was in the hamlet where Bhan was born.

Notes

1 William H, Chickering, "A War of their Own," *The New York Times*, June 9, 2017, https://www.nytimes.com/2017/06/09/opinion/a-war-of-their-own.html. Documents mentioned below as being "in the Les Kosem trove" are in the author's collection but should be findable as well at the Documentation Center of Cambodia in Phnom Penh.

2 A third suitcase appeared to have only family related materials. I was under time constraint and could not thoroughly sift through any of the suitcases. A fair amount may still await discovery at the Documentation Center.

3 Some (many?) of these appeared to correspond with documents referenced by Po Dharma and Mak Phoen (*Du FLM à FULRO: Une Lutte des Minorités du Sud Indochinois 1955–1975* (Paris: Les Indes Savantes, 2006)). I assume they exist in a different location.

4 Provisional Revolutionary Government (of Vietnam), the VC/NLF's official name (see note 8, below).

5 Another document from a year later—a proposed constitution written by Paul Y-Bun Sur and approved by Kosem (see p. 222)—does mention America as a country to be approached for aid.

6 Certainly not Y-Bham Enuol, whose French was not great, nor his private secretary, Y-Dhun. Both arrived in Cambodia after the manifesto was written, plus it is too militant. Probably not Paul, whose one known document (aside from a journal article) uses different language and has different concerns. None of the leaders who stayed behind (Y-Thih Eban, Nay Luett, or Paul Nur) were militant enough. The possibility always exists that it was written by a highly literate and politicized Montagnard other than Dhon, but it seems exceedingly unlikely such an individual would not otherwise have risen to visibility.

7 Odd Arne Westad, *The Global Cold War: Third World Interventions and the Making of Our Times* (Cambridge, UK: Cambridge University Press, 2007), 101. The Bandung conference also supported non-alignment with either East or West in the Cold War. Though it had definite leftist sympathies (e.g., China was one of the "non-aligned" attendees), one of its take-home ideas was that competition between the US and the USSR could be exploited.

8 The Algerian rebels declared independence, then—*despite controlling almost no territory*—announced a provisional government and got it recognized by the United Nations. This was a brilliant idea that no doubt inspired both the Viet Cong and FULRO (Matthew Connelly, "Rethinking the Cold War and Decolonization: The Grand Strategy of the Algerian War for Independence," *International Journal of Middle East Studies* 33 (2001): 222).

9 Fanon, *Wretched of the Earth,* published in 1961 as *Les Damnés de La Terre.* The full quote is, "The colonized man liberates himself in and through violence [p. 44] … At the individual level, violence is a cleansing force. It rids the colonized of their inferiority complex, of their passive and despairing attitude. It emboldens them and restores their self-confidence. [p. 51]"

10 Kpa Doh, interview with author, April 1973.

11 "*Declaration—du Haut Comité du Front Unifié de Lutte de la Race Opprimée,*" in *HISTORIQUE* (February 25, 1965), 18. The use of "*lutte*" (struggle) instead of "*libération*" is a sign as well of a more leftist origin. This document is available in Cornell's Southeast Asia Library.

12 Y-Tlur Eban, interviews with author over a 20-year span, 2003–2023. This is the take of the pro-Y-Bham-Enuol refugee community in North Carolina.

13 *Entretien avec son Excellence Etienne Manac'h, Ministre Plenipotentiaire des Affaires d'Asie ayant lieu le 7 septembre 1966 de 09h45 à 10h45*, in Les Kosem trove. Document regarding Y-Bham Enuol's meeting with de Gaulle's Director of Far Eastern Affairs, Etienne Manac'h. This may have been part bluster, but Y-Bham Enuol must have known the French had good intelligence

sources and could crosscheck it. This document is interesting as well because Manac'h gets right to the point by asking what is [FULRO's] attitude toward the Viet Cong, the Saigon government, and the Americans. Y-Bham Enuol replies that the Viet Cong, like the South Vietnamese, have a policy of genocide against [his] people. Later, after implying that De Gaulle believes that the Viet Cong will win, Manach'h circles back, asking about FULRO's attitude toward the Americans. Y-Bham Enuol replies approvingly about the US military training already received by 20,000 Montagnards. Manac'h tries one last time, vaguely suggesting a hypothetical in which FULRO had to choose between the Viet Cong and the Americans. Y-Bham Enuol avoids the question and gives a flowery reply about FULRO's trust in France. At which point, a probably exasperated Manac'h says he has another meeting to go to, but that their representatives will keep in touch.

14 Bhan, interviews with author, 2009 onward

15 Y-Bham Enuol, letter to Maxwell Taylor, June 9, 1965.

16 Dorsey Anderson (CIA Officer in charge of Montagnard affairs), letter to Y-Bham Enuol, June 30, 1965, expressing his conviction that "you and the Vietnamese government will come to an agreement satisfactory to both of you, in time," but with a handwritten comment below by Um Savuth saying "[this] letter has nothing to do with [Anderson's] thinking. It's a letter of camouflage ... [He] tells us not to listen to the promises of the South Vietnamese government and asks us to choose the places dates and times to meet." This sounds darkly conspiratorial, but it may simply have been realistic advice from a sympathetic American, because, at this point, the South Vietnamese were nowhere near negotiating seriously.

17 Father Roger Bianchetti, interview with author, April 1973.

18 Document dated May 13, 1965, entitled *Proces Verbal,* in the Les Kosem trove. Somewhat surprisingly, given the leftist rhetoric only three months before, the document also declares that FULRO's "political line is that of the Free World."

19 First document—dated July 1, 1965, entitled *Preparation,* in the Les Kosem trove. Second document—undated, with a doodled title page, *Miltaire,* in the Les Kosem trove. In the latter, it appears that he is enumerating FULRO partisans *within Vietnam* (forces coming out of Cambodia are mentioned separately). In Darlac, these consist of 650 "special forces" (CIDG?—if so, seems low), 300 armed villagers, and 1,850 other (probably RF/PFs). In Quang Duc, he lists 800+800+500 men from three ARVN battalions—evidently composed largely of Montagnards—plus 457 armed villagers. Either this is extremely wishful thinking—which does not sound like Kosem—or FULRO had a strong base within Vietnam almost from the beginning. That said, it is one thing to profess allegiance to FULRO, quite another to risk death fighting the Vietnamese.

20 Document in the CREST files (CIA-RDP79T00472A001800030005-5, September 29, 1965).

21 CIA, *The Highlanders of SVN,* p.8586-. The CIA tracked the captured soldiers and, somewhat convincingly, says that they eventually got split up into six units and assigned to coastal provinces.

22 Document dated August 1, 1965, entitled *Renseignements,* in the Les Kosem trove.

23 "Austrien" was Lon Nol's made-up name from the two language families, Austroasiatic and Austronesian, spoken by Chams, Montagnards, Cambodians, and possibly Burmese. The idea of an alliance against Indochina's bullies, the Vietnamese and Thais, struck racial chords, plus it dovetailed with proclaiming an ethnic "nation" to reclaim lands previously lost to them.

24 Document dated September 10, 1965, *Proces Verbal de la Reunion de l'Amicale des Peuples Austriens,* p. 4, in the Les Kosem trove.

25 Undated document but commenting on a recent September 14, 1965 meeting, entitled *Analyse du Proces Verbale de l"Entrevue entre les Organes Gouvernementaux Sud-Vietnamiens et Y-Dhe-Y Wik,* in the Les Kosem trove.

26 His cousin Y-Ghak Adrong visited him "in jail" sometime in October or November (Y-Ghak Adrong, interview with author, August 20, 2017). Incarceration until trial was the norm. "Jail" was usually a deep pit dug in the ground. Puih Hloanh (interview with author, December 29, 2015) surprised me by mentioning offhandedly he had been jailed that way by Bhan (!) sometime after December 1968 on suspicion of being a spy for the Y-Bham Enuol faction and that he had been freed subsequently by Les Kosem.

27 Dhon said the disputes were over his taking water from a spring reserved for Y-Bham Enuol, then over his commandeering FULRO soldiers to help repair his own hut. Old men in North Carolina heard about these as Dhon's having received a delivery of food before Y-Bham Enuol.

28 Y-Ton Nie. This might be one and the same as the Y-To Nie who "had become commander of Y-Bham [Enuol's] presidential guard."

29 Mike Benge, interview with author, March 24, 2014.

30 Until now, scattered terrorism and threats to join the NLF made some sense vis à vis the US, worrying them into pressuring Saigon, but now, with the America's clear commitment to military victory, it became increasingly clear this was folly.

31 Summary of the "Condemnation and Judgments Against the … [Prisoner]." To avoid confusion, I have removed references in this document to Y-Nhuinh Hmok, Dhon's devoted companion (see photo on p. 119). He was so in Dhon's shadow that I could learn little about him. The tribunals see-sawed between condemning him to death, mostly by association, and freeing him to something like house arrest. However, it is certain he was executed along with Dhon, in the same manner.

32 Y-Nam's suggestion of colluding with "foreigners" could mean France, America, South Vietnam, the communists, or, as we have seen, even Les Kosem. It is curious that Y-Nam is the only one to have mentioned it, while those who were more vehemently against Dhon did not.

33 K'Briuh (interviews with author spanning 10 years from 2014–2024) passing on what he was told by one Y-Wik (not the same Y-Wik whom Dhon savaged for negotiating weakly with Saigon).

34 Oscar Salemink argued the Green Berets did the Montagnards "immense and irreparable harm" by encouraging their aspirations to autonomy (*The Ethnography of Vietnam's Central Highlanders* (Honolulu: University of Hawai'i Press, 2003), 255). However, his argument is predicated on the assumptions that American defeat was inevitable *and* that this was obvious at the time, assumptions that ignore what Phillip Roth called "the terror of the unforeseen" as well as the possibility of alternative outcomes, most notably one like Cambodia's under the Khmer Rouge.

35 *Document #110*, in the Les Kosem trove. The fact Bhan, Y-Nam, and Paul Y-Bun Sur are mentioned but Dhon is not suggests it was written after Dhon's murder (or after he was taken away)—thus, January or February 1966. It has a FULRO flag logo, which, with the number, locates it within an official series.

36 Dharma and Phoen (*Du FLM à FULRO*, 89) have this move in February 1966. Early on, Bhan told me about this separate basecamp (Srei Preah?), but without any larger implications.

37 Phillipe Drouin, Chapter 10, note 34.

38 Y-Tlur Eban, interviews with author, from 2003–2023.

39 Y-Tlur Eban (Rhadé), Kok Ksor (Jarai), and Sen Tith (Cambodian Cham).

40 Two such, both involving burial to the neck, were: being trampled by elephants; and being used, along with two other unfortunates, as the tripod for a cooking fire. The first was an ancient punishment for *lèse-majesté*, the second a paranoid and false rumor in the 1970s of Vietnamese treatment of Cambodians, to stoke Cambodian hatred of Vietnamese.

41 Thanks to Roih Krah for this perception, in his 2021 journal article specifically about Paul, "La Mesure de l'Homme: Y Bun Sur (10/09/1939–21/04/1975): Vie et Mort d'un Jeune Mnong Rlam," *Siksacakr: The Journal of Cambodia Research*, no. 16 (2021).

42 Document with no title, first words "*Premiere Epoque*," with Kosem's inscription at the top left, in Les Kosem trove.

43 His signature looks real. However, deceptive signatures were not unknown, e.g., Bhan's signature is on the flag document from September 22, 1964, months before he came to Cambodia.

44 King Henry II, speaking of Becket, leading his overzealous followers to misinterpret his wishes and murder Becket.

45 Three years later, Y-Bham Enuol was officially removed from command of FULRO by a committee for having caused "baseless accusations against Brothers [and] summary executions of … patriots without good reason and without prior consultation with the [High] Committee." Document dated January 1, 1969, untitled, in the Les Kosem trove. This was immediately after The Split, thus its 32 signers are militants left behind after Y-Bham Enuol's followers had left. As such, it is one-sided.

46 Y-Ghak Adrong, a cousin who lived with him and his family for two years in Binh Dinh. He added that Y-Bham Enuol "knew how to talk to people" (Y-Ghak Adrong, interview with author, August 20, 2017.

47 Bhan did say, in 2023 shortly before communication became too difficult, something about contemplating sending some men to rescue Dhon from "prison" but deciding against it in order not to pit FULRO soldiers against each other.

48 Bianchetti, interview with author, April 1973.

49 Y-Tlur insists that Y-Nam was in Ban Me Thuot during the rebellion. As FULRO's top soldier at the time (Bhan still being far away, at Kan Nak), he was probably expecting to assume overall command of the converging forces after they had taken the town.

50 Y-Tlur Eban, interviews with author over a 20-year span, 2003–2023. For the protective effect to work, the wearer had to be pure, i.e., no sexual relations, no contact with menstrual blood, etc.

51 This characterization of the Cold War is a modification from Westad, *The Global Cold War*.

Epilogue

The central thesis of this book is that Montagnard ethnonationalism played a much greater role in the Second Indochina War than previously thought and that it was homegrown. This book is an explicit effort to correct history's picture of Montagnards as pawns or victims without agency.

My argument is that the Montagnards remained unsubdued by lowlanders until the end of the 19th century because they were protected by highland malaria in addition to topography, and that, although the Jarai and Rhadé Montagnards adopted Cham traits through cultural diffusion resulting from trade, the plateau itself remained unconquered.

This freedom and sovereignty over their lands, still a living memory at mid-20th century, was the seed of a militant ethnonationalism that sprang up spontaneously among Montagnards in 1955–56 when President Diem of South Vietnam flooded their lands—the Central Highlands—with Vietnamese settlers.

Given form as FULRO (*Front Uni pour la Libération des Races Opprimeés*, Liberation Front for Oppressed Races), Montagnard ethnonationalism saw all Vietnamese, North and South, as colonialists, and FULRO's partisans saw themselves as anti-colonialist revolutionaries. Indeed, in several ways they consciously imitated the Viet Cong (VC).

FULRO's founders set out in the late 1950s on a path that no Montagnard had ever trod before. From 1963–65, under intense pressure, they briefly stood toe-to-toe with Washington, Hanoi, and Paris.

The United States defanged FULRO within South Vietnam and tried unsuccessfully to turn it against the communists. The communists, being Vietnamese and seen as the oppressor, tried to divert Montagnards from joining FULRO by pointing to autonomous zones created for Montagnards in North Vietnam, but word filtered south that these were largely illusory. Cambodia, and likely France behind it, came closest to success, midwifing FULRO's birth and encouraging its militancy in order to cause problems for the Americans and South Vietnamese, but never quite controlling its inner councils because FULRO's leaders were their own men. Their single-issue focus—to win a country of their own—enabled them to ally with others whose methods overlapped with theirs. For a while, this meant Cambodia and France. But, contrary to Hanoi's efforts to paint them as puppets, their relationship with outsiders was transactional.

Most fatefully, FULRO's growing army needed arms and ammunition, military training, and, above all, modern combat experience, and there was only one place it could obtain all four: the American military. Thus, FULRO encouraged young Montagnards to enlist as irregular soldiers alongside US Green Berets. Evidence suggests that at its peak, FULRO had as many as 5,000 soldiers at its base in Cambodia and up to 20,000 irregular soldiers within South Vietnam. Because many of the latter were paid by the Americans, communist propaganda tarred them as mercenaries. However, the kind of risks they ran, especially in units at the tip of the spear, plus the fact that most were dues-paying members of FULRO, testify to a higher motive, analogous to that of the communists themselves—defending their homeland against a hated invader.

Montagnards did join the Viet Minh/VC and serve as auxiliaries with the North Vietnamese Army. In the mid-1940s, the *corvée* (labor tax) and abuse by individual Frenchmen played a role in this recruitment. However, a more positive driver was likely the Vietnamese revolutionaries' egalitarianism and dedication, hugely impressive to a people who had known only disdain. Much later, American bombing and resettlement drove recruitment.

At some point, however, ethnonationalist ideology, spreading into the furthest corners of the highlands, must have begun to outpace other motives. From FULRO documents, we have a window into what popular leaders really thought, thus some idea of the will of the Montagnard people. Logically, ethnonationalism would have been more appealing to Montagnards than Vietnamese nationalism/unification or even communism. Plus, there is indirect evidence the Montagnard Viet Cong were ready to join forces with FULRO in an expected final showdown with the Vietnamese.

Today's Montagnards have lost much of their land and are fast being assimilated. Their culture, now being folklorized, will soon be extinct—exactly what FULRO feared. In retrospect, the gears of history were impossible to jam. To do so, FULRO would have had to help the Americans win the war by cutting the Ho Chi Minh Trail and/or Sihanoukville Trail—easy to breezily imagine, almost impossible to do.

It can be argued that the highlanders' fight to save their home from the Vietnamese was as fiercely anticolonial and revolutionary—and felt to be as existential—as the Vietnamese's fight to save their nation from the Americans and French. Yet, despite the power of this motivation, FULRO faded away for no apparent reason in the mid-1960s. It flickered once more into history's spotlight during the fall of Phnom Penh in 1975, then disappeared forever.

Almost 50 years ago, I set out to find out why. This book is what I learned.

FULRO was at heart a Montagnard salvational movement in response to overwhelming change. Intellectually a radical liberation movement stimulated by a wave of Vietnamese settler colonialism in the mid-1950s, its emotional engine was millenarism, a recurrent phenomenon among Southeast Asian hill tribes. Its precursor in the late 1930s, the Python God movement, had arisen out of premonitions of change. By the early 1960s, thanks to the Indochina wars, overwhelming change and loss were coming on like a freight train. Both FULRO and the Python God movement had messianic leaders, though in FULRO's case, its principal leader, Y-Bham Enuol, mounted the messianic tiger reluctantly. In late 1965, in a confrontation with younger radicals, he either could not get off that tiger or chose not to, and FULRO succumbed to a spasm of atavism, split between the more educated Montagnards and the more traditional ones.

This idea is based on limited data, as are several educated guesses I have made in this book. These are its weaknesses, but history requires I try to fill in the blanks. The elephant in the room is the lack of data from either the CIA or its French equivalent, the SDECE. The CIA must eventually come through on a Freedom of Information Act request submitted in 2017, though I do not expect much in the way of revelations, either because the CIA did not have a good source at the heart of FULRO or because it now wishes to hide its role. It is possible France's files will tell us a lot more, but any claims by the French as to controlling FULRO will need to be read with some skepticism, as the Montagnards were aware of efforts to manipulate them.

As their principal leader, Y-Bham Enuol, said, "No foreigner can have any power."

He was central to the FULRO story and is a hero to the Montagnard diaspora. The devotion he inspired suggests Heroic caliber, no matter how he looked to the young militants. I would have said more about him in this book if possible, but, by the time I met him, he was greatly diminished, and by now he has been smoothed of all sharp angles, polished like a figurine.

FULRO is historically important.

Politically, its intentional mystique kept everyone guessing, especially early in the war, affecting decisions made by the Vietnamese of both camps as well as by the Americans.

Militarily, FULRO was both stimulus and cement to the CIDG program, which was often the sole force contesting enemy control of vast areas of southern Vietnam. As the program sprouted special operations units, FULRO's call to drive the Vietnamese invader from their homeland inspired young Montagnards to undertake missions into the heart of enemy sanctuaries that were as dangerous as they were sometimes devastating to the enemy. The French had created similar units, trying to capitalize on age-old Montagnard enmity toward the Vietnamese, but were ultimately unsuccessful. The crucial difference now was that the Montagnards were fighting on their own behalf, with an ideology all their own.

FULRO's effect on the Montagnard people was, and still is, inestimable. To those who thirsted for modernity, it offered a route that seemed more authentically Montagnard than Marxism or The American Way. Ironically, by also attracting those who were ambivalent about modernity, it self-destructed.

After 1975, FULRO's flame kept the Montagnard and Cham peoples' resistance alive and was instrumental in their diaspora. Even today it affects lives, rarely with violence but always reminding them, for good or for ill, of their determination—declared in its Manifesto—"to stay forever as [they] are … and not, in any way, turn into Vietnamese."

Excepting Y-Bham Enuol, the five FULRO leaders came by their ethnonationalism in their teens, with four of them showing signs of anti-Vietnamese militancy at an early age. They were all influenced by foreigners, but the spontaneity of their central motive argues against having been molded by them. If FULRO's ideology was indeed the most homegrown, then its story is as close to an indigenous history of the Vietnam War as is likely to be written.

Finally, FULRO's war was a unique decolonization war, one waged by ethnic minorities to throw off oppression and colonial occupation of their lands by an ethnic majority, as opposed to by Europeans. Viewed as an anticolonial struggle for dignity as well as for land, FULRO's embrace of violence united Montagnards and dispelled feelings of inferiority. Its war was also unique in that it took place within a much larger conflict, one that subjected ethnic minorities to far greater pressures than other decolonization wars but also presented them with a unique possibility—or mirage—of cultural survival.

An irony, of course, is that the larger conflict was framed by the communists, and seen by much of the world, as an anticolonial war of liberation against American imperialism. Some Montagnards and Chams could relate to that interpretation and, today, have streets named after them.

But a great many could not.

Anticipating an eventual Armageddon, they made principled, often risky, even noble, choices to fight against what they saw instead as forces of oppression.

Bibliography

Ahern Jr., Thomas L. *Good Questions, Wrong Answers: CIA's Estimates of Arms Traffic Through Sihanoukville, Cambodia, During the Vietnam War*. An Intelligence Monograph. Washington, D.C.: Center for the Study of Intelligence, 2004.

Anonymous. "Memorandum of Conversation at the US Embassy (Saigon), April 4th at 1600 hrs, G.D. Jacobson SAAFO, presiding." 1975.

Anonymous. "Heroic Saga in the Vast Jungle (Attack on Ka Nak Outpost, 7 March 1965)." Translated by Merle Pribbenow. *Gia Lai Online*, July 24, 2009. https://baogialai.com.vn/khuc-trang-ca-giua-dai-ngan-post95133.html.

Antoine, F-P. "Dominique Antomarchi (1901–1941)," *Bulletin de l'Ecole Française d'Extrême-Orient* 47, no. 2 (1955): 549–54. http://www.persee.fr/web/revues/home/prescript/article/befeo_0336–1519_1955_num_47_2_3741.

Beaumont, Jacques. "Letter to Sihanouk, October 1967." Phnom Penh: The Charles Meyer Collection, Khmer National Archives, 1967.

Benge, Michael D. "The History of the Involvement of the Montagnards of the Central Highlands in the Vietnam War." Presentation during Saigon Arts, Culture and Education Institute Forum, 2011.

Benzaquen-Gautier, Stéphanie. "The Relational Archive of the Khmer Republic (1970–1975): Re-visiting the 'Coup' and the 'Civil War' in Cambodia Through Written Sources." *South East Asia Research* 29, no. 4 (2021): 450–68.

Bizot, François. *Le Portail*. Paris: Editions de la Table Ronde, 2000.

Bizot, François. *The Gate*. Translated by Euan Cameron. London: Vintage, 2004.

Bourotte, Bernard. "Essai d'histoire des Populations Montagnardes du Sud Indochinois jusqu'à 1945." *Bulletin de la Societé des Etudes Indochinoises* XXX, no. 1 (1955, translated by USAID, 1967): 17–116.

Brinkley, Joel. *Cambodia's Curse*. New York: Public Affairs Books, 2011.

Central Intelligence Agency. *The Highlanders of South Vietnam: A Review of Political Developments and Forces*. CIA-RDP80T01719R000300010003–8. Washington, D.C.: 1966.

Central Intelligence Agency. *Memorandum: The Situation in Vietnam, 22 May*. Directorate of Intelligence, 1967.

Central Intelligence Agency. Cable TDCS-314/05323–70, May 12, 1970.

Central Intelligence Agency. "Background leading up to the 18 March change of government in Cambodia." TDCS-DB-315/04151–70, August 14, 1970.

Chandler, David. *Brother Number One: A Political Biography of Pol Pot*. Boulder: Westview Press, 1999.

Chek Brahim. *Confession*. Catalogue #D02687 (1975–76), S-21 (Khmer Rouge torture center), Phnom Penh: Documentation Center of Cambodia (translated to English by Chenda Seang).

Chickering, William. "A War of Their Own." *The New York Times*, June 9, 2017. www.nytimes.com/2017/06/09/opinion/a-war-of-their-own.html.

Christie, Clive. *A Modern History of Southeast Asia: Decolonization, Nationalism and Separatism.* London: Tauris Academic Studies, 1996.

Colm, Sara, and Sorya Sim. *Khmer Rouge Purges in the Mondul Kiri Highlands.* Documentation Series no. 14. Phnom Penh: Documentation Center of Cambodia, 2009.

Conboy, Ken. *FANK: A History of the Cambodian Armed Forces, 1970–75.* Jakarta: Equinox Publishing, 2011.

Conboy, Ken. *The Cambodia Wars: Clashing Armies and CIA Covert Operations.* Lawrence: University Press of Kansas, 2013.

Connelly, Matthew. "Rethinking the Cold War and Decolonization: The Grand Strategy of the Algerian War for Independence." *International Journal of Middle East Studies* 33 (2001): 221–45.

Connor, Walker. *The National Question in Marxist-Leninist Theory and Strategy.* Princeton: Princeton University Press, 1984.

Corfield, Justin. *Khmers Stand Up!: A History of the Cambodian Government 1970–1975.* Melbourne, Australia: Center of Southeast Asian Studies, Monash University, 1994.

Cottingham, A. J. Jr., S. C. Boone, and L. J. Legters. "A Prospective Study of Malaria Incidence Among Indigenous and US Forces During Combat Operations." Annual Progress Report. Washington, D.C., and Ho Chi Minh City: Walter Reed Army Institute of Research and Institut Pasteur, 1967: 2–34, 35–68.

Courts, Phil. "Shootout on the Cambodian Border." 1966, accessed December 2017. www.vhpa.org/stories/Shootout.pdf.

Cupet, P. *Among the Tribes of Southern Vietnam and Laos.* Translated by Walter E. J. Tips. Bangkok: White Lotus Press, 1998.

Dam Bo (Jacques Dournes). "Les Populations Montagnardes du Sud-Indochinois," *France-Asie* 5 no. 49–50 (1950).

Dang, Vu Hieo. *Memory of Tây Nguyên (The Central Highlands).* Hanoi: The Gioi Publishers, 2012.

Darde, Jean-Noel. *Le Ministère de la Vérité: Histoire d'un Genocide dans le Journal L'Humanité.* Paris: Editions de Seuil, 1984.

Demeure, Françoise. *Memoires d'Avenir: La Fondation à Ban Me Thuot, Vietnam 1954–1975.* Paris: Bénédictines Missionaires de Vanves. 1er cahier 1953–56 (2005), 2eme cahier 1957–60 (2007), 3eme cahier 1961–67 (2010) and 4eme cahier 1967–75 (2013).

Department of Defense. Intelligence report #6028268769, May 11, 1969.

Dommen, Arthur J. *The Indochinese Experience of the French and the Americans.* Bloomington: Indiana University Press, 2001.

Dorgelés, Roland. *Sur La Route Mandarine.* Paris: Albin Michel, 1925. (English translation: Emerson, Gertrude Emerson. *On the Mandarin Road.* New York: The Century Company, 1926).

Dournes, Jacques. "Recherches sur le Haut Champa," *France-Asie* 20 no. 2 (1970): 143–62.

Dournes, Jacques. *Potao: Une Theorie du Pouvoir Chez les Indochinois Jorai.* Paris: Flammarion, 1977.

Dournes, Jacques. "Sam Bam, Le Mage et le Blanc dans L'Indochine Centrale des Années Trente," *L'Ethnographie* I (1978): 85–108.

Dournes, Jacques. *Minorities of Central Vietnam: Autochthonous Indochinese Peoples.* Report no. 18. London: New Edition, Minority Rights Group, 1980.

Drivas, Peter. "The Cambodian Incursion Revisited," *International Social Science Review* 86 (2011): 134–59.

Enuol, Y-Bham. Speech at the Indochina Peoples' Conference, Phnom Penh, March 4, 1965.

Faligot, Roger, Jean Guisnel, and Rémi Kauffer. *Histoire Politique des Services Secrets Français.* Paris: Editions La Découverte, 2012.

Fall, Bernard. *The Two Vietnams: A Political and Military Analysis.* London: Pall Mall Press, 1967.

Fanon, Frantz. *The Wretched of the Earth.* Translated by Richard Philcox. New York: Grove Press, 2004.

Farinaud, M. E. "The Use of Anti-Malarial Drugs as Adjuvants to DDT in Malaria Control in Vietnam." Paper presented at the WHO Malaria Conference for the Western Pacific and South-East Asia Regions, Taipei, WHO/MAL/106, 1954.

Fielding, Leslie. *Before the Killing Fields: Witness to Cambodia and the Vietnam War.* London: IB Tauris, 2008.

Ford, Daniel. *Cowboy: The Interpreter Who Became a Soldier, a Warlord, and One More Casualty of Our War in Vietnam.* Durham, NH: Warbird Books, 2018.

French Embassy of Phnom Penh. Monthly Report, November 5, 1966. Carton 14 S 367, Service Historique de l'Armée de Terre, Vincennes, Paris.

FULRO's High Committee. One of several manifestos dated September 20, 1964. Box 691, database no. 6308. Phnom Penh: The Charles Meyer Collection, National Archives, 1964 (11 pages missing).

FULRO's High Committee. HISTORIQUE 02/26/1965—in the Les Kosem Collection, Documentation Center of Cambodia.

Gay, Bernard. "New Perspectives on the Ethnic Composition of Champa." *Proceedings of the Seminar on Champa.* https://chamstudies.wordpress.com/2015/08/21/new-perspectives-on-the-ethnic-composition-of-champa/.

Global Witness. *The Cost of Luxury: Cambodia's Illegal Trade in Precious Wood.* London: Global Witness Limited, February 2015.

Grintchenko, Michel. *Atlante-Aréthuse: Une Opération de Pacification en Indochine.* Paris: Economica, 2001.

Guerin, Mathieu, and Jonathan Padwe. "Pénétration Coloniale et Résistance chez les Jarai: Revisiter le Rôle des Colonisés dans la Mise en Place des Frontières en Indochine," *Outre-Mers Revue d'Histoire* 99 (2011): 245–72.

Guinet, Pierre. Oral history obtained by Michel El Baze, 2015, http://ea58.free.fr/MichelElBaze/complements/PierreGUINETAveclecorpslegerinterventionaeroporteGUERREindochine1945–1946.html.

Guy, John S. "Artistic Exchange, Regional Dialogue, and the Cham Territories." In *Champa and the Archeology of My Son (Vietnam),* edited by Andrew Hardy, Mauro Cucarzi, and Patrizia Zolese. Singapore: NUS Press, 2009.

Hardy, Andrew. "Eaglewood and the Economic History of Champa and Central Vietnam." In *Champa and the Archeology of My Son (Vietnam),* edited by Andrew Hardy, Mauro Cucarzi, and Patrizia Zolese. Singapore: NUS Press, 2009.

Hastings, Max. *Vietnam: An Epic History of a Tragic War.* London: William Collins, 2018.

He, Jun-Dong, Min-Sheng Peng, Huy Ho Quang, Khoa Pham Dang, An Vu Trieu, Shi-Fang Wu, Jie-Qiong Jin, Robert W Murphy, Yong-Gang Yao, and Ya-Ping Zhang. "Patrilineal Perspective on the Austronesian Diffusion in Mainland Southeast Asia." *PLoS ONE* 7 (2012): e36437, doi:10.1371/journal.pone.0036437.

Hembree, Stephen C. "Malaria Among the Civilian Irregular Defense Group During the Vietnam Conflict: An Account of a Major Outbreak." *Military Medicine* 145 (1980): 751–56.

Heng, Piphal. (2021). Landscape, upland-lowland, community, and economy of the Mekong River (6th-8th century CE): case studies from the Pre-Angkorian centers of Thala Borivat and Sambor. *World Archaeology, 53*(4) (2022): 643–666.

Hickey, Gerald C. *Free in the Forest: Ethnohistory of the Vietnamese Central Highlands 1954–1956.* New Haven, CT: Yale University Press, 1982a.

Hickey, Gerald C. *Sons of the Mountains: Ethnohistory of the Vietnamese Central Highlands to 1954.* New Haven, CT: Yale University Press, 1982b.

Hickey, Gerald C. *Shattered World: Adaptation and Survival Among Vietnam's Highland People During the Vietnam War.* Philadelphia: University of Pennsylvania Press, 1993.

Hickey, Gerald C. *Window on a War.* Lubbock, TX: Texas Tech University Press, 2002.

Howard, John D. "The Revolt of the Montagnards." 2019, www.historynet.com/the-revolt-of-the-montagnards.htm.

Jackson, Karl D., ed. *Cambodia 1975–1978: Rendezvous with Death.* Princeton, NJ: Princeton University Press, 1989.

Jackson, Larry R. "The Vietnamese Revolution and the Montagnards." *Asian Survey*, 9 (1969): 313–30.
Jacq-Hergoualc'h, Michel. "L'Armee du Campa au Début du XIIIe Siècle." In *Le Campa et le Monde Malai: Actes de la Conférence Internationale Organisée à l'Université de Californie 30–31 Août 1990*, 1991.
Jaspan, Mervyn A. "Recent Developments Among the Cham of Indo-China: The Revival of Champa," *Asian Affairs* 1 no. 2: 170–76, doi.org/10.1080/03068377008729532.
Jeldres, Julio. "A Personal Reflection on Norodom Sihanouk and Zhou Enlai: An Extraordinary Friendship on the Fringes of the Cold War," *Cross-Currents: East Asian History and Culture Review*, E-Journal no. 4 (September 2012), http://cross-currents.berkeley.edu/e-journal/issue-4.
Jones Jr., Robert W. "A Team Effort: The Montagnard Uprising of September 1964," *Veritas* 3 (2007).
Joyaux, François. 'La Conférence des Peuples Indochinois," *Politique Etrangère* 30 (1965): 194–206.
Kamm, Henry. "Montagnards Who Fled Cambodia Get Little Aid," *The New York Times*, April 10, 1971.
Kelly, Francis X. *Vietnam Studies: U.S. Army Special Forces 1961–1971.* CMH Publication 90–23, Washington, D.C.: Department of the Army, 1973.
Khuc, Doan. *Review of the Resistance War Against the Americans to Save the Nation: Victories and Lessons.* Hanoi: National Political Publishing House, 1995.
Kiernan, Ben. "The 1970 Peasant Uprising in Kampuchea." *Journal of Contemporary Asia* IX (1979): 310–24.
Kiernan, Ben. "Orphans of Genocide: The Cham Muslims of Kampuchea Under Pol Pot," *Bulletin of Concerned Asian Scholars* 20, no. 4 (1988).
Kiernan, Ben. *The Pol Pot Regime: Race, Power, and Genocide in Cambodia Under the Khmer Rouge, 1975–79.* New Haven, CT: Yale University Press, 1996.
Kiernan, Ben, and Chan Boua. *Peasants and Politics in Kampuchea 1942–1981.* London: Zed Press, 1982.
Knoebl, Kuno. *Victor Charlie: The Face of War in Vietnam.* New York: Frederick A. Praeger, 1967.
Kpor, Y-Bhan. Handwritten autobiography, 2008 (author's personal collection).
Kurlantzick, Joshua. *A Great Place to Have a War.* New York: Simon & Schuster, 2016.
Kyheng, Savann. Personal testimony, recorded in late 1975 by François Ponchaud. Extraordinary Chambers in the Courts of Cambodia, document #00410372–376.
LaFont, Pierre-Bernard. *Campa: Géographie—Population—Histoire.* Paris: Les Indes Savantes, 2006 (translated by Jay Scarborough for Champaka/IOC-Champa, 2014).
Lansdale, Edward G. *In the Midst of Wars.* New York: Harper & Row, 1972.
Le Cao Dai. *The Central Highlands: A North Vietnamese Journal of Life on the Ho Chi Minh Trail 1965–1973.* Hanoi: The Gioi Publishers, 2004 (translated by Lady Borton).
Leslie, Jacques. *The Mark: A War Correspondent's Memoir of Vietnam and Cambodia.* New York: Four Walls Eight Windows, 1995.
Lewis, Norman. *A Dragon Apparent.* London: Jonathan Cape, 1951.
Lieberman, Victor. "A Zone of Refuge in Southeast Asia? Reconceptualizing Interior Spaces," *Journal of Global History* 5 (2010): 333–46.
Lind, Michael. *Vietnam: The Necessary War.* New York: Touchstone, 1999.
Lindsey, Fred. *Secret Green Beret Commandos in Cambodia.* Bloomington: AuthorHouse, 2012.
Locard, Henri. "Jungle Heart of the Khmer Rouge." NIAS Monographs no. 157. Copenhagen: University of Copenhagen, 2023.
Logevall, Fredrik. "De Gaulle, Neutralization, and American Involvement in Vietnam, 1963–1964," *Pacific Historical Review* 61 (1992): 69–101.
Long Boret, Public Library of US Diplomacy, 1975, wikileaks.org/plusd/cables/1975JAKART03915_b.html.
Maître, Henri. *Les Jungles Moi.* Paris: Larose, 1912.

Marr, David. *Vietnam 1945: The Quest for Power*. Oakland: University of California Press, 1997.
Maspero, Georges. *The Champa Kingdom*. Translated by Walter E. J. Tips. Bangkok: White Lotus Press, 2002.
McLeod, Mark W. "Indigenous Peoples and the Vietnamese Revolution, 1930–1975," *Journal of World History* 10 (1999): 2, 353–89.
Meinheit, Harold E. "Captain Cupet and the King of Fire: Mapping and Minorities in Vietnam's Central Highlands," *The Portolan,* Fall, 2012.
Meyer, Charles. *Derrière Le Sourire Khmer.* Paris: Plon, 1971.
Meyer, Charles. "Les Nouvelles Provinces: Ratanakiri-Mondulkiri," *Revue Monde en Développement* 28 (1979): 682–90.
Michaud, Jean. "The Montagnards and the State in North Vietnam from 1802 to 1975: A Historical Overview," *Ethnohistory* 44 (2000): 2, 333–68.
Morice, Jean. *Cambodge: Du Sourire à L'Horreur*. Paris: France-Empire, 1977.
Morris, Jim. *War Story*. Boulder: Paladin Press, 1979.
Morris, Jim. *The Devil's Secret Name*. New York: St. Martin's Press, 1990.
Nabias, Christine. "Neutralism in Indochina: A Comparative Study of Neutralism in Cambodia, Laos, and Vietnam, 1954–65." Master's thesis. Ithaca, NY: Cornell University, 1971.
Nakamura, Rie. "Cham in Vietnam: Dynamics of Ethnicity." Ph.D. dissertation. Seattle, WA: Department of Anthropology, University of Washington, 1999.
Nakamura, Rie. "Becoming Malay: The Politics of the Cham Migration to Malaysia," *Studies in Ethnicity and Nationalism* 19, no. 3 (2019).
Neale, Jonathan. *A People's History of the Vietnam War*. New York: The New Press, 2003.
Neveu, Roland. *The Fall of Phnom Penh, 17 April 1975*. Bangkok: Asia Horizons Book Co., 2015.
Ngoc, Linh, "Rong Yang Tower, a Treasure of the Cham People in the Central Highlands," *Tai Nguyen Moi Truong online March 5, 2022*, https://baotainguyenmoitruong.vn/thap-rong-yang-mot-bau-vat-cua-nguoi-cham-o-tay-nguyen-337438.html. Accessed December 2024.
Ngon, Vinh. *FULRO #1: A Criminal Organization*. Ho Chi Minh City: Cong An Nhan Dan, 1983 (translated by Merle Pribbenow, 2015).
Nguyễn, Huu An. *New Battlefields*. As told to Nguyen Tu Duong. Hanoi: People's Army Publishing House, 2002 (translated by Merle Pribbenow, 2nd printing).
Nguyễn, Thụy Phương. "L'école française au Vietnam de 1945 à 1975: de la mission civilisatrice à la diplomatie culturelle." PhD Thesis in Education Sciences. Université René Descartes, Paris V, 2013.
Noseworthy, William B. "Lowland Participation in the Irredentist 'Highlands Liberation Movement' in Vietnam, 1955–1975," *Austrian Journal of Southeast Asian Studies* 6, no. 1 (2013): 7–28.
Obsomer, Valérie, Pierre Defourny, and Marc Coosemans. "The Anopheles Dirus Complex: Spatial Distribution and Environmental Drivers," *Malaria Journal* 6, no. 26 (2007).
Office of the Historian. *Foreign Relations of the United States, 1961–1963: Volume II, Vietnam, 1962*. Washington, D.C.
Osborne, Milton. *Sihanouk, Prince of Light, Prince of Darkness*. Honolulu: University of Hawaii Press, 1994.
Osborne, Milton. *Phnom Penh: A Cultural and Literary History*. Oxford, UK: Signal Books, 2008.
Osman, Ysa. *Oukoubah*. Phnom Penh: Documentation Center of Cambodia, 2002.
Padwe, Jonathan. *Disturbed Forests, Fragmented Memories: Jarai and Other Lives in the Cambodian Highlands*. Seattle, WA: University of Washington Press, 2020.
Parmentier, Henri. *Inventaire Descriptif des Monuments Čam de l'Ànnam*. Publications d'EFEO, 1909.
Peang-Meth, A. "Understanding the Khmer: Sociological-Cultural Observations," *Asian Survey* 31, no. 5 (May 1991): 442–55.
Pearson, Thomas. *Missions and Conversions: Creating the Montagnard-Dega Refugee Community*. New York: Palgrave Macmillan, 2009.

Peng, Min-Sheng, Huy Ho Quang, Khoa Pham Dang, An Vu Trieu, Hua-Wei Wang, Yong-Gang Yao, Qing-Peng Kong, and Ya-Ping Zhang. "Tracing the Austronesian Footprint in Mainland Southeast Asia: A Perspective from Mitochondrial DNA," *Molecular Biology and Evolution* 27, no. 10 (2010): 2417–430.

Peterson, Barry. *Tiger Men: A Young Australian Soldier Among the Rhade Montagnards of Vietnam.* Bangkok: Orchid Press Publishing Ltd, 1988.

Phong, Dang. *Five Ho Chi Minh Trails.* Hanoi: The Gioi Publishers, 2012.

Po Dharma. "Le FULRO: Moment de l'Histoire ou Tradition de Lutte des Peuples du Sud du Campa." Contribution to the Deuxième Symposium Franco-Soviétique sur l'Asie du Sud-Est, Moscow, 1993. 270–76. Edited by P. V. Posner and O. V. Ribina.

Po Dharma, and Mak Phoen. *Du FLM à FULRO: Une Lutte des Minorités du Sud Indochinois 1955–1975.* Paris: Les Indes Savantes, 2006.

Ponchaud, François. *Cambodge Année Zéro.* Paris: Éditions René Julliard, 1977 (English translation: *Cambodia Year Zero*, Holt, Rinehart and Winston, 1978).

Pribbenow, Merle, translator. "Battles of the Ia Drang, Plei Me, and Sa Thay Discussion Page." *Vietnam Military History*, www.vnmilitaryhistory.net/index.php?topic=2047.20.

Pribbenow, Merle, translator. "[Battle of K'nak]." *Vietnam Military History*, August 13, 2008, www.vnmilitaryhistory.net/index.php?topic=16770.0.

Pribbenow, Merle, translator. "Source: Summaries of Campaigns Fought During the Resistance War Against the Americans to Save the Nation, 1954–1975." Compiled by the Military History Institute of Vietnam. Hanoi: People's Army Publishing House, 2003.

Quinn, Kenneth M. "Explaining the Terror." In *Cambodia 1975–1978: Rendezvous with Death*, edited by Karl Jackson. Princeton, NJ: Princeton University Press, 1989: 215–40.

Reed, Robert. "Jungle Frontiers," *Christian and Missionary Alliance Newsletter*, 1957.

Reed, Robert. "In December of 1965…" Personal account of the execution (2010). Passed on to the author by Juris Jurjevics.

Retboll, Torben. "Kampuchea and the Reader's Digest," *Bulletin of Concerned Asian Scholars* 11, no. 3 (1979): 18–23.

Rives, Maurice. "L'Armée Royale Khmère (1945–1954)," *Bulletin de l'A.N.A.I (Association Nationale des Anciens et Amis de l'Indochine)*, July–September, 1999.

Roger, R., E. Fife, and C. Webb. *A Prospective Study of Malaria Among Indigenous Forces in Vietnam with Observations on Incidence, Chemoprophylaxis and Immunology.* Annual report. Washington, D.C.: Walter Reed Army Institute of Research, September 1967 to June 1968: 108.

Roger, R., C. Webb, and J. Brown. *Studies of Malaria Prevalence in Western II and IV Corps Tactical Zone, Republic of Vietnam.* Annual report. Washington, D.C.: Walter Reed Army Institute of Research, September 1967 to June 1968: 86–107.

Roih Kra. "La Mesure de l'Homme: Y Bun Sư (10/09/1939—21/04/1975): Vie et Mort d'un Jeune Mnong Rlam," *Siksacakr: The Journal of Cambodia Research* no. 16 (2021).

Rumsby, Seb. "Rumours, Sects and Rallies: The Ethnic Politics of Recent Hmong Millenarian Movements in Vietnam's Highlands," *The Journal of Peasant Studies* (2018), doi: 10.1080/03066150.2018.1525362.

Salemink, Oscar. *The Ethnography of Vietnam's Central Highlanders.* Honolulu: University of Hawai'i Press, 2003.

Salemink, Oscar. "Trading Goods, Prestige and Power: A Revisionist History of Lowlander-Highlander Relations in Vietnam." In *Linking Destinies: Trade, Towns and Kin in Asian History*, edited by Peter Boomgaard, Dick Kooiman, and Henk Schulte Nordholt. Instituut voor Taal-, Land- en Volkenkunde 256, 2008.

Schanberg, Sydney. *Beyond the Killing Fields.* Washington, D.C.: Potomac Books, 2010.

Scheer, Catherine. "La Réforme des Gongs: Dynamiques de Christianisation chez les Bunong Protestants des Hautes Terres du Cambodge." Ph.D. thesis. Paris: Anthropology—The School for the Advanced Study of Social Sciences, 2014.

Scheer, Catherine. "Subaltern Soldiers: Overshadowed Bunong Highlanders in the Khmer Republic's Army, 1970–75," *Journal of Southeast Asian Studies* (2022): 1–30.

Schmid, Maurice. *Végetation du Vietnam: Le Massif Sud-Annamitique et Les Régions Limitrophes.* Paris: ORSTOM, 1974.

Scott, James C. *The Art of Not Being Governed.* New Haven, CT: Yale University Press, 2009.

Scupin, Raymond. "Historical, Ethnographic, and Contemporary Political Analyses of the Muslims of Kampuchea and Vietnam," *Sojourn* 10, no. 2 (1995): 301–28.

Seitz, Paul. *Men of Dignity.* Bar le Duc, France: L'Imprimerie Saint-Paul, 1975.

Sherman, Steve. Oral histories of US Special Forces, collected in the 1990s (1964 Montagnard Revolt).

Simpson, Charles M. *Inside the Green Berets.* New York: Berkley Books, 1983.

Sincere Jr., Clyde J. "II Corps Task Force Prong, 11/8/1966." MikeForceHistory.org, facebook.com/100064702057947/posts/1609864607757O5/ (2013).

Sliwinsky, Marek. *Le Génocide Khmer Rouge: Une Analyse Démographique.* Paris: Éditions L'Harmattan, 1995.

Slocomb, Margaret. *Colons and Coolies.* Bangkok: White Lotus, 2007.

Smith, Roger M., ed. *Documents of Political Development and Change.* Ithaca, NY: Cornell University Press, 1974.

Sochurek, Howard. "American Special Forces in Action in Vietnam," *National Geographic* 127 no. 1 (1965): 38–65.

Stanton, Shelby. *Green Berets at War.* New York: Dell Publishing, 1985.

Statler, Kathryn. *Replacing France: The Origins of American Intervention in Vietnam.* Lexington, KY: The University Press of Kentucky, 2007.

Summers, Laura. 'The Cambodian Civil War," *Current History* 63 (1972): 259.

Sur, Y-Bun (Paul). "Les Relations entre Montagnards et Vietnamiens au Vietnam Sud," *Vocation asiatique* no. 4 (1968), Paris, Lien-lac Van-hoa. Edited by Jean-Pierre Fontaine.

Swain, Jon. *River of Time.* London: William Heinemann Ltd, 1995.

Tarling, Nicholas. *Britain and Sihanouk's Cambodia.* Singapore: NUS Press, 2014.

Thayer, Nate. "Montagnard Army Seeks U.N. Help." *Phnom Penh Post,* September 12, 1992.

Thion, Serge. *Watching Cambodia.* Bangkok: White Lotus, 1993.

Torikata, Yuko. "Reexamining De Gaulle's Peace Initiative on the Vietnam War," *Diplomatic History* 31 no. 5 (2007): 909–38.

Tran, Ky Phuong. *Vestiges of Champa Civilization.* Hanoi: The Gioi Publishers, 2014 (2009 edition).

Vickery, Michael. *Cambodia 1975–1982.* Chiang Mai, Thailand: Silkworm Books, 1984.

Walker, Frank. *Tiger Man of Vietnam.* Sydney, Australia: Hachette, 2009.

Westad, Odd Arne. *The Global Cold War: Third World Interventions and the Making of Our Times.* Cambridge, UK: Cambridge University Press, 2007.

White, Terry. *Swords of Lightning: Special Forces and the Changing Face of Warfare.* London: Brassey's, 1992.

Whitmore, John Kremers. "The Last Great King of Classical Southeast Asia: 'Che Bong Nga' and Fourteenth Century Champa." In *The Cham of Vietnam: History, Society and Art,* edited by Ky Phuong Tran and Bruce M. Lockhart, Singapore: NUS Press, 2011.

Wong Tse Ken, Danny. "The Cham Arrivals in Malaysia: Distant Memories and Rekindled Links," *Archipel* no. 85 (2013).

Zhai, Qiang. *China & the Vietnam Wars, 1950–1975.* Chapel Hill, NC: University of North Carolina Press, 2000.

Index

Subjects

Page numbers in italics refer to maps and images.

Places

People